DORIS LESSING

Modern Critical Views

Henry Adams
Edward Albee
A. R. Ammons
Matthew Arnold
John Ashbery
W. H. Auden
Jane Austen
James Baldwin
Charles Baudelaire
Samuel Beckett
Saul Bellow
The Bible
Elizabeth Bishop
William Blake
Jorge Luis Borges
Elizabeth Bowen
Bertolt Brecht
The Brontës
Robert Browning
Anthony Burgess
George Gordon, Lord
  Byron
Thomas Carlyle
Lewis Carroll
Willa Cather
Cervantes
Geoffrey Chaucer
Kate Chopin
Samuel Taylor Coleridge
Joseph Conrad
Contemporary Poets
Hart Crane
Stephen Crane
Dante
Charles Dickens
Emily Dickinson
John Donne & the Seven-
  teenth-Century Meta-
  physical Poets
Elizabethan Dramatists
Theodore Dreiser
John Dryden
George Eliot
T. S. Eliot
Ralph Ellison
Ralph Waldo Emerson
William Faulkner
Henry Fielding
F. Scott Fitzgerald
Gustave Flaubert
E. M. Forster
Sigmund Freud
Robert Frost

Robert Graves
Graham Greene
Thomas Hardy
Nathaniel Hawthorne
William Hazlitt
Seamus Heaney
Ernest Hemingway
Geoffrey Hill
Friedrich Hölderlin
Homer
Gerard Manley Hopkins
William Dean Howells
Zora Neale Hurston
Henry James
Samuel Johnson and
  James Boswell
Ben Jonson
James Joyce
Franz Kafka
John Keats
Rudyard Kipling
D. H. Lawrence
John Le Carré
Ursula K. Le Guin
Doris Lessing
Sinclair Lewis
Robert Lowell
Norman Mailer
Bernard Malamud
Thomas Mann
Christopher Marlowe
Carson McCullers
Herman Melville
James Merrill
Arthur Miller
John Milton
Eugenio Montale
Marianne Moore
Iris Murdoch
Vladimir Nabokov
Joyce Carol Oates
Sean O'Casey
Flannery O'Connor
Eugene O'Neill
George Orwell
Cynthia Ozick
Walter Pater
Walker Percy
Harold Pinter
Plato
Edgar Allan Poe
Poets of Sensibility & the
  Sublime

Alexander Pope
Katherine Ann Porter
Ezra Pound
Pre-Raphaelite Poets
Marcel Proust
Thomas Pynchon
Arthur Rimbaud
Theodore Roethke
Philip Roth
John Ruskin
J. D. Salinger
Gershom Scholem
William Shakespeare
  (3 vols.)
  Histories & Poems
  Comedies
  Tragedies
George Bernard Shaw
Mary Wollstonecraft
  Shelley
Percy Bysshe Shelley
Edmund Spenser
Gertrude Stein
John Steinbeck
Laurence Sterne
Wallace Stevens
Tom Stoppard
Jonathan Swift
Alfred, Lord Tennyson
William Makepeace
  Thackeray
Henry David Thoreau
Leo Tolstoi
Anthony Trollope
Mark Twain
John Updike
Gore Vidal
Virgil
Robert Penn Warren
Evelyn Waugh
Eudora Welty
Nathanael West
Edith Wharton
Walt Whitman
Oscar Wilde
Tennessee Williams
William Carlos Williams
Thomas Wolfe
Virginia Woolf
William Wordsworth
Richard Wright
William Butler Yeats

These and other titles in preparation

Modern Critical Views

DORIS LESSING

Edited and with an introduction by
Harold Bloom
Sterling Professor of the Humanities
Yale University

CHELSEA HOUSE PUBLISHERS ◊ 1986
New York ◊ New Haven ◊ Philadelphia

© 1986 by Chelsea House Publishers, a division
of Chelsea House Educational Communications, Inc.
133 Christopher Street, New York, NY 10014
345 Whitney Avenue, New Haven, CT 06511
5014 West Chester Pike, Edgemont, PA 19028

Introduction © 1986 by Harold Bloom

Printed and bound in the United States of America

∞ The paper used in this publication meets the minimum
requirements of the American National Standard for Permanence
of Paper for Printed Library Materials, Z39.48–1984.

Library of Congress Cataloging-in-Publication Data
Doris Lessing.
  (Modern critical views)
  Bibliography: p.
  Includes index.
  1. Lessing, Doris May, 1919–   —Criticism and
interpretation. I. Bloom, Harold. II. Series.
PR6023.E833Z597   1986   823'.914   86–9707
  ISBN 0–87754–704–1 (alk. paper)

Contents

Editor's Note

This book brings together what I judge to be the most useful criticism yet published on the fiction of Doris Lessing, arranged here in the chronological order of its original publication. I am grateful to Nancy Sales and David Parker for aid in researching this volume.

The editor's introduction takes up the unhappy stance of dissenting from the judgments of many of the critics who follow. Centering upon the story "The Habit of Loving" and on *The Golden Notebook,* I suggest that there are acute limitations to Lessing's achievement, limitations caused by her too-literal distrust of her own language.

James Gindin begins the chronological sequence of criticism with a study of Lessing's intense commitment to social justice in her earlier work. *The Golden Notebook,* by common consent her most influential novel, is read by Dorothy Brewster as a composite image of our society's dilemmas, and by Paul Schlueter as an exercise in self-knowledge. Frederick R. Karl, surveying both *The Golden Notebook* and *The Four-Gated City,* suggests that Lessing's earnestness and ideological distrust of personality make her work rather too vulnerable to apocalyptic yearnings, despite what he judges to be her considerable achievements.

In a subtly balanced analysis of Lessing's characteristic dilemma, Patricia Meyer Spacks pictures "Lessing's heroines retreating from intolerable experience into the wider expanses of conscious or subconscious reshaping of it." Lynn Sukenick, examining the dialectic of feeling and reason in Lessing, insists that "the careless homeliness of her style" is more than compensated for by "an elusive quality called maturity," a defense that to this editor seems wholly ideological, whether applied to Lessing or to any other writer. Whether the esoteric elements in Lessing's ideology, such as the Sufism expounded by Nancy Shields Hardin, can help to persuade us when the narratives and their rhetoric cannot remains problematic. Barbara Hill Rigney, expounding *The Four-Gated City,* associates Lessing's dialectics of liberation with those of R. D. Laing, an association that parallels Laing's schizophrenia-as-salvation with Lessing's hysteria-as-sanity. In a similar defense of *Briefing for a Descent into Hell*, Roberta Rubenstein argues that the book is "an innovative and effective fusion of form and idea" despite its "stylistic lapses," which to me seem surely more than "occasional."

Lessing's speculative or science fiction is analyzed with a touch more detachment by Lorna Sage, who concludes that the novelist is ironically willing to confirm her own sense of cultural marginality by exploiting and indeed exhausting the available conventions of a popular genre. Catherine R. Stimpson, in an overview of the Martha Quest novels, shrewdly evades aesthetic judgment and implies that Lessing's "politics of mind" are inadequate, yet affirms that the saga of Martha provides us with "goads to growth." Finally, reviewing Lessing's *The Good Terrorist,* the novelist Alison Lurie finds in it "energy, invention, and originality," qualities palpably lacking in *Canopus in Argos.* Whether Lurie's optimism about Doris Lessing's future work, or my acute pessimism as to its continued stylistic decline, will prove to be justified cannot now be adjudicated. Certainly Lessing's work raises for all of us, in extreme form, the question as to whether ideological appeal now tends to substitute itself for the values intrinsic to narrative art.

Introduction

I

The best known of Doris Lessing's short stories, "The Habit of Loving," still serves to introduce both her authentic virtues and her very severe limitations as a writer of fiction. George Talbot, a London theatrical personage (sometime actor, occasional producer, sporadic reviewer), is gently but firmly jilted by "the love of his life," who has been in Australia during the years of the Second World War. A youngish sixty, he grieves, fails to win back his divorced wife, catches severe influenza, and is nursed back to health by a song-and-dance performer, "a small, thin, dark girl," named Bobby Tippett. George and Bobby marry; at thirty-five, she seems childlike to him. But to herself, and to her youthful lover of twenty, she seems already past fulfillment. Two passages between George and Bobby are wholly representative of Lessing's strength and weakness, early and late. The first turns upon the fine phrase of the title, "The Habit of Loving":

> In the morning she looked at him oddly, with an odd sad little respect, and said, "You know what, George? You've just got into the habit of loving."
>
> "What do you mean, dear?"
>
> She rolled out of bed and stood beside it, a waif in her white pyjamas, her black hair ruffled. She slid her eyes at him and smiled. "You just want something in your arms, that's all. What do you do when you're alone? Wrap yourself around a pillow?"
>
> He said nothing; he was cut to the heart.
>
> "My husband was the same," she remarked gaily. "Funny thing is, he didn't care anything about me." She stood considering him, smiling mockingly. "Strainge, ain't it?" she commented and went

1

off to the bathroom. That was the second time she had mentioned her husband.

That phrase, "the habit of loving," made a revolution in George. It was true, he thought. He was shocked out of himself, out of the instinctive response to the movement of skin against his, the pressure of a breast. It seemed to him that he was seeing Bobby quite newly. He had not really known her before. The delightful little girl had vanished, and he saw a young woman toughened and wary because of defeats and failures he had never stopped to think of. He saw that the sadness that lay behind the black eyes was not at all impersonal; he saw the first sheen of grey lying on her smooth hair; he saw that the full curve of her cheek was the beginning of the softening into middle-age. He was appalled at his egotism. Now, he thought, he would really know her, and she would begin to love him in response to it.

Poor George is quite mistaken; he never will really know her, and she never will love him. He is the archetypal Lessing male, in the habit of loving even as he is in the habit of living. Shrewdly observed by Lessing, nevertheless he is not *there* sufficiently to bear observation. Like most "realistic" representations, he is a reduction, and so a caricature, though a very effective one. Bobby begins as a caricature also, but her final, self-willed transformation reverberates with a mimetic force beyond caricature:

> One morning she announced she was going to have a birthday party; it would be her fortieth birthday soon. The way she said it made George feel uneasy.
>
> On the morning of her birthday she came into his study where he had been sleeping, carrying his breakfast tray. He raised himself on his elbow and gazed at her, appalled. For a moment he had imagined it must be another woman. She had put on a severe navy blue suit, cut like a man's; heavy black-laced shoes; and she had taken the wisps of black hair back off her face and pinned them into a sort of clumsy knot. She was suddenly a middleaged woman.
>
> "But, my darling," he said, "my darling, what have you done to yourself?"
>
> "I'm forty," she said. "Time to grow up."
>
> "But, my darling, I do so love you in your nice clothes. I do so love you being beautiful in your lovely clothes."

She laughed, and left the breakfast tray beside his bed, and went clumping out on her heavy shoes.

That morning she stood in the kitchen beside a very large cake, on which she was carefully placing forty small pink candles. But it seemed only the sister had been asked to the party, for that afternoon the three of them sat around the cake and looked at one another. George looked at Rosa, the sister, in her ugly, straight, thick suit, and at his darling Bobby, all her grace and charm submerged into heavy tweed, her hair dragged back, without makeup. They were two middleaged women, talking about food and buying.

George said nothing. His whole body throbbed with loss.

The dreadful Rosa was looking with her sharp eyes around the expensive flat, and then at George and then at her sister.

"You've let yourself go, haven't you, Bobby?" she commented at last. She sounded pleased about it.

Bobby glanced defiantly at George. "I haven't got time for all this nonsense any more," she said. "I simply haven't got time. We're all getting on now, aren't we?"

George saw the two women looking at him. He thought they had the same black, hard, inquisitive stare over sharp-bladed noses. He could not speak. His tongue was thick. The blood was beating through his body. His heart seemed to be swelling and filling his whole body, an enormous soft growth of pain. He could not hear for the tolling of the blood through his ears. The blood was beating up into his eyes, but he shut them so as not to see the two women.

One could read this as a parody, perhaps indeliberate, of a slogan in T. S. Eliot, thus rendered as: "Males cannot bear very much reality." Presumably Bobby's bitter self-reductiveness is Lessing's own. What is striking, and indubitably an aesthetic strength, is the extraordinary effect of the supposedly unbearable reality upon poor George. That is my second "poor George," reflecting the reaction of a fifty-five-year-old male literary critic to Lessing's "realistic" reduction of male attitudes. "Who is the interpreter and what power does he or she seek to gain over the text?" is a superb Nietzschean question. An answer, not un-Nietzschean, would be to remind the reader (and the critic) that the critic interpreting here is frequently assailed by feminist critics as "*the* patriarchal critic." Not un-Nietzschean also would be the related answer, reminding the reader that Doris Lessing is the interpreter, and that the power she seeks to gain over the text of life is always reductive: tendentious, resentful, historicizing. Do we know at the conclusion of "The Habit of Loving" what George Talbot is *really* like, simply because Lessing has told us, so vividly, the very worst things that can be said about him?

II

Lessing's one undisputable achievement remains her immensely influential novel *The Golden Notebook*. The oddity of this achievement is that the book is very much a transitional work, resembling neither her early social realism nor her later, rather grim ventures into speculative fiction. *The Golden Notebook* has mothered hordes of feminist novels, and yet it is hardly what would now be considered "feminist" writing by most critics of that persuasion. Not that Lessing is a contemporary version of George Eliot, a woman so strong as a novelist and so majestic as a moralist that her vision is not much more gender-oriented than was Shakespeare's. Critics who compare Lessing to George Eliot or to Turgenev do her an ill service, as she simply is not of that eminence. She is a contemporary George Gissing or Olive Schreiner, and inflating her importance, though inescapable in current literary and sexual politics, finally may sink her without trace. *The Golden Notebook* will survive, I think, because its rugged experimentation with form rises out of socially realistic concerns, and is therefore undertaken against the grain, as it were.

At the center of *The Golden Notebook* is Lessing's assumption that her Anna Wulf is a paradigm for all contemporary women. But is she? At one moment Anna gives us her erotic credo, which is presumably Lessing's also:

> The closest of all bonds; neurotic, pain giving, the experience of
> pain dealt and received; pain as an aspect of love; apprehended
> as a knowledge of what the world is, what growth is.

Whether or not this is a universal experience, its equation of pain, worldly knowledge, and growth is certainly the dialectic of experience in *The Golden Notebook*. Someone as removed as I am from Lessing's stance is in no position to challenge her dialectics, but only to wonder whether her own rhetoric is adequate to her proclaimed vision. About twenty-five pages from the end of the novel, Anna Wulf crawls into bed with the precise expectation of a particular dream:

> I also knew what I was going to be told. Knowing was an "illu-

mination." During the last weeks of craziness and timelessness I've had these moments of "knowing" one after the other, yet there is no way of putting this sort of knowledge into words. Yet these moments have been so powerful, like the rapid illuminations of a dream that remain with one waking, that what I have learned will be part of how I experience life until I die. Words. Words. I play with words, hoping that some combination, even a chance combination, will say what I want. Perhaps better with music? But music attacks my inner ear like an antagonist, it's not my world. The fact is, the real experience can't be described. I think, bitterly, that a row of asterisks, like an old-fashioned novel, might be better. Or a symbol of some kind, a circle perhaps, or a square. Anything at all, but not words. The people who have been there, in the place in themselves where words, patterns, order, dissolve, will know what I mean and the others won't. But once having been there, there's a terrible irony, a terrible shrug of the shoulders, and it's not a question of fighting it, or disowning it, or of right or wrong, but simply knowing it is there, always. It's a question of bowing to it, so to speak, with a kind of courtesy, as to an ancient enemy: All right, I know you are there, but we have to preserve the forms, don't we? And perhaps the condition of your existing at all is precisely that we preserve the forms, create the patterns—have you thought of that?

What this passage manifests (despite Lessing's intentions, I suspect) is that Anna Wulf is a failed writer, who cannot master "Words. Words." Lessing could be defended only by the assertion that Anna Wulf does not speak for her author, here or elsewhere, which is improbable. Certainly Lessing's speculative fiction *Canopus in Argos: Archives* perpetually relies upon the "terrible shrug" of saying:

> The people who have been there, in the place in themselves where words, patterns, order, dissolve, will know what I mean and the others won't.

Novels, like poems, cannot be written with rows of asterisks, a circle perhaps, or a square. As a prophet of consciousness, Lessing increasingly is humanly impatient in regard to language, an impatience that sometimes she can render with poignancy. Ultimately, it is her refusal to sustain or be sustained by societal ideas of order that drives her on towards speculative fiction, and towards speculative doctrines, as in Martha Quest's reading preferences in *The Four-Gated City*:

> books on Rosicrucianism and the old Alchemists; Buddhist books
> ... Yoga ... Zoroastrianism and esoteric Christianity ... the I
> Ching; Zen, witchcraft, magic, astrology and vampirism; schol-
> arly treatises on Sufism; the works of the Christian mystics ...
> everything rejected by official culture and scholarship.

The impulse is ancient and honorable, and recapitulates a tradition that goes from the Gnostics on through Blake and Yeats to such of our contemporaries as James Merrill and Thomas Pynchon. Yet Pynchon's Kabbalists, working out his doctrine of sado-anarchism, thoroughly exploit the limits of language, as do Merrill's occult personages and celebrants. Lessing's visionary fiction has some cognitive strength and considerable pathos, but the reader must fight through to them against Lessing's own language, which is, all too frequently, a kind of drab shrug. Doubtless the novel itself is a societal idea of order, a repressive convention that a prophet must transcend or circumvent in the struggle towards moral and spiritual liberation. Consider D. H. Lawrence, who achieved prophetic authority while remaining a strong novelist in *The Rainbow* and *Women in Love,* but who then became impatient, and so gave us *The Plumed Serpent* and the other novels of his final phase. Lawrence was a great poet, with preternatural verbal gifts, and so a fairer comparison for Lessing is her exact contemporary, Iris Murdoch. How do Lessing and Murdoch compare, as novelists and as seers?

Both may be called Platonic novelists, though only Murdoch is actually a Platonist, while Lessing is a post-Marxist materialist who has wandered into Sufism in the honorable spirit of the fierce Spanish anarchists who fought against Franco, while seeking a religion in Rosicrucianism and other assorted dank crankeries. Murdoch is a great storyteller, master of double plots and of endless surprises, while if you read even *The Golden Notebook* for the story then you may as well hang yourself. Neither Murdoch nor Lessing is proficient at depicting memorable personages, Murdoch because she runs to recurrent, set types, and Lessing because she cannot be bothered, since she has ceased to believe that we have (or ought to have) individual personalities anyway. Murdoch is an admirable comic writer, while there is not the slightest evidence that Lessing and her characters have any sense of humor whatsoever. The largest difference is that Murdoch trusts words, and has the discipline to order them.

Since both Murdoch and Lessing have the same underlying subject, which is the erotic war between men and women, Murdoch's superiority is palpable in representing the almost infinite nuances of the sexual agon. Men and women fall in love in Murdoch, as they frequently do in reality, but in Lessing they almost invariably deceive or are deceived, in a quest for power over others. Though clearly I prefer Murdoch, Lessing has the stronger extra-literary appeal in an age of ideologies, all of them promising liberation. Yet *The Golden Notebook* and certain moments in the Martha Quest novels should endure, because Lessing is very much a representative writer for our time. She has the spirit, if not the style, of the age.

JAMES GINDIN

Doris Lessing's
Intense Commitment

Among young contemporary English writers, Doris Lessing is the most intensely committed to active persuasion to reform society. In a series of loosely connected essays, entitled *Going Home* (1957), published after she had returned to her early home in British colonial Africa for a visit, Miss Lessing frequently advocates direct participation in political action. She talks of the "sense of duty" that makes her join organizations, defends (on biographical rather than ultimate grounds) her own support of communism, and ends her essays by unfurling a qualified banner:

> In this book I have made various statements about the possibility of Communism becoming democratic. Since writing it the Soviet intervention in Hungary has occurred. It is hard to make adequate political assessments on notes added hastily to galley proofs as a book goes to press. But it seems to me that during the last three years the great words liberty, freedom and truth have again become banners for men to fight under—in all the countries of the world. It seems to me wrong that so many people should be saddened and discouraged by this sudden violent crisis we are all living through: it is a crisis in the battle of truth against lies, of honesty against corruption, of respect for the goodness of people against cynicism.

From *Postwar British Fiction: New Accents and Attitudes.* © 1962 by the Regents of the University of California. University of California Press, 1962.

Miss Lessing's interest in the battle permeates most of her short stories and novels. Frequently the theme of the work is whether or not, despite a hostile or indifferent society, strong commitment to a particular cause or political doctrine is justifiable.

The issue of commitment is most tersely stated in Miss Lessing's play, *Each His Own Wilderness* (first presented in 1958). The play presents a violent conflict between mother and son. The son, Tony Bolton, just discharged from the army, returns to his mother's London home while she is preparing for one of her frequent rallies to champion worthy causes. Tony, whose first memory is the bomb that killed his father in World War II, is skeptical about causes and rallies, bitter that so much of his mother's energy has been given to Spain and Hungary and other world problems. In one argument he rails at his mother: "You're so delightfully old-fashioned. Getting killed for something you believe in is surely a bit of a luxury these days? Something your generation enjoyed. Now one just—gets killed." His contemporary, Rosemary, talks of six big men somewhere who could blow up the world any time they wished, a concept that renders all protest against the H-bomb useless. Tony is no closer to his mother on the subject of domestic politics:

> Why are you sitting there looking so tortured? You've got what you wanted, haven't you? Well? You've spent your life fighting for socialism. There it is, socialism. You said you wanted material progress for the masses. God knows there is *material* progress. Hundreds of millions of people progressing in leaps and bounds towards a materially-progressive heaven. . . . Do you know what it is you've created, you and your lot? What a vision it is! A house for every family. Just imagine—two hundred million families— or is it four hundred million families? To every family a front door. Behind every front door, a family. A house full of clean, well-fed people, and not one of them ever understands one word anybody else says. Everybody a kind of wilderness surrounded by barbed wire shouting across the defences into the other wildernesses and never getting an answer back. That's socialism. I suppose it's progress. Why not? To every man his wife and two children and a chicken in the pot on Sundays. A beautiful picture—I'd die for it. To every man his front door and his front door key. To each his own wilderness.

The conflict between generations is not only political, for Tony, a highly Oedipal young man of twenty-two, becomes furious whenever his liberated mother mentions one of her love affairs. He shrieks that she lives "like a pig," yet he would rather live in her house than find a flat on his own. Similarly, the mother finds Tony a bore, a stupid "insufferable prig," yet she is willing to sell all her possessions to provide him with an allowance for self-discovery. The final exchange of the play summarizes both the political and the personal conflict, focuses on the issue of the sort of commitment a person ought to make. Tony's mother speaks first:

> I'm nearly 50—and it's true there's nothing much to show for it. Except that I've never been afraid to take chances and make mistakes. I've never wanted security and safety and the walls of respectability—you damned little petty-bourgeois. My God, the irony of it—that we should have given birth to a generation of little office boys and clerks and . . . little people who count their pensions before they're out of school . . . little petty bourgeois.

After his mother leaves, Tony turns to Rosemary to deliver the final lines of the play:

> Rosemary, listen—never in the whole history of the world have people made a battle-cry out of being ordinary. Never. Supposing we all said to the politicians—we refuse to be heroic. We refuse to be brave. We are bored with all the noble gestures—what then, Rosemary? . . . Leave us alone, we'll say. Leave us alone to live. Just leave us alone.

Even though Tony is given the last speech, his point of view is not that of the author. Tony is made too childish, too petulant, to represent anything more than a contemporary phenomenon. Rather, the play simply states, without resolving, different attitudes toward political and social commitment.

Some of Miss Lessing's novels, however, develop these issues a good deal further. The series of novels that deals with Martha Quest's growing-up (a sequence, as yet unfinished, which includes *Martha Quest*, 1952; *A Proper Marriage*, 1954; and *A Ripple from the Storm*, 1958) demonstrates a strong endorsement of the heroine who is anxious to change society, to work actively for a more humane and just world. Martha, the heroine, encounters difficulty in attempting, within the severely restrictive society of colonial Africa, to define herself both personally and politically. The books by Havelock Ellis she has read as an adolescent do not square with the attitudes toward sex she finds around her; the books about socialism and economics have little to do with the problem of the color bar she sees every day. Martha's books, her associations, her kind of perception, have all helped to make her very different from her mother, the representative of conventional colonial society.

The conflict between mother and daughter begins early, and, like the conflict between mother and son in *Each His Own Wilderness,* covers both political and sexual issues. Martha is disgusted with her mother's combination of purity and calculation about sex, her mother's Victorian propriety and constant assumptions concerning the laziness and the dishonesty of all African natives. Her mother, on the other hand, finds Martha blasphemous and immoral. But the two, like Tony and his mother, cannot simply ignore each other. Mrs. Quest, though continually rebuffed, keeps returning to her daughter, trying to help Martha and give her unwanted advice, as if the bitter quarrels had never occurred. And Martha, when seriously ill, wonders why her mother has never really loved her. Her emotional attachment to her mother is deeper than that to either of the two husbands she marries in unsuccessful attempts to discover herself.

Martha, in her quest for values, joins the Communist party early in World War II, but finds the party, with all its interminable bickering and its anxiety to remain a force within a hostile society, unable to do anything about colonial Africa's principal problem, the division between white and black. Yet, despite her many mistakes, Martha never retreats into the indifferent complacency or the assumption of eternal rightness which she sees all around her in colonial society. Martha searches for herself and battles for what she believes.

Julia Barr, the young heroine in *Retreat to Innocence* (1956), represents a more complex treatment of Miss Lessing's kind of commitment. In ways, Julia, who frequents espresso coffeehouses and wears black sweaters, is like Tony Bolton. Both are products of the new generation, born in the mid-thirties to liberal and aristocratic parents, handed educations their mothers had to fight for, wanting only to find some personal meaning to hang on to. Julia, too, fights the parents she cannot break from and bitterly opposes what she calls her parents' "messiness" about politics and sex. Her desire for stability and her wish to disassociate herself from political issues seem priggish and selfish to her concerned father: "A more self-centred, selfish, materialistic generation has never been born into this unfortunate old country. All you want is to cultivate your own gardens. You really don't give a damn for anyone but yourselves, do you?" Julia, who offers less childish defenses for her attitudes than Tony Bolton does, feels that her parents' political concerns have kept them from understanding and appreciating human beings. She recalls that on a trip through Spain with her mother, after a peasant had mended a puncture in their tire and they had spent several hours talking with the peasant's family, all her mother could speak of was the need for "a sensible English town Council and a birth control centre."

Julia, unlike Tony Bolton, develops as the novel progresses. She falls in love with a Communist refugee writer, Jan Brod, a man more than twice her age, long since defined by political forces Julia can barely comprehend. Julia, the product of a wholly different time and place, cannot share Jan's deep involvement in politics. But this involvement, this overwhelming concern, gives him an energy, a force, an attraction that Julia cannot find in any of the agreeable and socially acceptable young men she knows. Julia argues with Jan about politics, and makes him acknowledge his awareness of all the purges and iniquities the Communists have created. Yet she can also understand and feel the emotional force of Jan's ultimate defense of the Communists:

> But don't you see, when people formed themselves together in the Party, for the first time in history, without God, without excuses, relying on themselves, saying: We accept the responsibility for what we do, we accept all the good and the evil of the past, we reject nothing—then for the first time in history man became free; he became free because he rejected nothing.

Jan's defense stands as the affirmative battle cry in the novel. Jan himself, however, cannot remain in England, for the established hypocrisy will not grant him citizenship. Julia is not sufficiently converted to follow him back to central Europe, for the affair with Jan is part of her means of self-discovery. But she is able to realize that her shelter and comfort have something hollow about them and that in losing Jan she has lost more than she has gained. Julia, being herself, has no genuine alternative. Still, Miss Lessing makes it clear that Julia and her generation are lesser beings than their predecessors because they lack the energy and the purpose of a Jan Brod.

Miss Lessing's commitment usually involves opposition to the reigning precepts of English or Anglo-colonial society. Both Julia and Martha Quest, despite their different political attitudes, are enormously attracted to an aristocrat, a representation of the society's model. Martha is fascinated by Mr. Maynard, the magistrate who, although reactionary, maintains a steady and biting wisdom about Africa. Julia is strongly drawn to her father, that liberal, tolerant, stable representative of the basic English virtue of fair play. Yet, in both instances, the aristocrat betrays the faith placed in him. Mr. Maynard runs a vigilant spy service directed against radicals which belies his pose of sardonic intelligence; more directly, he lies about Martha's close friend in order to cover up his failure to persuade her to lose by abortion the child fathered by Maynard's dissolute son. Julia, too, is betrayed by her father, the benevolent liberal and patron of the arts, living on the income earned in the family business now managed by a "competent commercial person from the Midlands." Julia asks her father to help secure British citizenship for Jan. Her father promises but, after making a casual inquiry, refuses to push the matter further and retreats into the shell of upper-class complacency, sure that the government must know what it's doing, confident of the judgment of the British Home Office. Julia's father's liberalism is hollow, despite the appearance he gives of genuine concern. Even Tony Bolton's mother, who had seemed fine and elegant and truly solicitous of others, stupidly wounds another person and betrays Tony by selling their house, his symbol of security and permanence. The liberals, the people who apparently manifest concern about social and political problems without objecting to the fundamental society itself, and the aristocrats, those sustained and honored by the society, stand revealed holding shoddy or dishonest poses.

Yet many of Miss Lessing's heroines, disillusioned by their own societies, can find themselves through an older person denigrated by most of society. Martha Quest, for example, has her first affair with a Jewish orchestra leader much older than herself, who is patronized with sneers by most of her colonial friends. His very difference, the fact that he cannot be defined in terms of the society, is part of his attraction for Martha. Similarly, the young actress in "The Habit of Loving" (a story in a volume of the same title, published in 1957) marries a much older actor who cannot understand the contemporary quality of her lost-gamin routine, who believes the theater should contain violent, bombastic gestures. The young actress requires definition outside the world by which she has been conditioned. Julia Barr, too, in loving Jan, has reached outside the society established for her, embraced the alien and the unexpected. Women define themselves through the sexual relationship, and Julia, Martha, and others all demonstrate their partial or essential rejection of their own societies by affairs with the ineligible and the unexpected. And conversely, in Miss Lessing's fiction, the aristocrats and the halfhearted liberals, those endorsed by the society, are apt to be worth little as men.

Doris Lessing has consciously sought the socially rejected. When she moved to England in 1949, her sense of social responsibility and her distrust of those who sanction and are sanctioned by the reigning society led her to search for her values and for her literary material among the working classes in London. As she herself explains in a recently published documentary (*In Pursuit of the English,* 1960):

I propose to admit, and voluntarily at that, that I have been thinking for some time of writing a piece called: In Pursuit of the Working-Class. My life has been spent in pursuit. So has everyone's, of course. I chase love and fame all the time. I have chased, off and on, and with much greater deviousness of approach, the working-class and the English. The pursuit of the working-class is shared by everyone with the faintest tint of social responsibility: some of the most indefatigable pursuers are working-class people.

But the pursuit, as Miss Lessing describes it in her documentary, did not uncover any unanimity of repressed nobility among the London proletariat. Miss Lessing reports her difficulties in finding a place to live, her encounters with sharp operators and grasping landlords among the working classes. A poor clerk, Rose, finally helps her get settled, and the landlords, Dan and Flo, invite her to vast spaghetti suppers and round up the furniture she needs. Still, the same landlords are cruel to an old couple in the house, whom they want to evict, and neglect their own young daughter so badly that authorities threaten to take the child to a state home. Some of the people Miss Lessing encounters do reinforce conventional ideas of a concerned and humane working class:

> Two houses down on the opposite side lived an old man on the old-age pension, who was reading for the first time in his life. He was educating himself on the *Thinker's Library*. He had been a bricklayer, his wife was dead and he was now half-crazed with loneliness and the necessity to communicate what he had so slowly and belatedly learned. He lingered on the pavement at the time people were coming home from work, made a few routine remarks about the weather, and then whispered confidentially: "There's no God. We aren't anything but apes. They don't tell the working-man in case we get out of hand."

But few of the Londoners described would provide so fertile material for a potential uprising among the proletariat. In fact, most of them become capitalists themselves whenever they get the opportunity. Dan, the head of the household, first began to acquire extra cash in the war when he was personal servant to a surgeon commander and received tips for squiring the commander's mistress in and out of quarters. Right after the war he stripped washbasins and baths from bombed houses and sold them. With these two sources of income, he was able to buy and furnish the house he now owns. An enterprising capitalist, Dan has solid hopes of increasing his holdings and becoming a fairly wealthy landlord. Though able with his hands and skillful at remodeling furniture, Dan has no thought whatever of emulating William Morris.

Miss Lessing also shows the insularity of these people. They often hate the French and hate the Jews, and are aware of little outside their own corners of London:

> Flo's London did not even include the West End, since she had left the restaurant in Holborn. It was the basement she lived in; the shops she was registered at; and the cinema five minutes' walk away. She had never been inside a picture gallery, a theatre or a concert hall. Flo would say: "Let's go to the River one fine afternoon and take Oar." She had not seen the Thames, she said, since before the war. Rose had never been on the other side of the river. Once, when I took my son on a trip by river bus, Rose played with the idea of coming too for a whole week. Finally she said: "I don't think I'd like those parts, not really. I like what I'm used to. But you go and tell me about it after."

These people have little respect for British institutions and the justice of the law courts. In one of the funniest episodes in the book, the family goes to court to evict the old tenants from their house. In the antechamber their lawyer coaches them to lie consistently, to make a coherent case out of a long history of mutual grudges, cruelty, and complaints about dirty bathrooms. They win the case only because the old couple are even more incoherent and gratuitously foul-mouthed than they. But the point of the scene is that all the parties—the family, the old couple, the lawyer, even the judge himself—make the whole notion of the supposed fair play of British courts seem ludicrous. The people from the working class are simply less verbally skillful, less proficient in handling the forms, less sophisticated versions of their counterparts who compose the Establishment. No one is adequate to carry the banner for the revolution.

In portraying the working class, Miss Lessing often uses women to present the argument in favor of restricting one's activity to the comfortable, the sheltered, the safe. In the short novel called "The Other Woman" (one of a series of short novels published as *Five* in 1953), a young working-class girl chooses to break her engagement when her mother is killed by a lorry just before World War II. She decides to stay with her father in the basement they have always known, rejecting any outside influence. She chides her father for wasting his time at political meetings where nothing is ever accomplished, berates Parliament periodically, and lumps Hitler, Churchill, Attlee, Stalin, and Roosevelt together as people who make her sick. Her small security is blown up when her father is killed in a bombing in the war. She clings to the demolished basement as long as she can, until a kind young man almost carries her out by force. Once out of the basement, she can live with the man quite easily, clinging to that which is most readily available. She discovers that her young man has been married before, and his attentions soon begin to wander toward a third woman. The girl and the young man's first wife, accepting the male's infidelity without scenes or recriminations, finally agree to start a cakeshop in another basement and leave the young man to his newest mistress. The heroine does not search for romance or for passion: she simply accepts conditions around her and tries to work things out as safely and securely as she possibly can.

Rose, one of the central figures in *In Pursuit of the English,* is much the same kind of person. A hard life has taught her to fend for herself, to value her daily round, her drop of tea, her security. She, too, is skeptical about and indifferent to political parties or slogans. Her view of political personalities has little to do with the policies or the programs the personalities supposedly represent:

> Rose would listen to Churchill talk with a look of devotion I entirely misunderstood. She would emerge at the end of half an hour's fiery peroration with a dreamy and reminiscent smile, and say: "He makes me laugh. He's just a jealous fat man, I don't take any notice of him. Just like a girl he is, saying to a friend: No dear, you don't look nice in that dress, and the next thing is, he's wearing it himself."
>
> "Then why do you listen to him?"
>
> "Why should I care? He makes me remember the war, for one thing. I don't care what he says about Labour. I don't care who gets in, I'll get a smack in the eye either way. When they come in saying Vote for Me, Vote for Me, I just laugh. But I like to hear Churchill speak, with his dirty V-Sign and everything, he enjoys himself, say what you like."

Rose also objects to the false film versions of the Cockney and to any kind of slogan concerning brotherhood. Yet she sentimentally misses the warmth and the comradeship of the war when the usual class barriers were down and people all felt closer to one another. Rose's attitude toward politics, like that of the heroine in "The Other Woman," is handled somewhat sympathetically because she's had a hard life, she's a woman, and she's a member of the working class. Because of these, Miss Lessing can make Rose's insistence on her own narrow world and her rejection of all political questions both faintly comic and sympathetic.

People without Rose's warrant who still hold the same attitudes receive much more biting treatment. The younger generation has had a much easier time, and their choice in favor of limiting experience to the secure is made much more selfish and materialistic. In *Retreat to Innocence,* Julia is frequently labeled as selfish, and the young Cockney lad who tends the coffee bar is made to say:

> My old man, he was a proper old Bolshie he was. I don't hold it against him, mind. They had it tough when he was young. And he was on to me when I was a nipper, giving me the *Herald* and all that. I've been raised on William Morris and Keir Hardie and all that lot. And I wouldn't say a word against them—grand old boys they were. But I says to my dad, I says, what's in it for me?

Yet Miss Lessing treats the middle-class woman of limited and nonpolitical interests with even more sharpness. Working-class people have, at least, the excuse of a certain amount of economic and educational deprivation. But the middle classes often receive no sympathy whatsoever. A middle-class couple spending a holiday abroad appear in "Pleasure" (another story in the volume called *The Habit of Loving*). The young couple are interested only in spear fishing, in impressing their neighbors with the fact that they've been abroad, in justifying everything English to themselves and to anyone else they happen to meet. Not a shred of sympathy enters the one-dimensional characterization of the empty couple in "Pleasure," and the woman seems singled out to bear the brunt of Miss Lessing's disapproval. This commonplace middle-class woman is treated with a fierce contempt, an attitude far more shrill than any leveled against stupid, materialistic Cockneys or patronizing and deceptive aristocrats or those nasty, bigoted, lonely colonial women on farming outposts in Africa.

Miss Lessing's commitment to a sense of social responsibility and to a pursuit of those oppressed by society also infuses her fiction about colonial Africa, where she spent most of her first thirty years. In Africa the pursuit centers on the color bar, and, in all Miss Lessing's fiction dealing with Africa—her first novel, *The Grass Is Singing* (1950); the three novels dealing with Martha Quest; a volume of short stories called *This Was the Old Chief's Country* (1951); and four of the short novels collected as *Five*—the division between white and black is central. Often, in Miss Lessing's fiction, the white man is an interloper, attempting to wrest independence or security from the African soil or asserting himself in a colonial office established to govern the alien country. The white man carries his European culture and attitudes with him, preserves his religion and his heavy oak Victorian furniture, and brings up his children as he would in England. The child, from whose point of view the story "The Old Chief Mshlanga" is told, is living in British Africa:

> This child could not see a msasa tree, or the thorn, for what they were. Her books held tales of alien fairies, her rivers ran slow and peaceful, and she knew the shape of the leaves of an ash or an oak, the names of the little creatures that lived in English streams, when the words "the veld" meant strangeness, though she could remember nothing else.
>
> Because of this, for many years, it was the veld that seemed unreal; the sun was a foreign sun, and the wind spoke a strange language.
>
> (*This Was the Old Chief's Country*)

In many of the stories, the white settler's assertion of his inherited culture is, in this new land, his means of establishing his difference from the black men all around him. Some of the white settlers, like Dick Turner in *The Grass Is Singing,* have been failures in English society and have come to Africa in order to reestablish themselves; others, like the old farmer in "The De Wets Come to Kloof Grange," are motivated by an urge to bring new land into cultivation.

Most of Miss Lessing's alien white settlers, and their more shrill and insistent wives, regard themselves as sensitive, aware, and responsible, and look at the blacks as happy, amoral, and irresponsible. In one story in *This Was the Old Chief's Country,* a black woman is missing and the clues surrounding her disappearance point toward possible suicide. But the whites hesitate to endorse this supposition: "Later, we talked about the thing, saying how odd it was that natives should commit suicide; it seemed almost like an impertinence, as if they were claiming to have the same delicate feelings as ours." Farmers and businessmen grumble about the useless and ignorant blacks as regularly as they discuss the crops, the weather, or the prospects of business; the women complain that the household blacks are lazy, dishonest, fully deserving of the cuffs they get, and then wonder why the blacks are not more grateful for their civilized servants' jobs. In *The Grass Is Singing,* a successful neighboring farmer helps Dick Turner, for whom he has little love and less respect: "He was obeying the dictate of the first law of white South Africa, which is: 'Thou shalt not let your fellow whites sink lower than a certain point; because if you do, the nigger will see he is as good as you are.' '' Any kind of human relationship between white and black, within the strictures of this environment, is impossible.

The Grass Is Singing traces the horror that can result from a subterranean relationship between white and black within colonial African society. Mary, a thirtyish office worker in an African town, marries as her last chance Dick Turner, the inept and inefficient farmer. Gradually Mary shrivels in the midst of their futile battle to achieve security from the land. Only the Negro houseboy has the energy and the skill to force Mary's attraction, yet she, having always lived in Africa, is also repelled by the sight of him. She cannot bear to look him in the eye, fears even talking to him, while she unconsciously reveres his competence, strength, and grace. Mary would like to preserve her sanity by discharging the boy, but she has been unable to handle servants before and her husband insists that she keep this one. The conflict within Mary, the alternating love and hate toward the Negro, the frightening awareness that she possesses the one emotion her society most violently condemns, leads to her murder. She is destroyed by her inability to reconcile a human emotion with her own deep commitment to the rigid line her society maintains between white and black.

Like Mary Turner, many of the colonials feel a deep fear, a constant emotional apprehension about living in Africa. They are aware that they are interlopers, white aliens in a black world. The little girl in "The Old Chief Mshlanga" fears the isolation of her whiteness as she walks through the brush to the native village. Her wealthy father can force the natives to move, but he cannot control the mounds of mud, the rotting thatch, the tangled growth of pumpkins, and the hordes of white ants which the natives leave behind them. And the girl is frightened. Most often it is the woman, like the poor farmer's wife in "The Second Hut," or the wealthy farmer's wife in "The De Wets Come to Kloof Grange," who feels this fear, this inability of the white man to control the black, lush growth around him, yet men, too, sometimes have these moments of perception. The able farmer in " 'Leopard' George," a man who has never married because he thought himself in perfect control over his native mistresses, is surprised when a young, hitherto discreet mistress embarrasses him in front of white guests:

> In that moment, while he stood following the direction of his servant's eyes with his own, a change took place in him; he was gazing at a towering tumbling heap of boulders that stood sharp and black against a high fresh blue, the young blue of an African morning, and it was as if that familiar and loved shaped moved back from him, reared menacingly like an animal and admitted

danger—a sharp danger, capable of striking from a dark place that was a place of fear. Fear moved in George; it was something he had not before known.

(*This Was the Old Chief's Country*)

The apprehension that the sensitive white feels in Africa is the mark of his failure to impose himself and his standards completely on the dark, fertile continent he inhabits. The fear is also, simultaneously, the sign of his own awareness in contrast to his denser, more complacent fellow colonials. Martha Quest, the perceptive heroine of *A Proper Marriage,* who has made a bad, hasty first marriage with a young colonial, uses the black of the native as the image of her own awareness:

> There were moments that she felt she was strenuously held together by nothing more than an act of will. She was beginning to feel that this view of herself was an offence against what was deepest and most real in her. And again she thought of the simple women of the country, who might be women in peace, according to their instincts, without being made to think and disintegrate themselves into fragments. During those first few weeks of her marriage Martha was always accompanied by that other black woman, like an invisible sister, simpler and wiser than herself; for no matter how much she reminded herself of statistics and progress, she envied her from the bottom of her heart.

For Miss Lessing, the recognition of the black's simplicity and value is the admission of the white settler's failure to civilize Africa.

Not all the white settlers are identical in Miss Lessing's fiction. As in her work dealing with the English, her fiction about Africa frequently relies on a conflict of attitudes between different generations. In *Going Home,* Miss Lessing praises the motives of the older generation of white colonials:

> It seems to me that this story of the man who preferred to die alone rather than return to the cities of his own people expresses what is best in the older type of white men who have come to Africa. He did not come to take what he could get from the country. This man loved Africa for its own sake, and for what is best in it: its emptiness, its promise. It is still uncreated.

Newer settlers, in contrast, are likely to be more dedicated to hard cash or to redeeming previous failures. The comparison between generations is not, however, always so one-sided. In "The De Wets Come to Kloof Grange," the older generation may have established a more comfortable and peaceful settlement, but the younger generation is more willing to try to meet Africa on its own grounds, to swim in its streams and talk to its natives. In another story, "Old John's Place," the newer generation is rootless, an example of those who use Africa to find a security they have been unable to find in Europe. Yet in this story the older community, dogmatic, sure of itself and its moral standards, can find neither room nor sympathy for the new, more morally flexible immigration. In a few isolated instances the new generation can even, personally and temporarily, break down the color bar. In "The Antheap," one of the short novels in *Five*, a white boy and a black boy, born on the same farm, manage to remain close friends despite the older generation's constant attempts to remind each that he owes allegiance only to his own color. The two boys finally win and go off to the university together. Martha Quest herself, brought up in Africa, tries to break through the color bar, an aim that appalls her parents. But Martha does not represent the majority of her generation. Her contemporaries rebel against their parents, but in a very different way. They build a club,

> and inside it, nothing could happen, nothing threatened, for some
> tacit law made it impossible to discuss politics here, and Europe
> was a long way off. In fact, it might be said that this club had
> come into existence, simply as a protest against everything Europe
> stood for. There were no divisions here, no barriers, or at least
> none that could be put into words; the most junior clerk from
> the railways, the youngest typist, were on Christian-name terms
> with their bosses, and mingled easily with the sons of Cabinet
> ministers; the harshest adjective in use was "toffee-nosed," which
> meant snobbish, or exclusive; and even the black waiters who
> served them were likely to find themselves clapped across the
> shoulders by an intoxicated wolf at the end of the dance: "Good
> old Tickey," or "There's a good chap, Shilling," and perhaps even
> their impassive, sardonic faces might relax in an unwilling smile,
> under pressure from this irresistible flood of universal goodwill.

But clapping the waiters on the back is only part of the story. At a later party some of these drunken colonials try to force a Negro waiter to perform a "war dance," making rather malicious sport of him. Their parents engage in a different sort of cruelty, a more tight-lipped and morally defended white superiority. The younger generation never bothers to defend white superiority; the young club members simply, and casually, assume it.

Miss Lessing's African fiction, like her other fiction, often shows her scorn for the halfhearted liberal, the aristocratic do-gooder who does not really commit himself to the downtrodden. The newly arrived colonial woman in "A Home for the Highland Cattle" (one of the short novels in *Five*) is anxious to treat her native houseboy with justice and humanity. She is even willing to steal her landlady's huge picture of prize highland cattle so that the houseboy can legitimize his mistress by buying her as a wife. The white woman tries to understand the way black society operates, and the boy genuinely appreciates her efforts, but still, at the end of the story, the white woman, now no longer living in the rented flat, fails to recognize her former houseboy as she watches the police marching him off to jail. She is too busy buying a table for her new house, although her gifts have led to his prison sentence. In "Little Tembi," a white woman's special fondness for a black boy whose life she once saved turns the boy into a wheedling thief. The boy is unable to accept his position in the black society and yet he is not, despite the special favors, allowed full equality with the whites. His ambivalent position destroys him, while the kindhearted white woman sits by wondering what has happened. Both these women ultimately betray those they tried to help. But Miss Lessing strongly endorses those more systematically committed to working for the socially oppressed. In "Hunger" (another of the short novels in *Five*), a young Negro leaves his native village for the jobs and the lights of the large city. He is sent to some Communist whites who try to help him. But he neglects their advice; he lies, steals, falls in with prostitutes and professional thieves, and is finally carted off to jail for trying to rob the Communists' home. Yet the Communists stick with him and send him a letter, telling him so. From prison, the Negro returns the following message:

> Tell him I have read it with all my understanding, and that I thank him and will do what he says and he may trust me. Tell him I am no longer a child, but a man, and that his judgement is just, and it is right I should be punished.

The attempts of the person fully committed are apt to have impact and meaning.

Not all Miss Lessing's Communists are similarly effective. In *A Ripple from the Storm,* the third novel in the series dealing with Martha Quest, Martha's Communists, whose interminable debates take up about half the novel, are severely split over whether to follow their sympathies and fight the color bar or attempt to gain acceptance among the white population. What should be the crucial question for African reformers is abandoned as the party attempts to work its way into colonial society. The Communists' failure here is an example of the way history operates: the forces of time and place prevented the Communists from reconciling their beliefs with their possibilities. The same doctrine, carrying for Miss Lessing the same intrinsic worth, might well have succeeded somewhere else, at some other time, under different circumstances.

Miss Lessing maintains a consistent interest in time and place. Both the use of the social class as a significant part of the identity of the individual, and the fact that conflicts are so frequently depicted as conflicts between generations, between the products of one time and another, indicate Miss Lessing's addiction to historical categories. Frequent parenthetical historical references fill all the fiction. An attitude stemming from the twenties or from World War I is accurately pinned down and labeled. Martha Quest is characterized in terms of details relevant to her time and place; she categorizes herself, and is categorized by others, as a socialist and an atheist, labels that stick with her throughout the novels. Early in the first novel, *Martha Quest,* Miss Lessing fixes Martha:

> She was adolescent, and therefore bound to be unhappy; British, and therefore uneasy and defensive; in the fourth decade of the twentieth century, and therefore inescapably beset with problems of race and class; female, and obliged to repudiate the shackled women of the past.

Similarly, early in *Retreat to Innocence,* Julia is fixed as a young London girl of 1955 in terms of black sweaters, frequent attendance at espresso coffee bars, and constant objection to the "phony." Minor characters are also defined by time and place, often in an introductory biography that leaves little for the character to do or say once he appears on the scene. Willi, the haunted revolutionary in *Retreat to Innocence,* is fully explained as soon as he momentarily appears. The case history of Miss Privet's career as a prostitute is documented in *In Pursuit of the English* to an extent hardly merited by a minor character. This extensive detailing of character detracts from Miss Lessing's effectiveness in two ways: it sometimes breaks the fiction into a series of journalistic essays or case histories, and it limits the author to the view that all people are almost completely conditioned by time and place, by historical environment.

The historically conditioned character sometimes suggests the cause of an aesthetic shortcoming in Miss Lessing's novels. (The short stories, on the other hand, emphasizing a single relationship, a single conditioning, or the impact of a particular commitment, are often much more effective.) For example, *The Grass Is Singing,* the novel concerning Mary Turner's destruction, begins and ends with an account of Tony Marston, a young Englishman with the usual progressive ideas who has just come to Africa and finds his first job on the Turner farm. Tony serves a valid function in the plot, for he stumbles on a scene in which the Negro is dressing a strangely transfixed and hypnotized Mary. Mary cannot bear the white discovery of her fascination with the Negro, and this incident precipitates her destruction. Yet Tony himself reacts exactly as a young Englishman with vaguely progressive ideas, the product of his place and generation, might be expected to react: he falls right in with all the usual white clichés, sanctioned by the wisdom of experience, about maintaining the color bar. What might have been a device to extend the point of view, to provide additional insight toward the events of the novel, turns instead, because of the interest in fixing Tony, into the dullness of another case history. Historical accuracy, in this novel, cuts off a possible dimension of human perception.

Frequently, Miss Lessing's journalistic essays do not deal with specific characters but rather furnish sociological descriptions of what it was like to be in a specific place at a specific time. The Martha Quest series is full of such descriptions: the African legal office in the thirties; the change in the colonials' club at the beginning of World War II; the coming of British airmen to African bases, and the difference this creates in the town; the Communists' trying to sell their paper in the native quarter: the predictable seediness and irrelevance of the Left Book Club's meeting. A few of the short stories are entirely dependent upon this kind of sociological description. "The Eye of God in Paradise" (a story in *The Habit of Loving*) is an illustration, seen from the point of view of a pair of British doctors, of the various forms and echoes of Nazism still evident in Germany in 1951. Some of the sociological essays in *Going Home*, like the one defending the character of the Afrikander or the one pointing out that the Union of South Africa is no more discriminatory and at least more honest than is the British government of Southern Rhodesia, are both intelligent and unconventional. But essays are one thing and fiction is another. Too often Miss Lessing's fiction is dissolved in a long sociological or journalistic insertion, like the accounts of communistic tactics and wrangles in *A Ripple from the Storm* or the long, dull, clinical study of discovering that one is pregnant which takes up about seventy pages of *A Proper Marriage*. Her politics are one-sided, her characters are limited in conception, and her world revolves in a simple pattern.

The same flaw is evident in the first novel of another young author. Margot Heinemann, in *The Adventurers* (1960), carefully documents a good deal of history concerning the Welsh miners after World War II. Much of the sociological description carries enormous interest, but the characters become simply sociological representations: the young miner's son who rises as a journalist and betrays his old tribal loyalties; the young miner, for whom force of character takes the place of education, who remains loyal to his fellows; the upper-class sympathizers who stick to a Communist ideal that is no longer relevant to conditions among the working class. All these characters are completely determined by the forces that have molded them, completely predictable once the background has been established. Then, the course set, the novel simply reports, with journalistic accuracy, what the conference or the strike or the industrial campaign was like. Miss Heinemann's novel, like some of Miss Lessing's, is not only rooted in the social scene but becomes, completely and merely, the reflection of that scene.

Doris Lessing's intense feeling of political and social responsibility is carefully worked into specific historical situations. But the positive convictions can become heavy-handed, and the specific situations journalistic, while the strict allegiance to time and place can limit the range of perception about human beings. Miss Lessing's kind of intensity is simultaneously her greatest distinction and her principal defect. She produces an enormously lucid sociological journalism, honest and committed, but in much of her work she lacks a multiple awareness, a sense of comedy, a perception that parts of human experience cannot be categorized or precisely located, a human and intellectual depth. Intense commitment can cut off a whole dimension of human experience.

DOROTHY BREWSTER

The Golden Notebook

EACH HIS OWN WILDERNESS

In *Each His Own Wilderness,* produced at the Royal Court Theatre in 1958, there are interesting foreshadowings of characters and situations in *The Golden Notebook,* and of the feminist theme of "free women." Two middle-aged women, Myra and Milly, widowed or divorced, each have a son whom she has brought up, Tony and Sandy, respectively. The two women, politically and socially conscious, veteran fighters in many good causes, were described in a review of the play in the *Spectator* (March 28, 1958) as "oddly endearing amalgams" of Beatrice Webb and Molly Bloom. There is a sharp rift between the mothers and the sons. The boys and girls of twenty or so in the decade of the 1950s are totally uninterested in politics, causes, demonstrations, and casual love affairs; security is what they want, and orderliness. The mothers are so anxious not to be possessive that they refuse to guide their sons. In act 2, Milly having just returned from a trip to Japan with a delegation of women, they discuss their sons. Myra had sent Tony to a progressive school, hoping it would turn him into an integrated personality, whereas Milly had sent Sandy to a public school, with the result that he has beautiful manners and never does anything that is not calculated—he even falls in love where it does him most good. She rather expected him to drop her after completing his expensive education, but he opted to stay with her. Why? One day she heard him say to one of his "posh" friends, "You must

From *Doris Lessing.* © 1965 by Twayne Publishers, Inc.

meet my mother, she's such a character." She obligingly played the role of a woman of the people with a heart of gold: "I'll be an asset to him in the Labour Party." Tony has long arguments with his mother; when he listens to conversations between his mother and the older men, he comments aside for the benefit of young Rosemary: "One half of this lot are bogged down emotionally in the thirties with the Spanish Civil War, and the other half came to a sticky end with Hungary."

At another point in the play Tony remarks to his mother: "I've spent a good part of what are known as my formative years listening to the conversation of the mature. . . . You're corrupt. You're sloppy and corrupt. I'm waiting for that moment when you put your foot down about something and say you've had enough. But you never do. All you do is watch things—with interest." Tony's notion of the vision his mother and her lot have created gives the play its title:

> A house for every family . . . to every family a front door. . . . A house full of clean, well-fed people, and not one of them ever understands one word anyone else says. Everybody a kind of wilderness surrounded by barbed wire shouting across the defences into the other wildernesses and never getting an answer back. That's socialism. I suppose it's progress. . . . To every man his front door and his front door key. To each his own wilderness.

Tony, for all his cynicism about politics and causes, is a little Hamlet; he is emotionally upset by his mother's love affairs; he has grown up accustomed to "uncles." He clings to the house she owns—where all the happenings of the play take place—as a symbol of security; when he learns that she has sold it in order to have money to promote his career in anything he wants to do, he becomes hysterical. All he had wanted was to be with her in that house and to live with some sort of dignity; he was so tired of "all the brave speeches and the epic battles and the gestures." And his mother, bewildered, proclaims her own life a failure, since she had spent most of it bringing him up; but at least she had not been afraid to take chances and make mistakes. "The irony of it—that *we* should have given birth to a generation of little office boys and clerks and . . . little people who count their pensions before they're out of school." And off she goes—rather like Nora of *A Doll's House*—leaving young Rosemary wondering, "What's the matter with being safe—and ordinary?" and Tony saying, "Leave us alone to live."

When we meet Tommy in *The Golden Notebook*, we remember Tony. The son-mother relationship is explored on a deeper level, and the son finds a strange but convincing way out of his psychological impasse. To understand

Tommy, it is not necessary to have met Tony in Doris Lessing's world, but it helps.

FREE WOMEN AND MOTHERS

A generation ago, Virginia Woolf, writing her feminist book, *A Room of One's Own,* was agreeably surprised to find among the first words of a new novel written by a woman that Chloe liked Olivia: "Sometimes women do like women." Chloe and Olivia share a laboratory as well as domestic interests. Doris Lessing's pairs—the two in the play and Molly and Anna in the novel—share politics and causes as well as domestic interests and the problems of motherhood. They are often together without any men around. "When women are alone," wrote Virginia Woolf, "unlit by the capricious and coloured light of the other sex," what are their gestures, their half-said words? And she noted how long accustomed women have been to concealment and suppression when they thought themselves observed. Looking back at the relationships between women in the English novel, she found them all too simple, with too much left out; women were shown almost always in relation to men. There is, continued Mrs. Woolf, a spot the size of a shilling in the back of the head, so they say, which no one can see for himself, and men for ages have pointed out to women that dark place at the back of their heads. A true picture of man as a whole cannot be painted until a woman has described to men that spot in the back of men's heads. Did Virginia Woolf do it perhaps in Mr. Ramsay—or Orlando? Has Doris Lessing done it with what some male reviewers consider her men victims in *The Golden Notebook?*

Developing her feminist theme, Mrs. Woolf recalled how women have sat indoors in many societies for millions of years, and how those rooms must have been permeated by woman's creative force. Doris Lessing's marked interest in rooms is not just the novelist's usual concern with background. An astonishing number of rooms in her world come to mind: that fascinating room of her childhood; the big living room in "Winter in July," with the African night outside; the cramped, shabby, suffocating little bedroom in *The Grass Is Singing* where Mary Turner slowly decays; the blitzed but cosy basement which Rose in "The Other Woman" hated to leave; Room Nineteen, where Susan drifts off down the dark river of her suicide; the swaying tower room of "Dialogue"; the spacious workroom where Anna's four notebooks—black, blue, red, and yellow—are spread out upon the long trestle table; and many others. In any search for symbolic meanings, here is a field for exploration.

The Golden Notebook opens with a conversation between Anna and Molly in the summer of 1957, after a separation. A review compared this opening with that of D. H. Lawrence's *Women in Love,* which is a dialogue between Ursula and Gudrun. Lawrence, a rash man, was not afraid to set two young women talking together, unobserved. Doris Lessing's two women are close upon forty, and they are articulate upon all sorts of matters in a way that would have enraged Lawrence. Besides this opening conversation, there are three other brief sections of dialogue between them, each preceding extracts from the four notebooks, and a concluding conversation—five in all. It would not be amiss to put up a notice, "Danger! Free Women talking!"—like the warning at street excavations, "Danger! Men working!" For what these two experienced women say is often explosive.

"The two women were alone in the London flat." It is a sunny spring day, the windows are open, and men are delivering milk and selling fresh strawberries from the country in the street. Tommy, Molly's son, is in his room upstairs. It is a cheerful opening scene, but two reasons for uneasiness soon appear: Tommy is a problem, and Anna, with a successful first novel promising a literary career, seems unable to write. They eat strawberries and cream and drink wine in the sunlight, and catch up on what has happened to them during the year of separation. Richard, Molly's ex-husband and the father of Tommy, comes in and they discuss Tommy, who presently joins them. Richard is now married to Marion. It is a very cleverly constructed scene, with casually scattered clues to past events and future developments. As they remember and reflect upon their lives and opinions, the two women find many things rather odd. Molly is particularly sensitive to the oddity of things. At the end of the book, when Molly and Anna are looking at the roads ahead of them, it is Molly who says, "It's all very odd, isn't it, Anna?" And so it is, but continuously interesting, this story of "free women."

What, in the third quarter of the twentieth century, are the advantages, the opportunities, and the handicaps of women determined to be free? In 1929 Virginia Woolf specified a room of one's own and five hundred pounds a year for a woman writer. Wherever the income came from, it was to keep coming in without effort on the recipient's part. Anna has earned her income in the past; it derives from the royalties of her successful first novel; so, for a time at least, she can work at what she pleases, regardless of pay. Logically, it should be at another novel, but she has a "writer's block." As long as she is a member of the Party, she does volunteer work in the main office, reads the manuscripts submitted, and so on. When she leaves the Party, she is busy with her notebooks and with personal relationships that need a lot of attention. The sessions with her psychoanalyst alone must have taken up many hours. Molly, an artist in the theater, plays minor comedy parts. Her son, being grown, does not require the attention needed by Anna's little daughter. She has a house in London, in which Anna and Janet live until Anna takes a house of her own not far away, renting out a room when she can find a suitable tenant. One tenant, Ronnie, who figures in a vivid little episode with his homosexual friend, is very undesirable.

Other women in the novel include wives (there have to be wives so that there can be husbands to stray from home); a woman editor of a woman's magazine, a woman talent scout for the cinema, a woman worker in the Party office; but there are no women doctors or lawyers or teachers or members of Parliament. Since Virginia Woolf wrote *Three Guineas,* complaining of the narrow field for women's activity, women in the professions have greatly increased in numbers in England. The people Anna meets at parties or at work include interesting exiles from the Continent, an African or two, Americans in England for business or professional reasons, and American exiles—an export from the United States, thanks to the investigating activities of Congressional committees. The experiences Anna has with several of them lead her to generalizations about American men on this rather narrow personal basis. By having Anna working on a novel with a heroine named Ella, Mrs. Lessing introduces Ella's father, a retired army officer; Ella's lover Paul, a doctor; and several other characters. And by having Anna, though born and brought up in London, spend some of the war years in Southern Rhodesia, she can add Africa to the background, and Royal Air Force trainees and others to the cast.

Now what is it like to be "free and responsible, a woman in relation to men and other women, and to struggle to come to terms with one's self about these things and about writing and politics"—to quote from a *New Statesman* review of April 20, 1962? As for men, Molly and Anna "remain interested in men with a curiosity that is almost archaeological; as if there were so few good ones left that it is necessary to hunt for them amid the ruins," as Irving Howe writes. Mr. Howe's comment is supported by one of Anna's observations: "I am always amazed in myself and in other women at the strength of our need to bolster men up. . . . Women have this instinctive need to build a man up as a man. . . . I suppose this is because real men become fewer and fewer." At this point Anna is looking back on her life, realizing that a period of years shapes itself into a certain kind of being that can be rolled up and tucked away, or "named"; and being still within that period, one can foresee that, when it is over, one will glance back and say, "Yes, that is what I was." And the following quotation describes what Anna thinks she was at a moment of awareness that a new period was beginning which she must live through: "I was a woman terribly vulnerable, critical, using femaleness as a sort of standard or yardstick to measure and discard men. . . . I was an Anna who invited defeat from men without even being conscious of it. . . . I was stuck fast in an emotion common to women of our time, that can turn them bitter, or Lesbian, or solitary." This estimate of herself is no mere statement; her love affairs are acted out. But perhaps the most thought-provoking reflection about "free" women is simply this: "What's the use of us being free, if they [men] are not?"

Both Molly and Anna are responsible mothers. Molly's son Tommy is a problem, and his story develops within a complicated web of influences and counterinfluences, involving his mother; Anna; his father, Richard, important in the world of Big Business; and his father's second wife, Marion, whose friendship with Tommy brings about a very odd but credible solution for both his problem and hers. What happens to the children of "free" women? Tommy is one of the answers. His attempt at suicide leaves him blinded, and the blindness blocks off some of his troublesome complexes, leaving him a fragment of what he had the potentiality of being—but a self-consistent fragment. Fragmentation of the personality is a problem of our time along with alienation and loss of identity. Molly finds it very odd when her blind son becomes friendly with his father's second wife and they virtually take over Molly's flat: "My husband's second wife moving into my house because she can't live without my son. . . . I was sitting upstairs quiet as a mouse, so as not to disturb Marion and Tommy and thinking I'd simply pack a bag and wander off somewhere and leave them to it, and I thought that the generation after us are going to take one look at us, and get married at eighteen, forbid divorces, and go in for strict moral codes and all that, because otherwise the chaos is just too terrifying."

Anna's daughter is an anchor rather than a problem, and Anna is held back from going to pieces as long as she has to shape Janet's day from early morning to night into a healthy routine. It comes as a shock to the "free" woman that Janet, at thirteen, wants to go to the most conventional of boarding schools, wear an ugly uniform, walk in a "crocodile," and live the life depicted in vapid books about girls' schools. She seems destined by nature for an unproblematical life, this child of a mother who had no time for people "who haven't experimented with themselves, deliberately tried the frontiers." But Anna yields, and, when Janet goes, an Anna begins to come to life "who died when Janet was born."

ARTIST'S SENSIBILITY

Anna's problem, her writing block, leads her obviously enough to a psychoanalyst. Of this interesting woman doctor, whom Anna and Molly call

Mother Sugar, Mrs. Lessing draws a fascinating portrait. The sessions with her expose both private and public neuroses. Or, to quote Irving Howe again, Doris Lessing "grasps the connection between Anna Wulf's neuroses and the public disorders of the day." The connection is too much for Anna, and the novel is about how she cannot write a novel. On the last pages of *Remembrance of Things Past*, Proust's narrator begins to write the novel Proust has already written. Towards the end of *The Golden Notebook*, Anna's departing lover gives her the first sentence of the novel Doris Lessing has already written: "The two women were alone in the London flat." André Gide's alter ego, the novelist Edouard in *The Counterfeiters*, is living through his experiences and turning them into a novel at the same time. What is the relation between fiction and life? In the old days, as Sir Philip Sidney put it, the storyteller came with a tale that kept children from play and old men from the chimney corner. Now he comes with *Finnegans Wake*. In an interview published in *The Queen*, Mrs. Lessing says: "If a writer writes a book like *Tom Jones*, and says 'Look at this young man,' it is quite a different thing from when, let us say, Jack Kerouac writes *On the Road*. He is saying, 'This is my sensibility, and it's what I believe in.'"

Mrs. Lessing had other things to say in this interview. It is always worth while to listen to a writer's explanation of what he is trying to do, compare it with what he did, and perhaps discover that he did something else that even he himself did not know he was doing. Like many other novelists today, Mrs. Lessing has felt that the formal novel was not doing its job any more. So why not write the short formal novel and also put in the experience it came out of, and escape from that feeling writers have when they have finished a nice, tidy little book: "My God, that novel is supposed to be summing up all this!" Therefore, put in the short formal novel and *all this*. "I also split up the rest into four parts to express a split person. I felt that if the artist's sensibility is to be equated with the sensibility of the educated person, then it is logical to use different styles to express different kinds of people." The particular form she chose enabled her to say things about time, memory, and the human personality—"because personality is very much what is remembered; also it enabled me to say to the reader: Look, these apparently so different people have got so-and-so in common, or these things have got this in common. If I had used a conventional style, the old-fashioned novel, which I do not think is dead by any means ... I would not have been able to do this kind of playing with time, memory and the balancing of people."

Doris Lessing, who has proved in many stories and novels that she can come to us quite simply with a tale, had reached the point when she was not satisfied with that. But embedded in the structure of *The Golden Notebook* are two tales equal to her best. Isn't it a little odd to remember that in the tradition of the English novel—a tradition which she says, in that interview, she is outside of—tales were introduced by Fielding and by Dickens in the most cheerfully obvious manner. If one has the storytelling gift, one will get the story in somehow. In the notebook with the black cover, Anna reviews experiences of her African years, and it is in these sections that two beautifully written episodes occur that could find a place in *African Stories*. I shall come back to them later.

The artist's sensibility as a mirror for our time has been explored by Proust, Joyce, Lawrence, Mann—the list is Mrs. Lessing's—and she calls this exploration one of the mainstreams of the modern novel. And to her Mann is the greatest. "If one were going to write after Thomas Mann who has said everything that can be said about the artist practising, what next? Mann's whole message was that art is rooted in corruption—in illness, above all." Mrs. Lessing thinks, however, that art is rooted in an overwhelming arrogance and egotism: "There is a kind of cold detachment at the core of any writer or artist." The artist has to be ruthless. But suppose he has a conscience about artistic creation? Tolstoy had, of course, because he came to the conclusion—at least as old as Plato—that artists are liars. But suppose one's conscience is concerned with being a good human being—what then? This viewpoint has crept into the socialist and communist attitudes to artists: "They say straight out or by implication that the writer has to serve society." A writer might be blocked by this kind of reasoning: "It's bad to spend my time writing books because I ought to be doing something about the state of the peasants somewhere. It's immoral to write when people are suffering." Such a writer could easily develop beautiful rationalizations for not writing. How far away seems the time when a Dickens had no doubt that he could tell his tales and at the same time expose the wrongs of society!

In the interview from which we have been quoting, Mrs. Lessing told about a woman she had known who wrote one highly successful novel and then could not go on, for reasons suggested by the above analysis. Asked how much society really entered into it, Mrs. Lessing replied, "I don't know. I merely used the writer's block to say something about a certain way of looking at the world." And, asked to sum up *The Golden Notebook* in a few sentences, she answered: "It is a novel about certain political and sexual attitudes that have force now; it is an attempt to explain them, to objectivize them, to set them in relation with each other. So in a way it is a social novel, written by someone whose training—or at least whose habit of mind—is to see these things socially, not personally."

Doris Lessing, with an impressive list of books to her credit, is not suffering from a writer's block. So she cannot be identified with Anna Wulf, except in so far as Anna's creator, with her insight into many of Anna's emotions and attitudes, can imagine a writer being blocked by them. Are they her own emotions and attitudes? This is a tricky question for critics, and Mrs. Lessing expressed irritation with a review in the *Times Literary Supplement* which equated Martha Quest with Doris Lessing, and then compared Martha Quest with Anna Wulf, presenting the two women as combinations of the author and her characters. But it isn't surprising for a reader or even a critic to become perplexed about the character-creating process. Three leading characters in *War and Peace* were imaginatively projected out of the rich many-sided personality of Tolstoy—Andrey, Pierre, and Nicholas. Each resembles Tolstoy in certain basic characteristics and experiences, but this obviously did not bother Tolstoy. But suppose that Nicholas Rostov, created by Tolstoy as Anna was created by Doris Lessing, decides to write a novel about Ivan X. And this Ivan begins by resembling Nicholas, but then takes on a different identity; and Nicholas becomes self-conscious about what is going on in himself. Doris Lessing launches Anna Wulf into *The Golden Notebook*, and Anna decides to write a novel about Ella. "I see Ella, walking slowly about a big empty room, thinking, waiting. I, Anna, see Ella. Who is of course, Anna. But that is the point, for she is not. The moment I, Anna, write: Ella rings up Julia to announce, etc., then Ella floats away from me and becomes someone else. I don't understand what happens at the moment Ella separates herself from me and becomes Ella." Well, who does?

One of the truths about Anna at this stage is that she is going to pieces. It is the author's intention that she should go to pieces, but not to the point of suicide—only to the point of devastating self-knowledge. Anna's preoccupation with social problems comes from the kind of education (in the Western world), vaguely humanistic, in which it is assumed that "everything is for the best, justice will prevail, that human beings are equal, that if we try hard enough, society is going to become perfect, that people are fundamentally good. These are attitudes that seem increasingly absurd in the world as it is now." The absurdity may become, however, more than one can stand. Mrs. Lessing seems to believe that these humanistic attitudes, good in themselves, can swing over into their opposite and become profoundly destructive. Anna becomes split by the conflict within her; the split is symbolized by the four notebooks—the African memories, the experience with Communism, the diary, and the short novel. The possible fusing together of the fragmented parts in a new whole is symbolized by the golden notebook, which, oddly enough, Anna gives to her last or latest lover, who is even more divided within himself than she is. One of the briefly summarized story ideas in the novel outlines this situation: "Same theme as Chekhov's *The Darling*. But this time the woman doesn't change to suit different men, one after another; she changes in response to one man who is a psychological chameleon, so that in the course of a day she can be half a dozen different personalities, either in opposition to, or in harmony with him."

In the last of the yellow notebook entries, of which the first three have been devoted to the novel about Ella, Ella has disappeared, and, instead of a coherent narrative, there are nineteen fragments of possible stories, of which the above quotation is one. Then follows Anna's diary in the blue notebook, recording among other things the course of her affair with an American, Saul Green. This affair seems to contain in embryo many of the stories. Just why Mrs. Lessing puts the story ideas first and then follows with the experience out of which they might have come, isn't clear, but the sequence convinces the reader that Anna's confusion is pretty serious. Dates, in other parts of the book carefully noted, are omitted. Saul Green has no sense of time when he is in some of his chameleon phases, and Anna appears to have joined him. A group of paragraphs, numbered 1 through 18, each headed with the phrase "a short story" or "a short novel," appears in the yellow notebook. It is as if Anna had read through it, seeing eighteen possible stories. Or did she jot down the story ideas first, and then have the stages of the affair to order? She may know how to transform fiction into life. She does dream to order while undergoing psychoanalysis. These dreams are remarkable. Some of them recall the nightmares of destruction recorded in *Going Home*. They are also developing dreams in sequence, as in that delightful story, "Two Potters." In one of the latest, when Anna is nearest to a complete breakdown, a tiger appears, quite a memorable beast. He turns up during the disastrous love affair with Saul Green, and the tiger image is used again in Mrs. Lessing's drama, *Play with a Tiger*. There is nice hunting here for the explicators of symbols.

NIGHTMARES AND OBSESSIONS

What are some of Anna's nightmares and obsessions? Several of them are also Martha Quest's. Martha was haunted by the specter of repetition, of being part of a cycle, of being her mother over again, and of repeating the experience of generation after generation. That specter takes shape after she is married and feels trapped. Much earlier, when a young girl, she experienced a timeless moment of complete depersonalization. She was walking home at sunset from an errand at the station, a white girl alone on the veld, an unusual experience in itself. The natural beauty around her induced a mood of ecstatic union with nature, for which she was prepared by her absorbed reading of English poetry. "The bush lay quiet about her, a bare slope of sunset-tinted grass moved gently with a tiny rustling sound. . . . She stood quite still, waiting for the moment, which was now inevitable. There was a movement at the corner of her eye," and a small buck came out from the trees and stood quietly flicking its tail a few paces away. "The buck gazed at her; and then turned its head to look into the bush, laying its ears forward. A second buck tripped out from the trees, and they both stood watching her; then they walked daintily across the ground, their hooves clicking sharp on the stones, the sun warm on their soft brown hides. They dropped their heads to graze, while their little tails shook from side to side impatiently, with flashes of light." The feeling in Martha deepened: "There was a slow integration during which she, and the little animals, and the moving grasses, and the sun-warmed trees, and the slopes of shivering, silvery mealies, and the great dome of blue light overhead, and the stones of earth under her feet, became one, shuddering together in a dissolution of dancing atoms." During a brief space of time—"which was timeless"—she understood quite finally "her smallness, the unimportance of humanity. In her ears was an inchoate grinding, the great wheels of movement, and it was inhuman, like the blundering rocking movement of a bullock cart." What it meant continued to perplex her in memory (*Children of Violence*).

In one of Anna Wulf's sessions with Mother Sugar, Anna, rejecting the remedy for pain that consists in putting it away where it cannot hurt by turning it into a story or into history, declares herself convinced that there are whole areas of herself made by the kind of experience women have not had before. Mother Sugar smiles. "Never?" And behind her voice Anna hears the sounds always evoked at such moments—"seas lapping on old beaches, voices of people centuries dead." Mother Sugar insists that the details change but the form is the same; she calls up the artist-women, the independent women of the past who insisted on sexual freedom, a line stretching back into history. But Anna argues that they did not look at themselves as she does or feel as she does.

> I don't want to be told when I wake up terrified by a dream of total annihilation, because of the H-bomb exploding, that people felt that way about the cross-bow. It isn't true. There is something new in the world. . . . I don't want to be told when I suddenly have a vision . . . of a life that isn't full of hatred and fear and envy and competition every minute of the night and the day that this is simply the old dream of the golden age brought up to date. . . . The dream of the golden age is a million times more powerful

because it's possible, just as total destruction is possible. Probably *because* both are possible. . . . I want to be able to separate in myself what is old and cyclic, the recurring history, the myth, from what is new, what I feel or think that might be new.

If she meets a man who is cracked, split across, it might mean, Anna thinks, that he is keeping himself open for something. She is not satisfied, as she accuses Mother Sugar of being, if she recognizes in a dream this or that myth or folk tale and has thus gone beyond the childish, transmuted it, and saved it by embodying it in a myth. She is not satisfied to fish among her childish memories and to merge them with the art or ideas that belong to the childhood of a people. In this process "the individual recognizes one part after another of his earlier life as an aspect of general human experience." But does he become free when he can say that what he did or felt is "only a reflection of that great archetypal dream, or epic story, or stage in history?" He has separated himself from the experience, or fitted it like a piece of mosaic into a very old pattern. Is he then free of the individual pain of it? Anna is not convinced.

Anna's obsession with repetition plays a part in her decision to leave the Communist party. Toward the end of her five-year affair with Michael, she tries to assess the quality of her life by writing down as truthfully as she can every detail of one day, say the 17th of September, 1954—a literary project that has tempted many since Joyce wrote *Ulysses* and Virginia Woolf, *Mrs. Dalloway.* She notes physical details with the power to shock—again reminiscent of Joyce. Then she realizes that we deal with physical aspects of living quite without conscious thinking, almost as we breathe; but start writing them down, and the balance between truth and fact is shifted. She spends the day at the office of the Party, in informal and formal conferences, talking freely with several of the workers, old and young, whom she knows best, realizing that some of this talk would be accounted treasonable in a Communist state; yet realizing, too, that, when she leaves the Party, she will miss "the company of people who have spent their lives in a certain kind of atmosphere, where it is taken for granted that their lives must be related to a central philosophy."

She has understood that the Communist party, like any other organization, "continues to exist by a process of absorbing its critics into itself. It either absorbs them or destroys them." But on this day she sees the process rather differently. There is the group of hardened, fossilized men, that is opposed by fresh young revolutionaries; they form between them a balanced whole until the young in their turn become the hardened and the fossilized, and a group of fresh, lively-minded, critical people send forth shoots of new life. But the old and sapless are kept in existence for some time. No right, no wrong, "a process, a wheel turning." And though everything in Anna cries out against such a view of life, it has the power to throw her back into a political-terrorist nightmare, which she relates with spine-chilling clarity and which owes much to the actual memories of her lover Michael—memories of relatives murdered in gas chambers, of close friends, Communists, who were murdered by Communists.

One of the duties of this day in the Party office is to decide whether or not to publish some manuscripts, politically correct but artistically bad, as the committee well knows; but they are "healthy" art. Anna is aware of her inconsistency in rejecting her own fiction as unhealthy and also rejecting "healthy" art when she sees it. Here is another block. But Anna is not blocked when she indulges herself in the writing of parodies or *pastiche* of the healthy Communist story, of the African story (*Blood on the Banana Leaves*), or of the avant-garde stories in American little magazines. She gives up in sheer disgust because what is actually published is itself parody. At a later stage of her breakdown, she forces herself to contemplate the horrors and absurdities and ironies of current history by tacking up on the walls of the room where her notebooks are spread out on the long trestle table newspaper headlines and clippings about the world's hideous disorders. This is a very effective device for inducing hysteria—one not to be recommended.

THE FILM SEQUENCE

In the section entitled "The Golden Notebook," almost at the end of the novel, Anna, looking back over her life, sees it in film sequences run off by a projectionist, and names each as it appears: the Mashopi film; the film about Paul and Ella; the film about Michael and Anna; that about Ella and Julia; that about Anna and Molly—all directed by Anna Wulf. And Anna is faced by the burden of recreating order out of the chaos her life has become. "Time had gone, and my memory did not exist, and I was unable to distinguish between what I had invented and what I had known, and I knew that what I had invented was all false. It was a whirl, an orderless dance, like the dance of the white butterflies in a shimmer of heat, over the damp sandy vlei."

The Mashopi film belongs to the period during the war when Anna Wulf spent the years 1939–45 in Salisbury, Southern Rhodesia. One wonders how Anna, born in a house in Baker Street, London, came to be in Salisbury, where she had married and divorced Max Wulf, a shadowy figure. In the

Mashopi episodes, Anna is Willi Rodde's girl, and Willi is a Communist refugee from Hitler's Germany. It is always a pleasure to have Doris Lessing back in Africa; and if she wishes to put Anna Wulf there, though Anna, unlike Martha Quest, did not grow up there, that is fine. The result is the Mashopi film, unrolled in two sections of the black notebook, and some of her most brilliant writing.

Recalling her African experiences, Anna writes: "In our own small town a year after Russia entered the war, there had come into existence a small orchestra, readers' circles, two dramatic groups, a film society, an amateur survey of the conditions of urban African children, and half a dozen discussion groups on African problems." For the first time the town enjoyed something like a cultural life, shared by hundreds who knew Communists only as people to hate. The little group of Communists, though they had inspired these activities, often paradoxically disapproved of them, but "a dedicated faith in humanity spreads ripples in all directions." People who do not even know it have been inspired or given a new push into life because of the Communist party. The tiny group in the colonial capital had no links at all with such African movements as there were, but operated in a vacuum, so that its debates and conflicts were internal; and within a year the group was split, equipped with splinter groups, with traitors, and with a loyal hard core that kept changing, except for one or two at the very center.

Several members of the group go for weekends to a country hotel about sixty miles from the town, at a small station called Mashopi: Willi Rodde, authority on Marxism; Anna Wulf; the beautiful Maryrose from a Cape family; and three young Englishmen in training at the Royal Air Force base. Paul and Jimmy are both from Oxford and Ted is from the London working class. Paul has great charm but a hidden arrogance that often leads him to malicious mockery of unsuspecting people; his is a class arrogance. Willi is equally arrogant in his intellectual certainties, and the two are antagonistic, but attracted to each other and very much alike. Jimmy, a homosexual, is hopelessly devoted to Paul, who does not respond except with irritation. To Maryrose, her brother, recently killed, had been a little more than kin. Ted Brown, a genuine Socialist, is always rescuing some promising young man from darkness. Paul is in love with Anna, and everybody is in love with Maryrose, who is friendly to them but can love no one but the lost brother. "We were all at various times in love with each other," as Paul said; it was obligatory in the times they lived in to be in love with as many people as possible. Anna tries to remember just what each was like. She draws up parallel columns of contradictory traits in Willi's character, but falls back on the fact that we remember someone we have known by a trick of gesture, a

smile, a look, that seems to hold the essence of his personality. Personality
is a unique flame. Anna would agree with D. H. Lawrence, who once wrote:
"I conceive of a man's body as a kind of flame, like a small candle flame,
forever upright and yet flowing."

The group quarreled on these weekends over Communist tactics. They
considered "black nationalism" a right-wing deviation, and only once, as
Anna recalls, did they come anywhere near the truth, and "that was when
Paul spoke in a spirit of angry parody," foretelling developments not unlike
those in Kenya a decade later. "All this while the ox-wagons rolled by in the
white dust of the sand-veld, the trains rocked by on the way from the Indian
Ocean to the capital, while the farmers drank in their khaki in the bar, and
groups of Africans, in search of work, hung around under the jacaranda tree,
hour after hour."

The hotel was right in the bush, complete with kopjes and natives, but
also with an English bar, dart boards, steak and kidney pie, and the Boothbys
to run it—Mrs. Boothby an ex-barmaid, and Mr. Boothby an ex-sergeant-
major. The servants were of course natives, and the cook occupied a privileged position, being allowed to live on the grounds with his family. A
frequent visitor was an older man, George Hounslow, an inspector of the
railroad, who had for his mistress the cook's wife and whose conscience was
oddly disturbed by his half-caste baby. Trouble grew out of this situation
and out of Paul's making friends with the cook; that sort of thing just wasn't
done, and it worried Mrs. Boothby, who liked Paul. The cook was as puzzled
as Mrs. Boothby. But, with the colony full of air force men from outside,
many Africans had become aware that a white man could treat a black man
as a human being. A moving part of the story is the unhappy outcome for
the cook and his family.

Other visitors to the hotel were the local farmers and trainees of the
nonintellectual variety, such as Johnny, a gifted jazz pianist, and Stanley, who
kept him supplied with cigarettes and beers so that he would not stop playing. Mrs. Lattimer, middle-aged but beautiful and promiscuous, attracted
Stanley; her husband took it out on her when he was drunk. There were
dances and festivals, several love affairs got under way, and one of them
ended in disaster, as Anna remembers; but actually what was painful about
that time was that nothing was really disastrous. "It was all wrong, ugly,
unhappy and coloured with cynicism, but nothing was tragic, there were no
moments that could change anything or anybody. From time to time the
emotional lightning flashed and showed a landscape of private misery and
then—we went on dancing." All this time her own group organized meetings, discussions, and debates; read and argued; cured souls and helped

people; and they earned their livings. The men being trained were under continuous nervous strain, and they all lived at this pitch for over two years, becoming slightly mad out of sheer exhaustion.

These memories of Mashopi occur in the pattern of the novel, the pattern Mrs. Lessing chose (as quoted above) because she wanted to say things about time, memory, and personality that did not fit into the neat structure of the well-made novel. The memories are not consecutive; the two main episodes are widely separated. Bits of them may turn up in dreams. The second episode comes back to her after she dreams of an incident on a London street when a man in a hurry kicked and killed a pigeon. Even in the dream she had struggled to recall what that had reminded her of. When she woke, she recaptured it in clear detail, and she was exasperated to realize—as we all do sometimes—that our brains contain so much that is locked up and unreachable until some trivial incident unlocks it. What she recaptured is a treasure of beauty and insight.

Because of the earlier recollections of the weekends at the hotel, we already know the characters in the little drama and the tensions that exist among them. Mrs. Boothby suggested one pleasant morning after a heavy rain that, if one of the boys could shoot, he could take Mr. Boothby's rifle, go to a spot not far from the hotel where pigeons were likely to congregate, and shoot enough of them for a pigeon pie. So Paul, who remarked in his bantering manner that his expensive education had not failed to include the niceties of grouse and pheasant murder, took the rifle; he collected Anna and Maryrose, Willi and Jimmy, and they set forth. Willi carried along *Stalin on the Colonial Question*. Because of the heavy rain the night before, there was now a festival of insects—a riot of white butterflies in the air, and on the grass and over the road millions of brightly colored grasshoppers.

They paused to watch the insects coupling: "the happy or well-mated insects stood all around us, one above the other, with their bright round idiotic black eyes staring." It was absurd, obscene, fascinating. Better to watch the butterflies, but they too were pursuing vile sex, as Paul remarked, not just celebrating the joy of life. Jimmy and Paul interfered with the grasshoppers, seeking with grass stems to persuade the ill-mated to regroup themselves into well-matched couples; the scientific approach, said Paul with satisfaction, admiring his rearrangement; but the insects soon changed back into their old positions. Jimmy saw no evidence that "in what we refer to as nature things are any better ordered than they are with us" and perhaps in this "riot of debauchery" males were with males, females with females. Paul, irritated, stepped on the couples he had organized. Anyway, all these insects would be dead by night. If they weren't, if they didn't kill each other and weren't eaten by birds, they would bury the hotel under a crawling mass, and swarms of butterflies would dance a victory dance over the deaths of Mr. and Mrs. Boothby and their daughter. This led to talk about the prodigality of nature and to analogies with human societies; when Paul said, "The point I was trying to make, comrades," Willi, the father-figure in the group, interrupted: "We know the point you are trying to make . . . let's go and get the pigeons."

Anna remembers them, five brightly colored young people, walking with the sun stinging their backs, in the grassy vlei, through "reeling white butterflies under a splendid blue sky." They settle down in a shady spot at the foot of a kopje, "a giant pile of pebbles," to await the coming of the pigeons. The kopje is "full of the earthworks and barricades built by the Mashona seventy, eighty years before as a defense against the raiding Matabele. It was also full of magnificent Bushmen paintings." Paul imagines a war scene as savage as the insect wars. A pigeon coos nearby; he shoots it down, and then remarks that "we need a dog to fetch it"—and Jimmy is the dog. Later Paul looks with distaste at a wounded pigeon and says, "Do you expect me to kill the thing in cold blood?" But this time Jimmy waits for Paul to prove himself; the pigeon obligingly dies first. The drama between Paul and Jimmy plays itself out along with the shooting of the pigeons and the battles between an anteater in the bottom of a sand pit and the victim ants and beetles. Meanwhile Willi reads steadily on, the corpses of the pigeons accumulate, and there is a smell of blood.

A file of natives, farm workers, passes on the track nearby, talking and laughing, but falling silent and averting their faces when they see the white group. And this introduces the colonial problem. Here in the little colonial society, on "this insignificant handful of sand on the beaches of time," a million and a half blacks and one hundred thousand whites exist to make one another miserable, when there is enough of everything, including talent, "to create light where darkness now exists." And why? Willi comes out with an answer so exactly what the others expect that they burst out laughing: "There is no need to look any further than the philosophy of the class struggle." They revert to the Mashona-Matabele days when men fought for land, women, food—for good reasons, not like us. "As a result," Paul predicts, "of fine comrades like Willi, ever ready to devote themselves to others, or people like me, concerned only with profits, I predict that in fifty years all this fine empty country we see stretching before us filled only with butterflies and grasshoppers will be covered by semi-detached houses filled by well-clothed black workers." Willi sees nothing the matter with that, and Jimmy, serious as ever, cannot see why the houses need to be semi-detached, for under Socialism. . . . The conversation is interrupted by a deadly fight between the anteater and a beetle, both disappearing under the sand, which heaves and eddies in "a suffocating silent battle." One of the group comments: "If we had ears that could hear, the air would be full of screams, groans, grunts, and gasps. But as it is, there reigns over the sun-bathed veld the silence of peace." They go back to the hotel with their bag of pigeons. "Our heads ached with the heat. We were slightly sick with the smell of blood."

In the brilliantly depicted African landscape and in an atmosphere heavy with the menace of war, the tensions—sexual, emotional, intellectual— among the three men and two women are dramatized in dialogue and action, stimulated by their half-reluctant and half-fascinated interest in the pigeon-shooting and in the life and death struggles of the insect world.

When Anna, living in a kind of nightmare, watched the film sequences of her life unroll themselves, she saw the Mashopi hotel explode in "a dancing whirling cloud of white petals or wings" of the butterflies which had chosen to alight on the building:

> It looked like a white flower opening slowly, under the deep steamy blue sky. Then a feeling of menace came into us, and we knew we had suffered a trick of sight, had been deluded. We were looking at the explosion of a hydrogen bomb, and a white flower unfolded under the blue sky in such perfection of puffs, folds and eddying shapes that we could not move, although we knew we were menaced by it. It was unbelievably beautiful, the shape of death; and we stood watching in silence, until the silence was slowly invaded by a rustling, crawling, grating sound, and looking down we saw the grasshoppers, their gross tumbling fecundity inches deep, all around us.

This pattern of images, repeated with variations, conveying both beauty and terror, helps to shape a novel that is complex, far-ranging, often difficult, fragmented like our society and our consciousness, challenging in its art and its ideas.

PAUL SCHLUETER

Self-Analytic Women:
The Golden Notebook

M rs. Lessing's protagonists, as intelligent, sensitive women in the midst of racial and political turmoil, necessarily find two areas, the racial and political, occupying much of their thought and activity, and as a corollary to this preoccupation, they become increasingly aware of their status in an essentially masculine world. While Martha Quest is not "emancipated" in the trite and stereotyped sense (i.e., so concerned with sexual equality that it becomes a morbid, dehumanizing obsession blocking out all other considerations), she does manifest such a degree of personal integrity that she cannot look passively on injustice and prejudice, just as her acuteness of perspective gives her a far more coherent method of evaluating the conflict between her own generation and that of her parents than is true of most adolescents and young adults. But Martha Quest, in some ways, seems an apprenticeship-effort for the creation of Anna Freeman Wulf, Mrs. Lessing's protagonist in *The Golden Notebook* and by far one of the most consciously self-critical and analytical women in modern fiction.

Unlike Martha, though, Anna senses the incoherence in her life to such a degree that she attempts to compartmentalize it, thus giving the reader individual glimpses of several distinct and unique sides to Anna's psyche. Anna's method in detailing her own gradual mental and psychological disintegration takes the form of four separate notebooks in which she systematically recounts the events and thoughts in four different time spans or

From *The Novels of Doris Lessing*. © 1969 by Paul George Schlueter, Jr., © 1973 by Southern Illinois University Press.

"moods" of her life: a black notebook (for the events in "black" Africa), a red notebook (for her time as a Communist), a yellow notebook (a fictionalized effort to see herself in perspective), and a blue notebook (primarily a factual diary-account of her life). These are in turn succeeded and superseded by another notebook, the golden one of the novel's title.

Thus while Anna, like her predecessors in Mrs. Lessing's fiction, finds racial and political concerns forcing a personal commitment, each is displaced by a successive commitment; only when the commitment that seems also to be Mrs. Lessing's is recognized and adopted—the commitment to individual artistic expression, such as through writing—does Anna achieve emotional and personal equilibrium. Thereafter she does not lose her concern for idealistic theory and practice, but she rechannels these drives into personally satisfying public forms; no longer, for instance, does she work surreptitiously and frustratingly for communism, but instead turns to more publicly acceptable political expression, to the British Labour party. And by turning from a private to a public use of language, she eliminates the incoherence in her personal emotional life.

Mrs. Lessing had suggested some of the same character types and emphases found in *The Golden Notebook* in a play produced at the Royal Court Theatre in 1958, *Each His Own Wilderness*. A brief examination of this play, I believe, can help lead to a greater understanding of the later novel. Two middle-aged women named Myra and Milly, both evidently divorced or widowed, work with high dedication in their particular social and political realms, but both experience difficulty in achieving harmonious relationships with their respective sons, who are alike in reflecting a malaise about life and an indifference toward the issues that concern their mothers so deeply. Not only is a conflict of generations present, but also a gulf that is never satisfactorily breached: the mothers, as fairly typical women of the 1950s, want their children to make up their own minds about life, while the sons long for a serene, settled way of life. Tony, Myra's son, for example, says to her,

> I've spent a good part of what are known as my formative years listening to the conversation of the mature. You set my teeth on edge. You're corrupt, you're sloppy and corrupt. I'm waiting for the moment when you put your foot down about something and say you've had enough. But you never do. All you do is watch things—with interest.

Another statement, the source of the play's title, concerns the generation of Tony's mother and the special kind of world it has created for his generation:

Do you know what you've created, you and your lot? What a vision it is! A house for every family. . . . A house full of clean, well-fed people, and not one of them ever understands one word anyone else says. Everybody a kind of wilderness surrounded by barbed wire shouting across the defences into the other wilderness and never getting an answer back. That's socialism. I suppose it's progress. Why not. . . . To every man his front door and his front door key. To each his own wilderness.

Much of the play concerns Tony's gradual estrangement from his mother, as he first discovers her sacrifice in aiding his education and Myra's ultimately leaving the house to her son, discouraged as she is at her sense of having wasted her life. For she has been promiscuous, she has, really, little to show (both in life and in her son) for her efforts, and she is far more dedicated as a human being than her son. Perhaps the trouble, in a word, is that she believes too much and he believes nothing.

In 1962, another play, *Play with a Tiger* (also written in 1958), was produced in the Comedy Theatre in London, and is somewhat more explicit in its relationship to *The Golden Notebook*. This play, whose title gives the novel one of its central symbolic motifs, again presents two people in an impassioned dialogue, an intellectual heroine and her younger American lover. The two are involved in the same kind of love-hate relationship Anna and Saul Green, the younger American writer with whom she for a time lives, have in *The Golden Notebook;* both are attracted to the other, but both realize the necessity of overcoming the other or of being overcome. While dramatically this play is no more satisfying than the other discussed, it does show an organic and thematic similarity to the novel itself, and serves as a kind of trying-out of some of the character relationships and incidents of the novel.

Even without relying too heavily upon these earlier plays as possible sources for *The Golden Notebook,* one can easily see affinities between Mrs. Lessing's own life and the characters and emphases of the novel. Instead, one complaint Mrs. Lessing has continually voiced since the novel's publication has been the tendency of reviewers and critics to confuse the fictional protagonist and the author herself. In an interview in the *Queen,* a British magazine, Mrs. Lessing said she was "appalled" at the "frivolity" and "amateurishness" of the reviews, since they were mostly interested in seeing an alleged Marxist or sexual orientation for the novel as a whole, or, worse, in seeing the book on the "gossip-column" level, with the author perfectly equated with the heroine. Indeed, as Mrs. Lessing said in another interview, some critics tried to turn the book into "The Confessions of Doris Lessing." And in a letter, Mrs. Lessing goes even further by saying that

> this autobiographical approach by critics is a very bad and indeed a very frivolous one. . . . Like every other writer, my novels are a mixture of straight (as far as anything can be) autobiography, and creation. . . . A young lady came to interview me from the Observor [sic] recently, and I said: Well at least they can't say Landlocked is autobiographical. Her reply was: But of course they say it is. "Why?" I ask. Because it is so convincing, she replies.
>
> I thought it was the job of a writer to make things convincing.
>
> This annoys me not because it is personally annoying, but because it means people don't read what I've written in the right way. The right way to read a novel is as if its [sic] a thing by itself, with its own laws, with due attention to its shape, not with reference back to possible autobiographical incidents.

One might go even further to say that The Golden Notebook, a book about a woman with a writer's block, could scarcely be the story of Mrs. Lessing herself, since she obviously has no writer's block. Hence one must consider the book not so much as an autobiographical or confessional novel, but more as a highly detailed examination of the forces which have gone into the complicated life of a real person who has some parallel characteristics with her fictional protagonist.

Mrs. Lessing has been keenly aware of the emphasis in twentieth-century literature on the artist's sensibility, and has singled out Thomas Mann as having devoted his entire life to an examination of this theme. But Mrs. Lessing says she has a "kind of hostility to the idea that an artist's sensibility should represent everyone," and that she wonders what, if anything, one could say about the theme after Mann's exhaustive examination. The "logical next step," she says, is that of a writer who cannot write. But this writer's block should result from "good intellectual reasons" such as political involvement; thus a development of such reasons, individually good as they are, would show how destructive they become when they lead to artistic inertia. In Anna Freeman Wulf, the protagonist of The Golden Notebook, Mrs. Lessing says, such a destructive emphasis causes the excessive "aggression, madness, cruelty, mixed up with love, kindness, and everything" that we find in the novel. "Not until the cruelty and aggression come out and are acknowledged," Mrs. Lessing adds, can Anna "start creating again." The writer's block itself, Mrs. Lessing says, is a way of saying something "about a certain way of looking at the world," a way which while not wholly Marxist is based in part on this political philosophy and such kinds of education as those assuming that "everything is of the best, justice will prevail, that human beings are equal, that if we try hard enough, society is going to become perfect, that people are fundamentally good." Thus *The Golden Notebook* is a novel about "certain political and sexual attitudes, that have force now; it is an attempt to explain them, to objectivise them, to set them in relation with each other. So in a way it is a social novel."

More integrally important than the immediate stimulus for this novel, though, is Mrs. Lessing's deep concern over form. She has said that its "meaning is in the shape," and that the particular shape was chosen because she "wanted to write a short formal novel which would enclose the rest in order to suggest what I think a great many writers feel about the formal novel; namely, that it's not doing its job any more. So I thought that the only way to do this would be to write the short formal novel and put in the experience it came out of, showing how ridiculous the formal novel is whan it can't say a damned thing. . . . So I put in the short formal novel and *all this*." Indeed, so insistent was Mrs. Lessing in setting this short novel (i.e., the passages labeled "Free Women" taken collectively) apart from the rest of the book that it is even set in a different typeface from the rest of the novel—"in a rather old-fashioned print, with rather flowery chapter headings, to suggest that this kind of novel is old-fashioned." Shape is, moreover, an integral part of the rest of the novel, since Mrs. Lessing says she "split up the rest into four parts to express a split person. I felt that if the artist's sensibility is to be equated with the sensibility of the educated person, then it is logical to use different styles to express different kinds of people. . . . Also this particular form enabled me to say things about time, about memory—which interests me very much; what we choose to remember—about the human personality because a personality is very much what is remembered. . . . If I had used a conventional style, the old-fashioned novel . . . I would not have been able to do this kind of playing with time, memory and the balancing of people." And elsewhere she has said that *The Golden Notebook* was a "very highly structured book, carefully planned. The point of that book was the relation of its parts to each other." Finally, Mrs. Lessing, for the original British edition of *The Golden Notebook,* made this statement (quoted from the book jacket):

About five years ago I found myself thinking about the novel most writers now are tempted to write at some time or another— about the problems of a writer, about the artistic sensibility. I saw no point in writing this again: it has been done too often; it has been one of the major themes of the novel in our time. Yet, having decided not to write it, I continued to think about it, and about the reasons why artists have to combat various kinds of narcissism. I found that if it were to be written at all, the subject should be, not a practising artist, but an artist with some kind of a block which prevented him or her from creating. In describing the reasons for the block, I would also be making the criticism I wanted to make about our society. I would be describing a disgust and self-division which afflicts people now, and not only artists.

Simultaneously I was working out another book, a book of literary criticism, which I would write not as a critic, but as practising writer, using various literary styles, in such a way that the shape of the book would provide the criticism. Since I hold that criticism of literature is a criticism and judgement of life, this book would say what I wanted to say about life; it would make, implicitly, a statement about what Marxists call alienation.

Thinking about these two books, I understood suddenly they were not two books but one; they were fusing together in my mind. I understood that the shape of this book should be enclosed and claustrophobic—so narcissistic that the subject matter must break through the form.

This novel, then, is an attempt to break a form; to break certain forms of consciousness and go beyond them.

Quoting Mrs. Lessing's statements of intention regarding *The Golden Notebook* at such length, then, ought to indicate the degree to which her accomplishment in the novel is deliberate and self-consciously one in which both form and content are necessarily closely linked—perhaps more so than in most novels of our or any time—and that the novel is considerably more than mere self-confessional.

A brief statement about the exact ordering of the materials in *The Golden Notebook* would not, perhaps, be wholly out of place here. All four of the major notebooks are written in the first person, and cover roughly the years from 1950 to 1957, with the fifth notebook (the golden one) describing only events during 1957, the year of its composition, and with Anna's one successful novel, *Frontiers of War,* having been published during or shortly after World War II. There are also five sections labeled "Free Women," written in the third person and, as we discover toward the end of the entire novel, purportedly written by Anna. These "Free Women" passages also describe events during the last year covered by the notebooks, 1957. The book opens with the first of the "Free Women" sections, followed by the four notebooks, in succession, black, red, yellow, and blue, with this pattern repeated four times and with the individual notebook sections varying from one page to some eighty pages in length. After the fourth repeating of this pattern comes the section based on Anna's last, the golden, notebook, and with the entire novel then concluded with a final "Free Women" episode.

But since the "Free Women" passages (comprising the "short formal novel" mentioned earlier) are an attempt at describing the thoughts and activities of an alter ego of Anna's, there are of necessity a number of inconsistencies in detail. Most obvious of these is the choice of endings: if we are to believe the final notebook entry, Anna, after she is given the first sentence of a novel by her young American lover, starts to write the first of the "Free Women" passages, while the ending of the final "Free Women" section presents Ella, Anna's alter ego, planning to "join the Labour Party and teach a night-class twice a week for delinquent kids." Furthermore, Tommy, Anna's son, is described in the opening "Free Women" section as being twenty years old in 1957 and seventeen years old in a notebook purporting to describe events in 1950; he later gets married, according to the notebooks, or travels to Sicily with his father's wife. While attempts at resolving such inconsistencies must ultimately be impossible, they seem to be part of the attempt on Anna's part to reflect and emphasize certain parts of life, not to mirror them perfectly in all respects. Thus one can read the "Free Women" sections as a kind of coda or variation on the themes emphasized in the notebooks, with Anna's controlled attempts at writing being the means by which she (but not necessarily her fictional alter ego) can achieve both a meaningful relationship with other people and an ordered personal identity. As a whole, then, these "Free Women" passages are a fictionalized effort by Anna to see herself in perspective, not a point-by-point parallel to her own life, and as such, their organic relationship to the story of Anna Wulf herself becomes clearer.

As has already been suggested, there is a pervasive awareness of the complex and constantly simmering racial struggle in central colonial Africa running throughout most of the writing of Doris Lessing. Even in those works, like *The Golden Notebook*, which are not directly set in Africa, there is a constant presence of Africa noticeable in many subtle but inescapable references and emphases. As was quoted earlier, Doris Lessing has said that she was

brought up in Central Africa, which means that I was a member of the white minority, pitted against a black majority that was abominably treated and still is. I was the daughter of a white farmer who, although he was a very poor man in terms of what he was brought up to expect, could always get loans from the Land Bank which kept him. (I won't say that my father liked what was going on; he didn't.) But he employed anywhere from fifty to one hundred working blacks. An adult black earned twelve shillings a month, rather less than two dollars, and his food was rationed to corn meal and beans and peanuts and a pound of meat per week. It was all grossly unfair, and it's only a part of a larger picture of inequity.

So explicit has Mrs. Lessing been in citing this injustice in detail, particularly (but not exclusively) in those works specifically concerned with Africa, that after a return trip in 1956 to Southern Rhodesia and South Africa, she found herself in the company of many of her friends in "being prohibited," as she has called it, that is, in being permanently exiled from the country in which she was raised. Thus she was not among those who were surprised at the dissolution of the Central African Federation in 1963, following a span of only a decade in which "the politics of partnership" was discarded as unworkable.

Anna's own constant thinking about the African situation most often takes the form of entries in the black notebook, in which she describes memories and her own innermost thoughts and convictions about the black-white struggle. Toward the end of the black notebook entries, she describes a dream she has had, a recurring dream, about the individuals she had previously known in Africa. This particular entry contains a series of news items, every one of which refers to "violence, death, rioting, hatred, in some part of Africa." Anna dreams that a television film is to be made about the people she had known at the Mashopi Hotel in the colony. Although the director tells Anna in the dream that the script would be "exactly what [she] would have written [herself]," she soon discovers that his choice of shots and timing changes the "story" as she recalls it, that she no longer recognizes the lines spoken or even the relationships described, and that the technicians and cameramen, all black, alter the cameras into machine guns. The director defends his version of the incident because "it doesn't matter what we film, provided we film something." In short, Anna no longer remembers the "real" past, and cannot say exactly why the version being filmed is "wrong."

Anna also recalls in her notebook entries several Africans she has met and has talked with in an earlier day. Of these, Tom Mathlong and Charlie

Themba are most prominent. Tom Mathlong especially becomes a kind of conscience for Anna, and even when not present except in her thoughts, his influence is pervasive and strong. When, for example, she and her friends, Marion and Tommy, express an interest in African nationalism, she tells them, first, that they must "stop this pretence of caring about African nationalism," and that they "both know quite well it's nonsense." She then immediately ponders,

> Well, what would Tom Mathlong say? She imagined herself sitting across the table in a cafe with Tom Mathlong telling him about Marion and Tommy. He would listen and say: "Anna, you tell me why these two people have chosen to work for African liberation? And why should I care about their motives?" But then he would laugh. Yes. Anna could hear his laugh, deep, full, shaken out of his stomach. Yes. He would put his hands on his knees and laugh, then shake his head and say: "My dear Anna, I wish we had your problems."

Indeed, Mathlong is a kind of saint, for he combines not only the idealism of the Communist party members mentioned above, but also an awareness of the ultimate rightness of his cause. He sees, in a word, not only the heights to which man's sense of ethicality can raise him, but also that sense of ethicality in perspective, in relation to those more sordid areas of life such as the inexorably slow progress visible in racial terms at any one moment. And although Anna, after pondering the meaning of the word, again says that Tom is a saint—"an ascetic, but not a neurotic one"—she recognizes, from his stoical acceptance of the inevitability of years in prison because of his nationalistic efforts, the degree to which he is perhaps too ideal for an imperfect world.

By contrast with Tom Mathlong, Charlie Themba, the other native discussed in detail in *The Golden Notebook*, demonstrates an opposite kind of character, one more approximating the opportunistic superiority of the whites in colonial Africa. No racial exclusiveness for him; he longs instead for political power as a means of personal aggrandizement and promotion. He had shown a similar high-mindedness to that of Mathlong's but ultimately becomes distrusted by his fellow natives. Anna describes Themba as a trade union leader, "violent and passionate and quarrelsome and loyal," and recently "cracked up" because of the pressure of politics—"full of intrigue and jealousness and spite." Themba, evidently paranoid and even psychotic, believes that Mathlong and others are intriguing against him, so he begins writing bitter, fantastic letters to people like Anna who know him.

These hysterical and incoherent communications show the degree to which a right-minded person, as a result of psychological and social pressures, loses not only his idealism but also his psychic balance.

But if Tom Mathlong represents the consistently ethical and trustworthy extreme, with Charlie Themba moving from that extreme toward one of opportunism and mental chaos, there is yet another type of native to be mentioned, the opposite extreme from Tom Mathlong. While this type is not singled out and named as an individual, he is described in terms generically applicable to purely opportunistic politicians the world around: "he's bombastic and rabble-rousing and he drinks and he whores around. He'll probably be the first Prime Minister—he has all the qualities—the common touch, you know."

These complicated and involved examples of the racial situation in Rhodesia show more than anything else the kind of commitment, admittedly a frustrating, futile one, that enlightened individuals like Anna Wulf dedicate themselves to during their African years. But just as the various natives described range from purely idealistic to purely opportunistic, so the whites too react in varying ways to the racial situation. Anna and others admit the wrongness of *apartheid* (even though this term is not used in the novel), but their ineffectual attempts at remedying the situation cause some to be so disillusioned that they give up, while others become cynically a part of the dominant power structure. As with both Mrs. Lessing herself and her earlier fictional creation, Martha Quest, Anna finds the frustrations and pressures too great to endure without signs of victory, so another commitment is made: to political action, particularly to Communist party activity.

In common with many other British and American intellectuals in the 1930s and early 1940s, Doris Lessing became a Communist as a result of sincere optimistic desires to see the world improved and to have the injustices of a supposedly inhuman competitive system of values eliminated. To a great extent, her decision to become a Communist appears now as naïve as many other youthful enthusiasms or commitments. She has said, for instance,

> when I became a communist, emotionally if not organizationally,
> in 1942, my picture of socialism as developed in the Soviet Union
> was, to say the least, inaccurate. But after fifteen years of uncom-
> fortable adjustment to reality I still find myself in the possession
> of an optimism about the future obviously considered jejune by
> anyone under the age of thirty. . . . Perhaps it is that the result
> of having been a communist is to be a humanist.

For the writer, uniquely equipped to communicate the political tensions of an era, has as his "point of rest" his "recognition of man, the responsive individual, voluntarily submitting his will to the collective, but never finally; and insisting on making his own personal and private judgements before every act of submission." Thus the same tension between the individual sense of responsibility and the collective emphasis on conformist thinking which has led so many idealists out of the party they considered a panacea for the world's economic and social ills is responsible for Mrs. Lessing's own disenchantment after some years' allegiance to the Communist party.

This allegiance, though, did not suddenly cease as if a radical experience such as a conversion had occurred. She has said that she

> decided to leave the party a good time before I finally left it. I didn't leave it when I decided to, because there was a general exodus, much publicized, from the British Party then, and the journalists were waiting for yet another renegade to publish his, her complaints against the C.P. [Communist Party]. To quote another old communist: "I find it nauseating when people who have been in the Party ten, twenty years, stagger out shouting and screaming as if they've been raped against their will." I left it because the gap between my own attitudes and those of the party widened all the time. There was no particular event or moment. The 20th Congress [in February 1956, at which Khrushchev denounced Stalin] shocked me, not because of the "revelations" but because I thought the "revelations" were long overdue, pitifully and feebly put forth, and no one really tried to explain or understand what had happened.

It is in Anna Wulf that Mrs. Lessing's subtle shifting of loyalty to communism is best illustrated, not only because of the later date of composition of *The Golden Notebook,* but also because of the fuller character portrayal we have of Anna than of earlier characters. Indeed, since *The Golden Notebook* is concerned most directly with the later stages in the political metamorphosis of Anna Wulf, we are given far more to support a person's leaving the party than his joining it. Anna once reflects that intelligent Communists believe the party "has been saddled with a group of dead bureaucrats who run it, and that the real work gets done in spite of the centre." Hence she and most other Communists mentioned in the book suffer a profound disillusionment, perhaps best illustrated by the bitter comment by Maryrose, a young Communist Anna had known in Africa: "Only a few months ago we believed that the world was going to change and everything was going to be beautiful and now we know it won't." And Anna herself, in one of her recurring dreams, tells about one particularly apocalyptic vision she has in which she foresees an end to the Communist system, at the very least for herself personally.

An end to communism, though, will result less from wishful dreaming than from the weight of the party's own weaknesses—none of which, really, have anything to do with party doctrine per se so much as the increasing bureaucratization and narrowness of thinking Anna sees around her. Thus the Communists portrayed in *The Golden Notebook* are consistently either those like Anna and Maryrose, disillusioned and despondent, or like Willi Rodde, who becomes part of the East German bureaucracy after the war; there seems to be no middle ground, such as impassioned dedication to the Communist cause, as can be found on occasion in Mrs. Lessing's earlier books.

Anna in particular notices with increasing distaste and disgust the official party falsification of truth whenever it seems expedient. Because of her work for John Butte, a Communist publisher, she is in a unique position to see at firsthand the exact ways in which such falsification takes place; indeed, it is the world of publishing that first interests her in joining the Communist party. But Anna soon finds out that the "truth" is not a very highly prized commodity in Communist publishing. She, as an editor, is given a novel by a faithful party member to consider for publication, which she evaluates as follows:

> This novel touches reality at no point at all. (Jack described it as "communist cloud-cuckoo spit.") It is, however, a very accurate recreation of the self-deceptive myths of the Communist Party at this particular time; and I have read it in about fifty shapes or guises during the last year. I say: "you know quite well this is a very bad book." . . . He [Butte] now remarks: "It's no masterpiece . . . but it's a good book, I think." . . . I will challenge him, and he will argue. The end will be the same, because the decision has already been taken. The book will be published. People in the Party with any discrimination will be even more ashamed because of the steadily debasing values of the Party; the *Daily Worker* will praise it.

After Butte, exasperated, says, "Publish and be damned!" Anna says,

> What you've said sums up everything that is wrong with the Party. It's a crystallization of the intellectual rottenness of the Party that the cry of nineteenth-century humanism, courage

against odds, truth against lies, should be used now to defend the publication of a lousy lying book by a communist firm which will risk nothing at all by publishing it, not even a reputation for integrity.

But Anna, herself sufficiently a person with integrity to admit the necessity of accepting her changing political views, can only protest; she cannot change the situation. For a time, though, she is temporarily recharged with enthusiasm and hope for the party, following the death of Stalin on March 5, 1953. Anna for a time believes that there is again a chance for a meaningful allegiance to communism. But the resurgence of hope does not last long; after she has been out of the party for over a year, she is invited back for a meeting at which the bureaucracy is supposedly to be removed and the party in Britain revitalized, "without the deadly loyalty to Moscow and the obligation to tell lies." But less than a year later, at another meeting, she realizes that she has accomplished nothing in all the "frenzied political activity" in which she has been involved. In short, Anna's renewed sense of purpose in the Communist party is short-lived, for she discovers that the situation she had sensed earlier, and which led her to her leaving the party, has not really changed at all.

Although Anna indicates at various times her reasons for leaving the party—its jargon, its dishonesty, its pettiness, and so on—she does specify in one passage in more detail her exact reasons for both becoming a Communist and for leaving the party. Jack, another party member, comments that society today is complex and technical that no one person can effectively understand it all. Anna answers him:

> "Alienation. Being split. It's the moral side, so to speak, of the communist message. And suddenly you shrug your shoulders and say because the mechanical basis of our lives is getting complicated, we must be content to not even try to understand things as a whole?" And now I see his face has put on a stubborn closed look that reminds me of John Butte's: and he looks angry. He says: "Not being split, it's not a question of imaginatively understanding everything that goes on. Or trying to. It means doing one's work as well as possible, and being a good person." I say: "That's treachery." "To what?" "To humanism." He thinks and says: "The idea of humanism will change like everything else." I say: "Then it will become something else. But humanism stands for the whole person, the whole individual, striving to become as conscious and responsible as possible about everything in the

> universe. But now you sit there, quite calmly, and as a humanist
> you say that due to the complexity of scientific achievement the
> human being must never expect to be whole, he must always be
> fragmented."

Her sense of this fragmentation is such as to demand of her a more coherent,
a more unifying life than has been possible through dedication to communism. Although party membership and activity can be a meaningful commitment, Anna discovers that it is too limited a commitment, too narrow in
its rewards and too dishonest in its demands upon the individual, to remain
for long the kind of commitment she needs for her own life. Again, she must
move on to a further level of commitment, that of an open and free acknowl-
edgment of her sexual nature, before she is able to move to what I believe is
her ultimate and most lasting commitment, to verbal communication through
writing for a public audience.

As Anna Wulf continues in her process of attempting to bring meaning
into the chaos of her life, we see how she gradually but perceptibly moves
from a purely objective area of concern (the racial), to an area with both
objective theory and personal application (the political), and now to the more
wholly subjective. That is, as an enlightened, liberal white, Anna is scarcely
as involved in the fight for racial justice as, say, Tom Mathlong; as a sensitive,
intelligent, and idealistic young woman, she cannot assimilate the inconsistencies and pettiness of communism; and now, we see another area of commitment in Anna's life, that collectively concerned with her views on sex and
marriage, and, concurrently, her need of psychoanalytic counselling. This
considerably more subjective commitment requires of Anna a correspondingly greater degree of insight into her own psyche and personality, as well
as a frank admission of the exact kind of woman she is.

As we first meet Anna and see her in her milieu, we notice the extent
to which she and her friend, Molly, seem conventionally "emancipated,"
particularly in the areas of sexual morality and their ability to move freely
through what is always an explicitly masculine world. The term they use to
refer to themselves, "free women," is itself the overall title for the short novel
Anna writes about her alter ego, and thus it is no surprise that the concept
of freedom occurs frequently in *The Golden Notebook*. But the concept itself
changes as Anna step-by-step becomes more fully aware of her identity.
Molly's statement early in the novel, "we're a completely new type of
woman," is fairly typical of the self-conscious "emancipation" the two
women adopt. Anna asks a bit later, "if we lead what is known as free lives,
that is, lives like men, why shouldn't we use the same language?" Molly

replies, "Because we aren't the same. That is the point." Anna's retort to this posits the essential contrast between the sexes evident throughout the book: "Men. Women. Bound. Free. Good. Bad. Yes. No. Capitalism. Socialism. Sex. Love." Despite this, Anna senses that women's "loyalties are always to men, and not to women"; she painfully realizes she is approaching middle age, and recalls that when she was younger, twenty-three or so, she suffered "from a terror of being trapped and tamed by domesticity." Now, though, she realizes the extent to which she is lonely. Molly reminds her in these terms of her loneliness:

> You choose to be alone rather than to get married for the sake of not being lonely. . . . You're afraid of writing what you think about life, because you might find yourself in an exposed position, you might expose yourself, you might be alone.

And later, when Anna canvasses for the Communist party, she notices the many lonely women who long for an audience for their personal problems, "going mad quietly by themselves, in spite of husband and children or rather because of them." Much later, when Anna leaves her lover (as described in the final "Free Women" section), she recognizes the price she must pay for being as free and independent and intelligent as she is: "that will be my epitaph. Here lies Anna Wulf, who was always too intelligent. She let them go." For the toughness Anna so proudly claims for herself is seen to be more attitude than actuality, as when she tells Molly about the kind of life the two are living:

> Both of us are dedicated to the proposition that we're tough. . . . A marriage breaks up, well, we say, our marriage was a failure, too bad. A man ditches us—too bad we say, it's not important. We bring up kids without men—nothing to it, we say, we can cope. We spend years in the communist party and then we say, well, well, we made a mistake, too bad. . . . Well don't you think it's at least possible that things can happen to us so bad that we don't ever get over them? . . . Why do our lot never admit failure? Never. It might be better for us if we did. And it's not only love and men. Why can't we say something like this—we are people, because of the accident of how we were situated in history, who were so powerfully part . . . with the great dream, that now we had to admit that the great dream has faded and the truth is something else—that we'll never be any use.

Indeed, Anna's American lover's charge that she has been trying to "cage the truth" is itself made near the end of Anna's series of notebooks and counseling sessions, and Anna, after the change is made, admits that "it's no good."

Anna's fictional alter ego, Ella, reflects, quite naturally, the same attitudes as her creator. We are told, for instance, of Ella's awareness that a free woman, having "positively disdained ordinary morality," is not acceptable to the majority of either sex. Ella's lover, Paul, tells her that the real revolution of the day is that of women against men. Ella herself realizes that her emotions are "fitted for a kind of society that no longer exists," a monogamous society, and that she ought to have been a man. Even more self-consciously than Anna, Ella prides herself on her independence, and is repeatedly reminded of this by her lovers. Ella comments to her friend, Julia, that "we've chosen to be free women, and this [i.e., sexual double standards and male indifference] is the price we pay." Julia's reply indicates the desperation both women feel: "Free! What's the use of us being free if they aren't? I swear to God, that every one of them, even the best of them, have the old idea of good women and bad women." The price paid, though, does not only include frustration and doubt, for Ella realizes that by being a "free woman," she has an advantage over wives, simply because she "was so much more exciting than the dull tied women." But, like Anna herself, who ultimately realizes that she is not free, Ella must accept responsibility to be either free or happy. Anna wishes she were married, for instance, saying that she doesn't like living the way she does, and Ella herself, we are told, "after years of freedom, is over-ready for a serious love."

Parenthetically, it should be mentioned that neither Anna nor Ella, in their self-conscious celebration of being "free women," approximates Mrs. Lessing's own attitude toward such freedom. She has said that she doesn't see herself as a "free woman" "only because I don't think anyone is 'free.'" She also observed that "to imagine free man . . . is to step outside of what we are," for

> There is no one on this earth who is not twisted by fear and insecurity, and the compromises of thinking made inevitable by want and fear. . . . Slaves can envy the free; slaves can fight to free their children; but slaves suddenly set free are marked by the habits of submission; and slaves imagining freedom see it through the eyes of slaves.

Hence this imagined freedom of Anna's and Ella's, as this chapter suggests, is not so much a total lack of individual responsibility as a series of gradually more intense and personal commitments, culminating, as the next part of this chapter will indicate, in the commitment to writing. Prior to that, though, we must consider the exact ways in which Anna's "emancipation" is expressed, through sexual attitudes and behavior, and through an obsessive self-understanding gained through psychoanalysis.

Throughout her life as recounted in the notebooks, and in her past youth as occasionally recalled in moments of stress or reminiscence, Anna thinks of herself in sexual terms, ranging from the trancelike "sexual obsession" felt at age fifteen (and which she would not go through again for an immense amount of money), to her subsequent simultaneous fear of and appeal for sexual experience, when she is first aware of her "emancipated" state, to the steps leading up to her defloration: petting and the initial act of sexual intercourse. In each of the several "lives" she experiences, she has lovers who more or less correspond in their meaning for her with the gradually changing sense of commitment she acknowledges. In colonial Africa, for instance, it is Willi (with whom Anna is sexually incompatible), a relationship that ends when Willi discovers that Anna has just had intercourse with another man and, full of hatred, forces her into one last act of intercourse. Later, involved with Michael, Anna moves into a more self-assured, yet still somewhat guilty, sexual relationship. The relationship itself seems based more on sex than on love, but does not last long. Then Anna meets the American Communist, Nelson, who has a "moral fear of sex," and who "could never stay inside a woman for longer than a few seconds." A friend of Molly's from Ceylon, DeSilva, further complicates Anna's wishes for a satisfactory sexual experience, for he, first, picks up a strange girl on the street with whom he wants only sex, no feelings, and, later, sleeps with Anna, who justifies the act on the grounds that "it didn't matter to me." This too ends, for DeSilva wishes to use one of Anna's rooms for sex with another woman, so that Anna could hear the couple in bed. Meeting an unnamed friend of Nelson's, Anna thinks, "A normal man at last, thank God," but this relationship ends because of the lack of warmth the man felt and because of his fear of his wife back home. All the men in this promiscuous sequence, quite clearly, are desperate choices for a love-partner for Anna, so it is small wonder that all the affairs end in a futile and sterile way.

But when Anna meets Saul Green, the American writer who aids in Anna's ultimate self-knowledge, she finds an entirely different sexual experience, even though there are the inevitable conflicts and arguments that affect their sexual rapport. Saul comes to Anna's apartment to rent a room, and upon their first meeting, gives Anna a close sexual examination. Their mutual attraction is shown in Anna's similar examination of Saul:

I saw his pose, standing with his back to the window in a way

that was like a caricature of that young American we see in the
films—sexy he-man, all balls and strenuous erection. He stood
lounging, his thumbs hitched through his belt, fingers loose, but
pointing as it were to his genitals.

Green subsequently refers to a "friend" (evidently himself) and the friend's
sexual problems, and in the process he and Anna discuss the language inevitably used in discussing sex, with Anna accusing Saul of having an unhealthy
attitude toward sex and Saul retorting by stating that he doesn't agree with
the typically masculine double standard; later the same day, they have their
first act of sexual intercourse. Anna senses that sex for Saul is a combination
of emotions, as it is for her: she sees him as making love out of fear (of being
alone), out of hatred (a hard, violent sex), and out of an indifference toward
Anna's feelings (after he has just returned from making love with another
woman). Anna realizes that Saul's lovemaking is not a sadistic act, but that
he does appear to be loving someone else while in the act. But sex with Saul
is warm and fulfilling, as it has not been with the other men in Anna's life,
and, important for Anna's psychological well-being, occurs spontaneously
and quickly.

Anna's other self, Ella, goes through somewhat the same sequence of
lovers and emotions prior to her achieving a fulfilling sexual experience. But
since Ella is a fictional creation of Anna's, Anna can put into Ella's consciousness and words many of the secret thoughts and socially embarrassing
ideas about sex that Anna does not mention. After her first act of intercourse
with a lover, Paul, Ella critically examines him and finds the experience
"beautiful," at least in part because he was the first lover she had had in
two years. They again make love, gradually more mechanically and less beautifully, even though she still senses the "instinctive warmth" radiated by Paul.
But Ella cannot accept statements made by Paul that make her unhappy, so
she mentally rejects his statement, "Odd isn't it, it really is true that if you
love a woman sleeping with another woman means nothing." Later, briefly
separated from Paul, she casually spends time with Cy Maitland, an American businessman. She is immediately attracted to Maitland, but for reasons
she cannot wholly analyze. His behavior in bed, though, is completely self-
centered and unconcerned for her feelings. Rapidly reaching orgasm, he repeatedly exclaims "Boy, Oh boy!" and talks of his wife. His attitude is
suggested by his statement to Ella: "That's what I like. No problems with
you," and "That's what I like about you—let's go to bed, you say, and that's
fine and easy. I like you." After the ending of this unsatisfactory affair, Ella
realizes that there is no point in her going to bed with anyone but Paul.

Later, Ella has intercourse with Jack, the efficient type of man who "has learned love-making out of a book. . . . [He] gets his pleasure from having got a woman into bed, not from sex itself." Ella's next step, the nadir of her erotic career, comes when feelings of despair hit her:

> Now something new happens. She begins to suffer torments of sexual desire. Ella is frightened because she cannot remember feeling sexual desire, as a thing in itself, without reference to a specific man before, or at least not since her adolescence, and then it was always in relation to a fantasy about a man. Now she cannot sleep, she masturbates, to accompaniment of fantasies of hatred about men. Paul has vanished completely: she has lost the warm strong man of her experience, and can only remember a cynical betrayer. She suffers sex desire in a vacuum. She is acutely humiliated, thinking that this means she is dependent on men for "having sex," for "being serviced," for "being satisfied." She uses this kind of savage phrase to humiliate herself.
>
> Then she realizes she is falling into a lie about herself, and about women, and that she must hold on to this knowledge: that when she was with Paul she felt no sexual hungers that were not prompted by him; that if he was apart from her for a few days, she was dormant until he returned; that her present raging sexual hunger was not for sex, but was fed by all the emotional hungers of her life. That when she loved a man again, she would return to normal: a woman, that is, whose sexuality would ebb and flow in response to his. A woman's sexuality is, so to speak, contained by a man, if he is a real man; she is, in a sense, put to sleep by him, she does not think about sex.

But despite these thoughts, she again succumbs to the temptation of a brief affair, this time with a Canadian scriptwriter; she again "feels nothing," and believes that the act was "something he set himself to do and that's all," i.e., an act of accomplishment, not an act of feeling.

In these furtive acts of intercourse, Ella, like Anna, discovers that although she can give pleasure, she does not receive it herself unles she has a deep emotional commitment to the man; indeed, Ella reflects, when she is with the Canadian writer, that she "has not had a real orgasm since Paul left her," and with Maitland, she realizes that it is even more complicated:

> Ella was thinking: But with Paul, I would have come in that time—so what's wrong?—it's not enough to say, I don't love this man? She understood suddenly that she would never come with

this man. She thought: for women like me, integrity isn't chastity, it isn't fidelity, it isn't any of the old words. Integrity is the orgasm. That is something I haven't any control over. I could never have an orgasm with this man, I can give pleasure and that's all. But why not? Am I saying that I can never come except with a man I love? Because what sort of a desert am I condemning myself to if that's true?

As an indication that the matter of orgasm is extremely central to the sexual commitment made by both Anna and Ella, Mrs. Lessing provides one lengthy passage in which both Anna and Ella occur. Anna mentions at first that the "difficulty of writing about sex, for women, is that sex is best when not thought about, not analyzed. Women deliberately choose not to think about technical sex. They get irritable when men talk technically, it's out of self-preservation: they want to preserve the spontaneous emotion that is essential for their satisfaction." After reflecting about a broken marriage, caused, as she was told, by the husband's too-small penis, Anna begins describing Ella's and her own sexual experiences in as clinical a tone as elsewhere in the book is condemned by Anna:

> When Ella first made love with Paul, during the first few months, what set the seal on the fact she loved him, and made it possible for her to use the word, was that she immediately experienced orgasm. Vaginal orgasm that is. And she could not have experienced it if she had not loved him. It is the orgasm that is created by the man's need for a woman, and his confidence in that need.
>
> As time went on, he began to use mechanical means. (I look at the word mechanical—a man wouldn't use it.) Paul began to rely on manipulating her externally, on giving Ella clitoral orgasms. Very exciting. Yet there was always a part of her that resented it. Because she felt that the fact he wanted to, was an expression of his instinctive desire not to commit himself to her. She felt that without knowing it or being conscious of it . . . he was afraid of the emotion. The vaginal orgasm is emotion and nothing else, felt as emotion and expressed in sensations that are indistinguishable from emotion. The vaginal orgasm is a dissolving in a vague, dark generalised sensation like being swirled in a warm whirlpool. There are several different sorts of clitoral orgasms, and they are more powerful (that is a male word) than the vaginal orgasm. There can be a thousand thrills, sensations, etc., but there is only one real female orgasm and that is when a

man, from the whole of his need and desire takes a woman and wants all her response. Everything else is a substitute and a fake, and the most inexperienced woman feels this instinctively. Ella had never experienced clitoral orgasm before Paul, and she told him so, and he was delighted. . . . But when she told him she had never experienced what she insisted on calling "a real orgasm" to anything like the same depth before him, he involuntarily frowned. . . . As time went on, the emphasis shifted in their love-making from the real orgasm to the clitoral orgasm, and there came a point when Ella realized . . . that she was no longer having real orgasms. That was before the end, when Paul left her. In short, she knew emotionally what the truth was when her mind would not admit it.

Just prior to the end of their time together, Paul leaves the country and Ella is thereafter incapable, as already mentioned, of achieving orgasm with any other lover. As she says later,

And what about us? Free, we say, yet the truth is that they get erections when they're with a woman they don't give a damn about, but we don't get an orgasm unless we love him. What's free about that?

The "new mood or phase" in which Ella finds herself, she says, "is only the opposite side of being possessed by sex"; she now says she "cannot believe she will ever feel desire again."

The "Free Women" sections of *The Golden Notebook*, finally, suggests even more of Anna's deep concern with the inadequacies of a sexual commitment. Marion, Anna's friend in these sections of the book, tells Anna that she hates going to bed, even though it was once the "happiest time" of her life, when she was still a newlywed. She indicates that Richard, her lover, has to "make himself" have intercourse with her, and asks Anna if she had ever slept with a man when she knew he was forcing himself to do so. Both Anna and Marion are concerned with what they call a "real man" (instead of the "little boys and homosexuals and half-homosexuals" in England), and Anna goes so far as to wish for such a man for her daughter's sake, evidently as a proxy father. Later Anna says to Milton, the American writer, that she has had her fill of "cold and efficient sex," after which he asks, "what's happened to all that warm and committed sex we read about in books?" He also says that "love is too difficult," to which Anna retorts, "And sex too cold." As if to support this statement by Anna, Milton shortly thereafter abruptly asks her, "Want me to screw you?" Anna replies that "there's something about a man with a whacking great erection that it's hard to resist," but they nonetheless separate, for Anna has made the discovery that "committed sex," as Milton calls it, is too insubstantial and dissatisfying a commitment for either her emotional security or her sense of identity.

It is, in fact, her search for her identity that leads Anna to go to and depend upon a lay psychoanalyst named Mrs. Marks, but who Anna usually refers to as "Mother Sugar." Anna recounts various dreams she has had to Mother Sugar, most of which are nightmares—of sheer terror, of sexual attack and sex-reversal, of the mad Charlie Themba, of a film projectionist showing her own life, and of her own death. The terrible dreams themselves parallel the emotional moods Anna experiences in her waking hours, and one dream in particular (in addition to the apocalyptic dream mentioned earlier of the Communist world) warrants fuller treatment:

> I dreamed I held a kind of casket in my hands, and inside it was something very precious. . . . There was a small crowd of people . . . waiting for me to hand them the casket. I was incredibly happy that at last I could give them this precious object. But when I handed it over, I saw suddenly they were all business men, brokers, something like that. They did not open the box, but started handing me large sums of money. I began to cry. I shouted: "open the box, open the box," but they couldn't hear me, or wouldn't listen. Suddenly I saw they were all characters in some film or play, and that I had written it, and was ashamed of it. . . . I was a character in my own play. I opened the box and forced them to look. But instead of a beautiful thing, which I thought would be there, there was a mass of fragments, but bits and pieces from everywhere, all over the world—I recognized a lump of red earth, that I knew came from Africa, and then a bit of metal that came off a gun from Indo-China, and then every-thing was horrible; bits of flesh from people killed in the Korean War and a communist party badge off someone who died in a Soviet prison. This, looking at the mass of ugly fragments, was so painful that I couldn't look, and I shut the box. But the group of businessmen or money-people hadn't noticed. They took the box from me and opened it. I turned away so not to see, but they were delighted. At last I looked and I saw that there was some-thing in the box. It was a small green crocodile with a winking sardonic snout. I thought it was the image of a crocodile, made

of jade, or emeralds, then I saw it was alive, for large frozen tears rolled down its cheeks and turned into diamonds. I laughed out loud when I saw how I had cheated the businessmen and I woke up.

While a precise and full analysis of this dream is clearly impossible, there are several points that must be made. In the first place, this dream of Anna's parallels her own life in several points. Some of the men with whom Anna (and Ella) have had affairs have been businessmen, and these have uniformly been unresponsive to feminine needs; they have, in a word, treated that which is beautiful and prized as a mercenary thing. Anna's own fragmented life is also suggested by this dream. And the crocodile is suggested by the letter from Charlie Themba, referred to above, in which he insanely envisions a crocodile devouring him. Thus this dream contains in capsule, symbolic form the several elements of Anna's own life, focused as they are in terms of a film or scenario with Anna as the author. Evidently death is the outcome of all the various earlier struggles—racial, political, sexual—that Anna has experienced, if, that is, she is able to "cheat" the "businessman." And this is, I believe, suggested by Anna's final dream, described in the last "Free Women" section of the novel:

> One afternoon she went to sleep and dreamed. She knew it was a dream she had often had before, in one form or another. She had two children. One was Janet, plump and glossy with health. The other was Tommy, a small baby, and she was starving him. Her breasts were empty, because Janet had had all the milk in them; and so Tommy was thin and puny, dwindling before her eyes from starvation. He vanished altogether, in a tiny coil of pale bony starving flesh, before she woke, which she did in a fever of anxiety, self-division and guilt. Yet, awake, she could see no reason why she should have dreamed of Tommy being starved by her. And besides, she knew that in other dreams of this cycle, the "starved" figure might be anyone, perhaps someone she passed in the street whose face had haunted her. Yet there was no doubt she felt responsible for this half-glimpsed person, for why otherwise should she dream of having failed him—or her?
>
> After this dream, she went feverishly back to work, cutting out news items, fastening them to the wall.

This dream appears to suggest that Anna's fragmented self has extended to her two children in the dream, with the "starved" one being any person with whom she comes in contact. Her sense of responsibility is focused on this "starved" person, whoever it might be at the moment, but responsibility, at this point, can only take the cathartic form of the frantic newspaper clipping and pasting discussed in the last section of this chapter; it is, in brief, a preliminary step in Anna's ultimate self-knowledge and acceptance of both herself and the world around her. It is significant, also, to note that there is one child in this dream that is "plump and glossy with health"; the obsessive terror and wasteland effects of most of her other dreams are ameliorated slightly by this image of fertility and plenty.

Mother Sugar's counseling of Anna is thus the specific means by which Anna is gradually able to see herself in perspective and to gain control of her own life. One lengthy exchange between the two women is central to any complete understanding of the forces that effect such a change in Anna, and is especially concerned with Anna's leaving the relative safety of her dreams and the world of "myth" they contain, and going forth on her own. No matter how horrible the dreams, Anna says, "all the pain, and the killing and the violence are safely held in the story and . . . can't hurt me." Anna sees that "the individual recognizes one part after another of his earlier life as an aspect of the general human experience," and (further supporting the obvious Jungian emphasis) that

> What I did then, what I felt then, is only the reflection of that great archetypal dream, or epic story, or stage in history, then he is free, because he has separated himself from the experience, or fitted it like a mosaic into a very old pattern, and by the act of setting it into place, is free of the individual pain of it.

After Anna says that she is "living the kind of life women never lived before," Mother Sugar asks,

> In what way are you different? Are you saying there haven't been artist-women before? There haven't been women who were independent? There haven't been women who insisted on sexual freedom? I tell you, there are a great line of women stretching out behind you into the past, and you have to seek them out and find them in yourself and be conscious of them.

After raising several objections, Anna says that she wants "to separate in herself what is old and cyclic, the recurring history, the myth, from what is new, what I feel or think that might be new. . . . Sometimes I meet people, and it seems to me the fact they are cracked across, they're split, means they are keeping themselves open for something." Mother Sugar's technique, quite clearly, is to ask Anna probing questions which force her to see herself in perspective and to see what she really is in the deepest recesses of her psyche. She does not leave Anna in the fragmented chaotic past, but instead, by the "shock of recognition," forces her to see the present and future as they really are, potentially coherent and ordered and fruitful.

Anna, though, cannot receive this ordered existence vicariously from Mother Sugar; she must work it out for and by herself, and this is done, through her obsessive concern with language and with putting on paper the ordered language constituting human discourse. Paralleling her sessions and conversations with Mother Sugar are Anna's frantic efforts to record, in fragmented form, all the experiences of her several disparate "selves," in the notebooks that constitute the bulk of *The Golden Notebook,* and gradually to go beyond the limitations of private communication to express to others, through a novel, her affirmation of on-going life and structured personal existence.

As Mrs. Lessing says in her personal credo, "The Small Personal Voice," commitment to writing is necessary because of today's confusion of standards and values; because of the compassion, warmth, humanity, and love of people to be found in the truly great novels; because the writer has a responsibility as a human being to choose for evil or to strengthen good; and—most important of all—because the writer's recognition of man as an individual is necessary if the novel as a genre is to regain greatness. To achieve greatness, Mrs. Lessing states that the novelist's "small, personal voice" must recreate "warmth and humanity and love of people," especially if a "great age of literature" like the nineteenth century is to result. Such a credo does not, Mrs. Lessing believes, necessarily become "propagandizing" for a cause, political or otherwise; nor does the novelist necessarily regress by so committing himself. Rather, the novelist "must feel himself as an instrument of change for good or bad," as an "architect of the soul." Not only can such ideas be said to apply to Mrs. Lessing herself, they also apply quite well to her protagonist in *The Golden Notebook,* Anna Freeman Wulf.

As *The Golden Notebook* opens, Anna Wulf is living as a divorcée in London, supporting herself and her daughter by the residual royalties from a successful novel, *Frontiers of War,* which is in turn based on Anna's earlier life in colonial Africa. As Anna attempts to make sense of her life, she puts down in four notebooks—black, red, yellow, and blue—her memories and feelings. In the black notebook, Anna writes her own account of her time in Central Africa during World War II, and the events leading up to the writing of *Frontiers of War.* Anna's feelings concerning this book are equivocal: she simultaneously depends upon the book's earnings, and knows it to be a failure. And later, when the many financial solicitations for her novel by film companies pour in, Anna's feeling of revulsion against the world of communism is made all the more pronounced. She ultimately does sell the film rights—three times, in fact—but never with any conviction that the book would be filmed; and on one occasion she refuses a studio's offer when the representative arrives. And, finally, when Anna does again write (the autobiographical novel called *Free Women*), she conceives of herself as being glad when one of her lovers said he did not like *Frontiers of War*.

As already mentioned, Anna's black notebook deals with her life in Africa and the red her life as a Communist. The yellow notebook, by contrast, is Anna's novelistic attempt to see herself in perspective, by means of a thinly disguised fictional alter ego, Ella, whose circumstances and personal life are quite like Anna's. Anna had mentioned earlier, in discussing the Communist party, that the ogre of capitalism—from a Communist viewpoint—could be "supplanted by others, like communist, or woman's magazine." It is no surprise, then, that Ella works for a woman's magazine, nor that she had written part of a novel. This fictional work in which Ella appears is entitled *The Shadow of the Third*, a reference, as Anna later explained it, to "the woman altogether better than I was." But this woman does not remain static; she is at first the wife of Paul, Ella's lover; then she becomes "Ella's younger *alter ego* formed from fantasies about Paul's wife," and she finally becomes Ella herself. The bulk of the yellow notebook, however, concerns Ella's gradual completion of her novel (it is barely half-finished as the notebook begins). The initial idea, she says, came "when she found herself getting dressed to go out to dine with people after she had told herself she did not want to go out." The difficulty she has with the writing, though, is not technical; we are told that "it was as if the story were already written somewhere inside herself." Just as Ella is Anna's alter ego, so Ella conceives of her novel as a reflection of herself, as "carrying on conversations with one's image in the looking-glass." Similarly, just as Anna can "read" Ella's story, so Ella sees her own novel as being already written and with herself reading it. Ella's novel is accepted for publication, and Ella sees it as having the same basic quality that Anna had earlier wished the Communist novels would have: honesty. For, as Anna herself says later concerning the yellow notebook,

> It frightens me that when I'm writing I seem to have some awful second sight, or something like it, an intuition of some kind; a kind of intelligence is at work that is much too painful to use in ordinary life; one couldn't live at all if one used it for living.

And just as those in Anna's Communist period who had experienced the most loneliness frequently turned to writing for meaning in an otherwise meaningless existence, so Ella too discovers that, for herself as well as for others, writing is a kind of therapy. Ella discovers, for instance, that her father, "alone, withdrawing from his wife into books and the dry, spare dreams of a man who might have been a poet or a mystic," is in fact both; but, significantly, his poems are about "solitude, loss, fortitude, the adventures of isolation."

For Ella, though, this isolation continues beyond the vicarious act of writing out, as a form of therapy, her emotions and sense of isolation. After the conversation with her father, she looks "for the outlines of a story" and finds, "again and again, nothing but patterns of defeat, death, irony." She refuses these; she fails to force "patterns of happiness of simple life"; but she finally finds it possible to "accept the patterns of self-knowledge which mean unhappiness or at least a dryness," and which could be twisted into a victory. That is, by searching in the negative "patterns," she can, she hopes, twist a positive "pattern" into shape. And by conceiving of a man and a woman, "both at the end of their tether," "both cracking up because of a deliberate attempt to transcend their own limits," a "new kind of strength" is found. She waits, we are told, "for the images to form, to take on life." But instead of "life," we are given a series of nineteen synopses of short stories or short novels, all of which are counterparts or summaries of events in the four notebooks or in the "Free Women" sections of *The Golden Notebook,* and all of which are expanded in the final portion of the yellow notebook, in the comments Anna makes (Ella has now been completely dropped from the narrative) about her relationship with Saul Green, an American. Saul is quite like Anna in his sense of defeatedness and spiritual and emotional isolation, and closely approximates Paul, in the earlier portions of the yellow notebook. He is particularly and acutely aware of Anna's attempt to make notations in a series of fragmented diaries (the four notebooks) a substitute for a direct encounter with her problems, with life, with her need to write. He asks, on one occasion, "Instead of making a record of my sins in your diary, why don't you write another novel?" Anna's retort that she has a "writer's block," of course, neither deters nor persuades Green; his comment has sufficiently disturbed Anna that she decides to begin a fifth notebook (the golden one mentioned in the novel's title), which Saul requests of her.

Instead of giving away the new notebook, Anna decides to pack away the other four notebooks and to start the new one—"all of myself in one book." In this golden notebook, the relationship between Anna and Green

continues and is finally broken off, but with each providing the first sentence
for a novel by the other; Green's finished novel, we are told, "was later
published and did rather well." But Anna's initial sentence serves as the
beginning of the *Free Women* novel which, like the four major notebooks,
is divided into parts; the fifth and last of these parts concludes *The Golden
Notebook,* and is her primary method of using writing as a therapeutic
measure.

The blue notebook, about which little has been said thus far, is primarily
a factual diary-account of Anna's experiences in analysis and of her near-
madness and is designed to be a contrast to the "fictional" qualities found
in the other notebooks. Anna Wulf is forced in this notebook to face her
nearly overwhelming fear of war and "of the real movement of the world
towards dark, hardening power," and as a result provides the novel's most
searing criticism of society. The diary entries run from 1950 to 1956 without
major omissions, but the eighteen months from March 1956 to September
1957 are described without dates and concern Anna's initial experiences
with Saul Green.

The "Free Women" portions of *The Golden Notebook* are in some
respects more enlightening than anything else in the book, and are certainly
to be considered an integral part of the major narrative of the novel, since
the events described in these portions (occurring in 1957) are chronologically
the closest to the present. Evidently ironically, Mrs. Lessing has said, "The
structure of the whole book says that this little novel (i.e., "Free Women")
came out of all that mass of experience." But since the point of *The Golden
Notebook* is, as Mrs. Lessing has said elsewhere, "the relation of its parts
to each other," the "Free Women" sections must be considered as relevant,
even if ironically so, as the notebooks themselves.

The first four (of five) parts entitled "Free Women" closely match what
is known of Anna from the notebooks, with the difference, as was mentioned
above, primarily one of chronology. These portions of the book deal particularly with a friend of Anna's, Molly Jacobs, and her son, Tommy, who is
closest to Anna in the sense that he knows her better than anyone else.
Molly's former husband (and Tommy's father), Richard, knows Anna well
enough to allude to her "complicated ideas about writing," and he also points
out that she is afraid of writing what she really thinks about life, since this
would make her expose herself emotionally and thus lead to isolation. Anna
says to Molly that her notebooks are "chaos," but to Tommy Anna admits
much more. To his question about her four notebooks ("Why not one notebook?"), Anna replies, "Perhaps because it would be such a—scramble. Such
a mess." And Tommy, aware of the pressures at work in Anna's mind (ev-

ident primarily because of similar pressures which lead to his own futile suicide attempt later), asks the question no one can state without self-incrimination: "Why shouldn't it be a mess?" Tommy also examines Anna's four notebooks, an act no one but Saul Green otherwise is described as doing. Anna explains her notebook habit by saying that she keeps "trying to write the truth and realising it's not true," to which Tommy retorts, "Perhaps it is true; perhaps it is, and you can't bear it, so you cross it out." Later, in an exhausted, near-delirious state, Anna sees herself,

> seated on the music-stool, writing, writing; making an entry in one book, then ruling it off, or crossing it out; she saw the pages patterned with different kinds of writing; divided, bracketed, broken—she felt a swaying nausea; and then saw Tommy, not herself, standing with his lips pursed in concentration, turning the pages of her orderly notebooks.

The ironic word "orderly" is of course unintentional because of Anna's mental condition at the time it was uttered, for if any one point is made repeatedly, it is that Anna's diaries (unlike Saul Green's, for example, which run chronologically) are chaotic, like her life. And when Saul later asks her the same question Tommy had asked earlier, about her four notebooks, she replies (putting away three of the four while speaking), "Obviously, because it's been necessary to split myself up, but from now on I shall be using one only." Anna had neglected her notebooks after Tommy's attempted suicide, and had wondered if his attempt had been "triggered off by reading her notebooks." But Anna herself has been reading Saul's diaries, until the moment when she knows she will never again do so, primarily because she has been able to manipulate the tangled lives of two isolated people, herself and Saul, and to find some meaning in life itself.

It is in Anna's frenzied efforts to find meaning in life that the most chaotic expressions of her obsession with writing and with words are to be found. Shortly after she was first advised to keep a diary, in 1950, Anna began the practice of cutting out and pasting—in the notebooks or on the walls of her room—carefully dated newspaper clippings. Seven years later, toward the novel's conclusion, Anna is still, and perhaps even more so, concerned with such clippings. Anna once again turns to her notebooks, neglected since Tommy's accident, but she feels alien to them, so, faster than ever, she cuts out newspaper clippings. Even though Anna, in these frenzied activities, approaches a psychotic state, she has always had the same obsession with masses of newspapers and magazines. But all these hysterical episodes with newspapers are but a prelude to the ultimate experience, which occurs toward the book's end.

After having missed the newspapers for a week (significantly, the things Anna realizes she has missed are "a war here, a dispute there"), Anna moves "forward into a new knowledge, a new understanding" based on her fear. In brief, this entire newspaper obsession serves as contrast or perhaps counterpoint to the major concern Anna senses with regard to her sanity, namely, the use and effects of written words. And while Anna's ultimate "cure" (if such is the word) for her malaise is her writing the novel entitled *Free Women,* much of the mental calm she achieves obviously comes through the medium of newspapers. For after she satisfactorily resolves her feverish obsession with newspapers, Anna looks at the blue notebook, in which these events are recorded, and thinks, "if I could write in it Anna would come back, but I could not make my hand go out to take up the pen." But after she discovers who she is, with the help of Saul Green, who is also lost and isolated, she is able to write again, with the result being, of course, the "Free Women" passages. Previously, Anna had turned "everything into fiction," which she then concluded was "an evasion." She also asks herself why she can not put down, simply, the real events in her life and in others' lives, with the answer that such fictionizing is "simply a means of concealing something" from herself. But after her return from the world of insanity and chaos, she finally does become capable of stating, through the medium of fiction, her true feelings and experiences.

The self-knowledge which seems to be at the heart of Mrs. Lessing's theme in *The Golden Notebook* is clearly, then, necessary for mental equilibrium and emotional stability, and is, at least in the case of Anna Wulf, capable of being gained through a psychological and mental descent into hell. But the written and printed word is especially important for Anna; hence the ultimate resolution of her particular mental and emotional problems is necessarily bound up in and with and through writing. Through writing— public writing, such as a novel, not private writing, such as the notebooks— Anna is able to relate meaningfully again to the world and to those she knows. Just as the earlier commitments Anna had made have proven false or insufficient or inadequate, so her final commitment proves true and sufficient and adequate. Although others can be committed to other causes, writers like Anna must, in Mrs. Lessing's words, recreate "warmth and humanity and love of people" in their writing. No longer can Anna remain neutral, uninvolved in the lives of others (as she certainly is in much of this book, particularly in the case of her passivity and unconcern at Tommy's attempted suicide), or unattached. She must become, again in Mrs. Lessing's terms, an "instrument of change for good or bad," an "architect of the soul." And since Anna, primarily through her commitment to writing, does find it possible to become these things, one can say with little hesitation, because of the personal struggle in which the protagonist is involved and the satisfactory victory that protagonist gains over her weaker self, that *The Golden Notebook* is very much in the line of the memorable nineteenth-century novels Mrs. Lessing cites as being the "highest point of literature"—those by Tolstoy, Stendhal, Dostoevsky, Balzac, Turgenev, and Chekhov.

Anna Wulf, then, is herself no more "free" than those she knew in the Communist party or in Africa or in any of several other earlier commitments; indeed, her very name suggests this symbolically, for she has ceased to be a "Free/man" when she married; then she became a "Wulf," not unlike the wolves of destruction she had earlier envisioned in her nightmares. But if absolute "freedom" is not possible in this world, then commitment is, and on this point Mrs. Lessing has been most explicit:

> The act of getting a story or novel published is an act of communication, an attempt to impose one's personality and beliefs on other people. If a writer accepts this responsibility, he must see himself . . . as an architect of the soul.

And in so communicating, Anna is paradoxically exercising the very quality mentioned above as impossible in our world, the freedom of the individual—the freedom to fight, to "push boulders," to write for others, to work responsibly to improve the world, to try to eliminate personal and social chaos, to see ourselves as we really are. The "commitment to freedom," then, is both relative and continually in need of reexamination and modification as life goes on. Even if such "freedom" is never attained, it is the goal which keeps us sane and able to handle the many pressures of human life responsibly. Mrs. Lessing has referred to a "resting-point, a place of decision, hard to reach and precariously balanced." She goes on to say:

> It is a balance which must be continually tested and reaffirmed. Living in the midst of this whirlwind of change, it is impossible to make final judgements or absolute statements of value. The point of rest should be the writer's recognition of man, the responsive individual, voluntarily submitting his will to the collective, but never finally; and insisting on making his own personal and private judgements before every act of submission.

Certainly Mrs. Lessing, in and through such profound and rich works as *The Golden Notebook,* has made this "recognition of man, the responsive individual." This is no small task for any writer, and Mrs. Lessing has generally succeeded in demonstrating in her longer fiction the extent to which she has mastered it. To be sure, there are points on which Mrs. Lessing can be criticized, as in her handling of character and situation, but these are, I believe, of less significance than her accomplishment in detailing the experiences and development of such highly sensitive, intelligent, and self-analytic women as Anna Wulf.

FREDERICK R. KARL

Doris Lessing in the Sixties:
The New Anatomy of Melancholy

The most considerable single work by an English author in the 1960s has been done by Doris Lessing, in *The Golden Notebook* (1962). It is a carefully organized but verbose, almost clumsily written novel, and if we were to view it solely as an aesthetic experience, we might lose most of its force. The book's strength lies not in its arrangement of the several notebooks which make up its narrative and certainly not in the purely literary quality of the writing, but in the wide range of Mrs. Lessing's interests, and, more specifically, in her attempt to write honestly about women. To be honest about women in the sixties is, for Mrs. Lessing, tantamount to a severe moral commitment, indeed almost a religious function, in some ways a corollary of her political fervor in the fifties.

While the English novel has not lacked female novelists, few indeed—including Virginia Woolf—have tried to indicate what it is like to be a woman: that is, the sense of being an object or thing even in societies whose values are relatively gentle. For her portraits, Mrs. Lessing has adopted, indirectly, the rather unlikely form of the descent into hell, a mythical pattern characterized by her female protagonists in their relationships with men, an excellent metaphor for dislocation and fragmentation in the sixties. Like Persephone, her women emerge periodically from the underworld to tell us what went awry—and it is usually sex. Within each woman who tries to survive beyond the traditional protection of housewife and mother, there

From *Contemporary Literature* 13, no. 1 (Winter 1972). © 1972 by the Regents of the University of Wisconsin.

exists a bomb which explodes whenever she tries to live without men, as well as when she attempts to live with them. Her dilemma is her personal bomb.

In a May 1969 interview at Stony Brook, New York, Mrs. Lessing spoke of the period in which *The Golden Notebook* takes place as a time when "everything is cracking up. . . . It had been falling apart since the bomb was dropped on Hiroshima." Then, in a statement which carries the full force of the self-hatred and driven quality we sense in Anna and Ella, two of her narrators, she says: "Throughout my life I've had to support parties, causes, nations, and movements which stink." She states further: "I feel as if the Bomb has gone off inside myself, and in people around me. That's what I mean by the cracking up. It's as if the structure of the mind is being battered from inside. Some terrible thing is happening." The Bomb metaphor recalls Donne's "Batter my heart, three person'd God; for you / As yet but knocke, breathe, shine, and seeke to mend, / That I may rise." The paradox is similar: one may be either destroyed or resurrected by the same experience. The difference is that Donne felt rape was another form of chastity, and Mrs. Lessing is afraid that rape is the final step. All her women, in one way or another, are raped. As if to confirm the paradox in her desire for experience, she says later in the interview: "Today it's hard to distinguish between the marvellous and the terrible." After the *The Golden Notebook,* Mrs. Lessing tried to plumb the terrible, for her next novel, *The Four-Gated City* (1969) is nothing but nightmare, the portrait of a city, London, in which all four gates are guarded by Cerberus.

To continue temporarily this metaphor, the four gates in that later novel all lead to houses of constriction, nightmare, impotence, not dissimilar to the four notebooks of the earlier novel. At each gate, Mrs. Lessing's Martha is seeking a path, similar to the faltering figure of Dante at the beginning of the *Inferno.* We remember that the protagonist undertaking the Perilous Journey in her five-novel series, *Children of Violence,* is named Martha Quest, whose last name suggests the motif. Accordingly, if we are to discuss Mrs. Lessing's work in the sixties—the period when her earlier ideas found suitable techniques—we must play off two books which converge and move away from each other, the experimental *Golden Notebook* and the even more tentative *Four-Gated City,* which crowns the *Children of Violence* series. Like asymptotes, the two books approach each other without touching, all the while utilizing common images and symbols: the gate, the door, the house or room, the descent into hell, the quest. To gain a sense of the underworld, where all quests lead to further frustration, we should begin with *The Golden Notebook.*

At first, it would seem that Mrs. Lessing has picked up where Joyce has ended, with Molly Bloom's somewhat ambiguous "yes I said yes I will Yes." After all, her women, Anna Wulf and Molly Jacobs, appear to be saying "yes" to themselves and thumbing their noses at convention. But this is only an initial impression. Actually, their uncertain state of survival fits well into the ironies, paradoxes, conspiracies, lies, and deceptions that attend the world around them. About midway through the book, in the "Red Notebook 2," Comrade Ted tells of his idyllic meeting with the father-figure Stalin, whose wise presence appears to see and know all. When Anna has read this tale of Ted's meeting with Stalin, she comments: "But what seemed to me important was that it could be read as parody, irony or seriously. It seems to me this fact is another expression of the fragmentation of everything, the painful disintegration of something that is linked with what I feel to be true about language, the thinning of language against the density of our experience."

In one sense, this tale, which can be read as either parody or as slavering devotion to an ideal, is the way we can read most human experience since the end of the Second World War. Mrs. Lessing tells us something about human experience in those years. She tells us, among other things, that experience is infinite, variable, and messy (neither Sartre's contingency nor Marx's necessity), that all is seeming, that we cannot measure life according to preconceptions, that indeed we cannot distinguish between subject and object, that, in many ways, we are our own self-made fools. To say this is not to wallow in endless guilt about our deficiencies, but to suggest that she gives us a way of seeing the familiar and the expected. Like Anthony Powell, who views his characters mythically against endless sweeps of time, even as emerging like saurians from primeval swamps, Mrs. Lessing presents her women as Protean, as endlessly trying to recreate themselves, only to see them fall back befuddled by men like Paul-Michael or Saul Green, who need women as mothers and/or scapegoats for their own weaknesses. The individual is always on the threshold of drowning in the collective consciousness, a political as well as a psychological point for Mrs. Lessing.

Again like Powell, with his insistent mythical-temporal references, Mrs. Lessing has mighty metaphors. The notebooks, four in number, are obviously facets of Anna's life, as clearly affirmations of her attempt to find unity as evidence of her fragmentation. "I keep four notebooks, a black notebook, which is to do with Anna Wulf, the writer; a red notebook, concerned with politics; a yellow notebook, in which I make stories out of my experience; and a blue notebook which tries to be a diary." In one way, these notebooks fulfill what the interior monologue does for Joyce: the derivations of this novel may be female novelists, George Meredith's feminist tracts, and Simone de Beauvoir's *The Second Sex,* but the structural conception is neo-Joycean, much as Powell's *Music of Time* is neo-Proustian despite its patina of Waugh and early Huxley.

Yet, despite these notebooks as outposts of achievement or sanity, as a means of holding on when everything else is blocked, Anna does not triumph through them. Rather, she must always return to her room—like Gregor Samsa's, her room is a fierce refuge against harsh men and events—and in her room she dreams endlessly. They are terrible things, her nightmares, which are almost comparable to Gregor's metamorphosis into a bug. One particular and recurring dream is of going under water, drowning in the very element she is trying to breast. Yet such dreams of anxiety mock Anna's conscious belief that, although ordinary, she is capable through personal exertion of moving society just a fraction. She refers herself to Sisyphus, another "boulder-pusher" who puts his shoulder hopefully to the stone even while suspecting it will roll back. One time it may not.

Her dreams and her will are always in conflict. In the "Blue Notebook 1," Anna tells her psychiatrist, Mrs. Marks ("Mother Sugar"), of her dream of the casket. Instead of the casket holding beautiful things, it is more like Pandora's box, letting out odiferous waves of war, blood, bits of flesh, illness. Then, suddenly transformed, the contents become a small, green, smirking crocodile, whose large frozen tears turn into diamonds. The precise image is unclear, but the sardonic crocodile mocks all of Anna's dreams, hopes, and illusions. One may assume that the casket and the malicious crocodile are Anna's burdens or obstacles, always there when she seeks good faith or release.

This dream is linked to several others involving a smirking dwarf-like old man, sometimes deformed, sometimes with a "great protruding penis," whose form originally took shape from a vase, like the crocodile in the casket. These interior, hollowed-out shapes, whether casket or vase, are surely vaginal, and therefore the misshapen, malicious figures who fill them are symbolic of the men intruding in Anna's life. These men are necessary for her at the same time they are inadequate, and the dreams are examples of anxiety. Late in the book, in a part that prefigures the section called "The Golden Notebook," Anna sees herself as the dwarf figure, as, what she calls, the "principle of joy-in-destruction." Perhaps she is right. What she means is that the anxiety regarding men is built into her own needs, that in some self-destructive way she is bound to seek out men who will remind her of the crocodile and the deformed dwarf with the protruding penis. All this would be consistent with her desire to live existentially, beyond the pale of normal supports.

In her Stony Brook interview, Mrs. Lessing spoke of how she uses dreams whenever she is stuck in a book. "I fill my brain with the material for a new book, go to sleep, and I usually come up with a dream which resolves the dilemma." Then she says, "The unconscious artist who resides in our depths is a very economical individual. With a few symbols a dream can define the whole of one's life, and warn us of the future, too. Anna's dreams contain the essence of her experience in Africa, her fears of war, her relationship to communism, her dilemma as a writer." While simplified, this is an honest attempt to create literary material out of Freudian analysis, although elsewhere Mrs. Lessing rejects the Freudian unconscious as too dark and fearful a place.

But the dream is a warning, whether it is sugar-coated by Mrs. Marks (a female "Marx") or whether Anna wishes to see it through. The dream always brings her back to the closeness of her room, just as Martha Quest in *The Four-Gated City* is nearly always enclosed in houses and interiors. Anna writes in the "Golden Notebook" section that: "My big room, like the kitchen, had become, not the comfortable shell which held me, but an insistent attack on my attention from a hundred different points, as if a hundred enemies were waiting for my attention to be deflected so that they might creep up behind me and attack me." This fear of attack or rape; the use of the room as refuge—as in the later book, the houses as lairs; the insistent need to withdraw into nightmares—all these are part of the descent into hell, that mythical and yet personal seeking after self. When Mrs. Lessing foresees that her imperfect female characters will always select an inadequate man to make themselves miserable, she is insisting that hell is within—a visceral time bomb—and it will not be simply exorcised by anything the external world can offer. With this, we have placed Mrs. Lessing with the nineteenth-century novelists whose protagonists are themselves piecing together fragments of experience and attempting to derive some unity; she is not with the later novelists who have taken patterns of fragmentation for granted.

Perhaps the closest we come to Mrs. Lessing's sense of the sixties is in Harold Pinter. At first, the two seem dissimilar, and the coupling of their names may appear bizarre. But both the playwright and the novelist are heir to a development in literature that has become insistent in the last fifty to sixty years. Since Kafka and Proust, there has developed what we may call a literature of enclosure. It is a type of fiction in which breadth of space is of relatively little importance. Space exists not as extension but only as a volume to be enclosed in a room, or a house, or even in a city. Joyce's Dublin has this quality—as though the city were not open to the sky but were a series of enclosures of houses and bars and meeting places. Such a city conveys not the sense of something unfolding, but of something accruing, like an internal growth which invisibly expands to tremendous size under cover of the flesh.

Kafka's use of rooms and houses is, of course, one of the prototypes of this kind of fiction. Another is, obviously, the room of Proust's Marcel, where he stifles in heat and frustration and self-hatred. A third is the cluttered rooms of Beckett's Murphy or Watt, who bitterly malign their fate and remain immobile. Such a development in literature may, at first, appear to be a direct response to the Freudian reliance on the regressive tendencies of the adult to return to the womb, that quasi-sacred place where needs are met without effort and without external threat. Such a response is certainly there, and it is questionable if such a literature would have developed, at least in this manner, without the influence of psychoanalytic thought. To follow this argument—which ultimately is not the major one—is to see that the room is the place in which one can dream, in which one can isolate himself as a consequence of neurosis or withdrawal symptoms, all as part of that desire to seek refuge from external onslaughts which are too much for the individual to withstand. All this is certain.

But there is a further argument for the preponderance of rooms and rooming houses in Pinter and Mrs. Lessing. I think we can say that the room or house signifies for them an entire culture, in particular England's shrinkage in the sixties from its postwar eminence to a minor "enclosed power." In *The Four-Gated City,* for example, Martha Quest uses Mark Coldridge's house as a way of settling her life and at the same time as an escape from a social and political world she cannot control. As a medieval family once hid behind drawbridge and moat, she hides behind the door, and thus self-concealment is both a physical and psychological fact.

Since enclosure is so significant in Mrs. Lessing's work, its features need detailed description: even though the room is a place of refuge, it is also the locale of one's descent into hell. Its physical desolation is indeed a counterpart of the character's psychological state. Further, the room serves as a tiny stage for those on a string in a puppet show. The enclosure fixes the limits of sexuality, threatens and reassures within bounds, freeing as it limits. As a consequence, the novel becomes personal, subjective, solipsistic, even when externals like political events are of significance.

The room bottles up rage, leaves no escape for anger except when it is directed back into the self. The lair is itself a physical symbol of impotence—lack of choice, will, determination; identity is indistinguishable from one's furnishings. (See Anthony Powell for this point also—most of his action takes place in living rooms and at parties; only Widmerpool has will—the rest are virtually impotent.) Clearly, the panoramic novel is snuffed out, for adventure is lost; there is no struggle. The room or house is a battleground. The family relationship is symbiotic. In such a room, eros becomes sex, spirit becomes physical, idea or theory becomes fact. Whereas space was once used for repetition of a holy act, the act of creation itself, now its repetition is one of staleness, of folding anxiety into neurosis. In the room a dumb waiter serves as a feedline, or people themselves are "dumb waiters."

Finally, in the novel of enclosure, the room is the ultimate of the profane world, negating Mircea Eliade's idea of space as being sacred. The room is geometric space, not the infinite space that Eliade sees as central to a reliving of the cosmogony: "It follows that every construction or fabrication has the cosmogony as paradigmatic model. The creation of the world becomes the archetype of every human gesture, whatever its plan of reference may be. We have already seen that settling in a territory reiterates the cosmogony. Now that the cosmogonic value of the Center has become clear, we can still better understand why every human establishment repeats the creation of the world from a central point (the navel)." Keep in mind Mrs. Lessing's "four-gated city" when Eliade writes: "On the most archaic levels of culture this possibility of transcendence is expressed by various images of an opening; here, in the sacred enclosure, communication with the gods is made possible; hence there must be a door to the world above by which the gods can descend to earth and man can symbolically ascend to heaven." When the room or house was sacred, one's conception of space was infinite, extending to the infinite space of the universe. Breathing in the air of this room, one could as it were breathe in something coexistent with the cosmos. Lessing and Pinter, like Beckett, provide rooms whose air is foul; space is not infinite, but geometric, and it signifies the final vestiges of the profane city.

All literature has had its enclosures, but never before has the interior been so intensely the depository of "normal" illness and anxiety. There is virtually no nature in Pinter or in the Lessing of these novels, and certainly not nature as relaxation or renewal. When Pinter wishes to speak of nature, he puts its joys, ironically, into the mouth of a killer like Goldberg, in *The Birthday Party*: "Because I know what it is to wake up with the sun shining, to the sound of the lawnmower, all the little birds, the smell of the grass, church bells, tomato juice—." Here we have the typical Pinter metaphysic: the juxtaposition of dissimilars as the image or symbol of dislocation. So, too, Doris Lessing. Scribbling away in her notebooks, Anna-Ella tries to deny the outside, to negate possible renewal through alignment with external forces. Just as all anxiety comes from within—after all, nothing very dreadful really happens to her—so, also, all surcease must come from within. Thus, the modern predicament: caught in our own existential stoicism, we cling to our miseries as the sole form of our salvation.

So much is clear. What is curious is that Mrs. Lessing has picked up many of D. H. Lawrence's injunctions about mechanical sex, about enervating marriages, about the boredom of non-vital relationships, and yet she has broken with his romanticism, in which human failings, or successes, are worked out in a natural climate. To illustrate how she accepts Lawrence's indictment of mechanical sex while still accepting the machine: at one point in *The Golden Notebook,* Mrs. Lessing speaks of the vaginal orgasm, as opposed to the superficial clitoral orgasm, as something "that is created by the man's need for a woman, and his confidence in that need." She says she can always sense when a relationship is dying, for the man begins to insist on giving her clitoral orgasms, and that is a substitute and a fake. The only female sensations occur "when a man, from the whole of his need and desire takes a woman and wants all her response."

Through some existential process of choice or search, Anna wants to deny the historical role of women; but in her rightful desire to destroy female bondage, she does not see that the world has itself entered a new phase. And the very qualities of tenderness and satisfaction equally given and equally accepted are no longer possible for men who have sublimated their human qualities for the practical advantages of civilization. Lawrence spoke of such enervation, and he felt it had arrived. Why should we doubt that it has? In fact, by 1969, with *The Four-Gated City,* Mrs. Lessing appears willing to admit that the question has answered itself. But, earlier, in *The Golden Notebook,* she has only drawn up to the edge. Probably, her commitment to the social possibilities of technology had blinded her to the steady erosion of individual consciousness.

Nevertheless, *The Golden Notebook* is one of the few English novels of the last decades to project outward rather than seek forms of settlement. Anna's quest, already doomed to futility and failure, must continue: as an emancipated woman, as an outsider, she must complete or doom herself with a male. She cannot be complaisant. Even as she may suspect that the male is becoming dehumanized—she is familiar with Freud—and is capable of relating only to profession, career, or materiality, she still asserts choice. To justify her existence, she must deny her historical and biological role. To justify her existence, she must start the descent that most women attempt to avoid or mitigate through conventional marriage.

While *The Golden Notebook* stops short of the apocalypse, *The Four-Gated City* embraces the beast. If the former limns a kind of limbo, then the latter is indeed hell. Yet Mrs. Lessing's statements in *Declaration* do not prepare us for the sense of doom in *The Four-Gated City*. In *Declaration*, she asserted her preference for the nineteenth-century realists—Stendhal, Balzac, Tolstoy, Dostoevsky—who despite their differences, stated their "faith in man himself." She said, further, that the writer must not plunge into despair, as Genet, Sartre, Camus, and Beckett have done, nor into the collective conscience, as the socialist country writers have done. "The point of rest [for the writer] should be the writer's recognition of man, the responsible individual, voluntarily submitting his will to the collective, but never finally; and insisting on making his own personal and private judgements before every act of submission." Particularly ironic is her statement that "there is a new man about to be born . . . a man whose strength will not be gauged by the values of the mystique of suffering."

By the time of *The Four-Gated City*, twelve years after *Declaration*, Mrs. Lessing has descended into despair. The four gates are four houses, and the four houses are all various circles of Dante's *Inferno*. The vision here is especially compelling because it appears to contradict the drift of her earlier work beginning with *The Grass Is Singing* and including even *The Golden Notebook*. In that first novel, concerned with the struggle between white interests and black survival, she demonstrated she could write a personal story against the background of complex social and political relationships. In fact, many of the attitudes and situations of that protagonist, Mary Turner, were later grafted on to Martha Quest of the *Children of Violence* series, chiefly the survival, or disintegration, of the individual amidst collective pressures. Mrs. Lessing catches superbly the degeneration of those whose relationships are based on subterfuge. Ostensibly about Mary Turner, the novel is prophetic: while trying to maintain his supremacy, the white declines, eventually fragments.

When Mary Turner "becomes" Martha Quest, tensions intensify between individual need and social rejection, between individual flexibility and social rigidity so that the first four volumes of the series, before *The Four-Gated City*, maintain an uneasy balance between stability and threat, order and potential violence. Martha herself grows up amidst the distrust between English and Africans and their mutual hatred of blacks, Jews, and change. These emotions, which she is aware of from childhood, become the major conflicts she confronts in the larger world. Already refusing the constricted role her mother forced herself to play, Martha drifts toward socialism and atheism, becomes pro-black, and attempts anything that will lead to substantial personal values. She is, of course, seeking her identity as a woman and as a person.

The first four volumes unfortunately often become trivial, especially when the main line of the narrative becomes lost in political details or in inconsequential personal acts. Mrs. Lessing knows certain things very well— the land, family relationships which have soured, the frustration of meaningless affections, the way parents hang on to their children when neither can really bear the other—but when she details the dogma of the Marxist-Trotsky-Stalin axis, the reader has no place to go. There is, nevertheless, in those early novels a curious psychological play, for those blacks hovering as dark presences in the background of white settlements are curious embodiments of Martha's slowly emerging other self. Like the black natives, waiting to break out to claim consciousness, she, too, is twisting and turning in her appointed, non-conscious roles as daughter and then wife. As "Mattie," she is a girl who will fit into the colonial pattern; as Martha, she is her own woman seeking consciousness.

Closely related to the dialectic of her roles is the recurring image of the black women who refuse to be fragmented by vague choices and who breed contentedly; they are essential women, avatars of Martha's own potential future. But Martha knows that these women do not live in a blissful, untroubled paradise, that they are diseased, that they die young, that they have given themselves over completely to a natural process without sufficient individual will. And yet she envies their instinctual mode of survival, their indifference to consciousness. The temptation is to be Mattie. And yet she also knows how impossible it would be for her to try to emulate the black women. She must become Sisyphus.

These first volumes in the series, very much a product of the 1950s in their linear political and social aspirations, were evidently part of Mrs. Lessing's own experience in Southern Rhodesia and parallel in many ways arguments and attitudes put forth by Simone de Beauvoir in *The Second Sex* (1949). One might go further and say that *Children of Violence*, except for its ideology, is a working out of entire chapters in the de Beauvoir book: Childhood, The Young Girl, Sexual Initiation, Lesbianism, The Married Woman, The Mother, Social Life, The Narcissist, The Woman in Love, The Independent Woman, et al. In the latter chapter, in fact, Simone de Beauvoir writes apropos of Martha: "When she [woman] is productive, active, she regains her transcendence; in her projects she concretely affirms her status as subject; in connection with the aims she pursues, with the money and the rights she takes possession of, she makes trial of and senses her responsibility."

Yet as the series continues, Doris Lessing clearly refuses for her characters the role of existential female, as later she rejected the polemics of women's liberation for a larger, more political view of life. Mrs. Lessing's Martha fears recurring history, knowing that she "could take no step, perform no action, no matter how apparently new and unforeseen, without the secret fear that in fact this new and arbitrary thing would turn out to be part of the inevitable process she was doomed to." This sense of nightmarish repetition, of destiny repeating itself inexorably, is of course very much part of the literature of enclosure. With spatiality, one can avoid repetition through novelty of choice or act, but enclosure negates personal expansion.

The Four-Gated City begins with suffocation and strangulation. The key images in the first pages are of grime, globules of wet, browny-grey textures, oilcloth with spilled sugar, gritty smears, grease, thumb marks. All these are "inside" images and forerun the theme of enclosure. Possibly the chief scenic effect of the book, as befitting Mrs. Lessing's continued descent into a fiercely populated hell, is either Bosch's *Garden of Earthly Delights* or his *Last Judgment*. In both paintings, as in Mrs. Lessing's novel, there is the mixture of sacred and profane, of realism and fantasy, of the loving and the obscene, of large vision and carping detail, of panorama and locale. There is no single style, but a comprehensive, somewhat mannered tone. There is, also, as a sexual by-product, the desire to wound and be wounded—both to gain delight from watching others roast over a slow fire and to be roasted oneself over the same fire. The theme of torture is never far from either Bosch or Mrs. Lessing. Both put a roof over hell. Durrell's Alexandria was also hell, but frantic sensuality was at least a temporary escape. And while Anthony Powell's seriatim novels are filled with mythical hells, whether from Homer or from Wagner, his central character, Nicholas Jenkins, remains relatively isolated from the deterioration around him. His descents are pratfalls, while others have indeed fallen. In Mrs. Lessing's novel, Martha succumbs. The theme is not so clearly decline and disintegration—as in Camus's *The Fall*—as it is the effort of sensitive human beings to survive schizophrenia.

Amidst the various denizens of Mrs. Lessing's hell, the key one is possibly Lynda Coldridge, the wife of Mark; it is to Mark's house that Martha goes seeking a refuge from external events which are themselves mad. Lynda has proven too sensitive for normal contacts—among other things, sexual relations—and her waking hours are spent in trying to hold on. At first, she survives by eating pills, but periodically she gives up these props in order to seek inner support. Yet in some curious way—and she is not particularly sympathetic—she is a seer, one who has a sense of impending disasters, and Martha evidently cannot forgo her presence. In fact, Lynda's very ability to "hear voices" and to experience visions is, in her society, a sign of her sickness. In other societies where such talents were indicative of the majority, she would not be sick or else her extravagances would serve a social function. One is reminded of R. D. Laing's injunction to those who would work with psychotics: "One has to be able to orientate oneself as a person in the other's scheme of things rather than only to see the other as an object in one's own world." A man who suddenly kneels down amidst a crowd to pray fervently is insane; in church, he is considered devout.

What is of interest here, however, is not simply Lynda. By herself, she is not a compelling person. Mrs. Lessing has moved beyond trying to create attractive characters whose point of view creates empathy. What is compelling is the fact that Martha Quest has given up the quest. She will never reach the Holy Grail, nor even continue the perilous journey, for she is seeking security at any level, and finds that it is easier to remain in the Coldridge house—behind that locked gate—and relate herself to Lynda's mad state. As long as Lynda is mad, Martha has Mark, while Lynda herself needs Martha's sense of order. All attachments are symbiotic. Again Laing proves instructive: "Generally speaking, the schizoid individual is not erecting defences against the loss of a part of his body. His whole effort is rather to preserve his *self*." This is, by now, Martha's effort: to preserve a person who is herself "precariously structured," the overall symbol of which is Lynda's tenacious attempt to hold on without returning to the hospital.

There is some warning of this deteriorative process in *The Golden Notebook,* during Anna's affair with Saul Green and shortly after with her dream of the dwarfed man with the protruding penis: "Sitting there I had a vision of the world with nations, systems, economic blocks, hardening and consolidating; a world where it would become increasingly ludicrous even to talk about freedom, or the individual conscience. I know that this sort of vision has been written about, it's something one has read, but for a moment it wasn't words, ideas, but something I felt, in the substance of my flesh and nerves, as true." Her affair with Saul Green, destructive in virtually every way, is a forerunner of nearly all relationships Martha has in *The Four-Gated City.*

More specifically, those four gates to the four houses where Martha stays are themselves microcosms of English society, and, ultimately, of the world as Mrs. Lessing envisages it. It is a society that follows the holocaust of the Second World War and which immediately precedes the apocalyptic vision that ends our present notion of the world and the book. Yeats's rough beast has arrived. Whereas once gates were entrances that one opened while seeking something or someone, they are now barriers which close off exits or prevent egress. The four bleak houses of England are the restaurant at the beginning, where Martha would be "Mattie" (a "good fellow") and would be expected to lose herself in a dull marriage; second, the house of Mark Coldridge, a writer somewhat close to the center of power, but besieged by predatory journalists and a center of madness, inactivity, frustration, as well as some kindness; third, Jack's house—literally, that Jack built—where girls go to be broken in for their future as prostitutes, where Jack sits like a spider catching them on the fly; and finally, Paul's house—Paul is Mark's nephew—where derelicts and misfits, sexual cripples and the maimed, as in some James Purdy story, congregate under Paul's protective wing.

The connecting link to all the houses, to all the gates, is Martha herself. At the opening of the novel, she arrives at the restaurant when she comes to post-war London, a continuation of the earlier *Landlocked.* She then seeks a job as a secretary, but accepts temporarily a post as Mark Coldridge's housekeeper. As the house becomes a walled-in medieval fortress which protects her against further action, even further thought, the job turns into a way of life. The house is Bosch's hell, Gregor Samsa's room, the Invisible Man's basement cell, but it is also a refuge. Perhaps a modern view of hell is no more than this, Sartre'e *No Exit,* a place in which one loses himself, his will, his determination, and exchanges choice for a lair. Dostoevsky pressed this option in the Grand Inquisitor scene, and the contemporary response is clear. Freedom, as Martha once quested after it in the stifling atmosphere of the white man's Africa, is not worth the struggle; we are, she appears to accept, all caught in a larger scheme anyway, and it is better to be besieged than to besiege. Using Mark's house as a base of operations—settling in for the rest of her useful years—Martha occasionally ventures out, to have casual sex with Jack and to continue the debasement of her former intentions. Or else she gravitates to Paul's house, a kind of live-in encounter group, in which the maimed attempt to support each other; all experience there is "tripping," hallucinatory.

Shut in, besieged, surrounded by madness, frustration, sickness, inadequate, furtive sex, gated, with hyena-like journalists howling outside, with nuclear bombs in production, with marches and countermarches, with threats always looming—whether Russia, fission, or personal schizophrenia—Martha has to put herself together in some fashion. If she is enclosed in four houses, she is also Janus-faced: the softness of Mattie is the reverse of the questing Martha. The houses are both integrative and disintegrative, much as the notebooks in *The Golden Notebook* represented two opposing strains: those parts of Anna-Ella which could be consolidated and those pieces which defied stabilization. The apocalyptic epilogue of *The Four-Gated City* represents, in some ways, the "golden notebook" section in that book. The content of both is seeking form. In geometry, the circle indicates perfection, completion. But Mrs. Lessing utilizes not circles, but "fours": four notebooks, four gates or houses, and epilogues or "golden" episodes. The "fours" indicate all directions, negate completion, baffle expansion, intensify the enclosed quest. There is no magic in four. And the content finally achieves a form that allows no exit, except through the apocalyptic vision of a new, technological world which ends the novel.

The hopeful, striving Martha of the earlier books in the series is clearly very different from the Martha of this novel and also different from the Anna-Ella of *The Golden Notebook*. Like the rest of us, Mrs. Lessing has changed her former vision, in which political and social action—the image of Sisyphus pushing that boulder—was possible, even though results were miniscule and possibly not even visible in one's own lifetime. Now the world has turned upon itself, in a repetitive cycle of violence: *Children of Violence* ends in a final disaster in which radioactivity, lethal gas, nerve gas, and the other by-products of a runaway society have ended life as we know it. Like Anthony Powell, as his series darkens, Mrs. Lessing gets gloomier and murkier, heading toward that vision which has rarely been sympathetic to the English temperament. It is chiefly a continental design, the sense of final things in Mann, Kafka, Conrad. Deeply humanistic, Mrs. Lessing takes up the familiar question of technology in conflict with the rest of life and foresees, in striking images of disintegration, science as inexorable, while human values, never more than tenuous, are trapped in Atreus-like houses in which people devour each other.

The symbol of breakdown in morality and in humanity is Jimmy Wood, a mild-mannered scientist and writer of space fiction who is a human computer. Jimmy represents the bland forces of military, science, and government which, with velvet glove, offer salvation while they are missing a human dimension: "It was as if Jimmy had been born with one of the compartments of the human mind developed to its furthest possibility, but this was at the cost to everything else." Jimmy specifically has been designing machines which can tamper with the human mind, making improvements on existing machines which destroy part of the human brain by electric charges. In addition, he has developed on government request machines to destroy the brains of dangerous persons, who would then vanish without protest. Further, Jimmy has worked on and perfected a machine for "stimulating, artificially, the capacities of telepathy, 'second sight,' etc." So that the machine would always have fuel, it is necessary for governments or the military to have on hand a "human bank" which the machine could utilize. Such a human radio or telephone, or whatever, would provide an extension to the machine and prove more flexible; after that, it is up to the military to find a specific use.

In a way, Jimmy Wood's invention works, for certain people do have psychological reactions as telepaths. The drift is toward the interchangeability of people and machines, until life itself is indistinguishable. The final sections of the novel concern a letter from Martha, now old and worn-out, addressed to Francis Coldridge, Mark's son. At the time Martha is barely surviving in Robinson Crusoe style on a "contaminated island" off the coast of Scotland. Britain has been poisoned; the political center has shifted to Africa and to the Chinese. The time is less than thirty years from now. In her *New American Review* interview, Mrs. Lessing spoke of *The Four-Gated City* as a prophetic novel. "I think that the 'iron heel' is going to come down. I believe the future is going to be cataclysmic."

In *The Golden Notebook,* the key issue was human relationships, especially the relationships between men and women as a key image of modern humanity or inhumanity. Sexual liberation, from the female side, and sexual restructuring, from the male, were necessary. But in 1969, Mrs. Lessing said: "I'm impatient with people who emphasize sexual revolution. I say we should all go to bed, shut up about sexual liberation, and go on with the important matters." Her turn upon herself is curious, for this conflict between collective politics and personal matters had been the crux of her work of the last two decades. Anna's psychiatrist, in fact, suggested that her political activity was an avoidance of personal blockage. The conflict was real. Now, the conflict has been "resolved." The incredibly difficult question of man-woman relationships becomes "going to bed," and sexual liberation seems an act of conscious choice, whereas before the very question of liberation raised all the familiar problems of identity and will.

The Four-Gated City is, in several ways, a curious finale to the *Children of Violence* series. It appears to cap the "enclosure" theme, so that Martha ends up, in Mark's house, as exhausted and otiose as the narrator in Proust or one of Beckett's dying gladiators. Up to this point, Martha, like Powell's Nicholas Jenkins, had been involved in a *Bildungsroman.* Far more than Jenkins, however, Martha has rubbed her nose into the filth of events. Observer more than participant, Jenkins moves easily in his own version of the dance of time. But while he waltzes or relaxes into old familiar motions, as appropriate to someone who glides through an established society, Martha contorts her body into the brittle shapes of modern dance, as befitting someone who must always create the society in which she is to move.

Self-evidently, she is involved in constant assertions of her mind and body, while Powell's protagonist has a ready-made group into which he always fits. And although he acts as a voice of decency and constraint among those who indulge in desperate ventures, he is too reserved to take any chances for himself. (We remember he is Sloth in the tableau of the Seven Deadly Sins.) Mrs. Lessing, born in Persia of British parents, then coming to England as an alien from Rhodesia, where she had lived from her fifth through her thirtieth year, is herself the prototype of the unsettled artist. Not unusually, her Martha must go through all the awkward, anxiety-producing movements of the dance of time. There is no point at which she can stop to say: "I have arrived, I can see all around me." For her, all experience is a series of new starts. Powell's Jenkins need never start anew, for all the flotsam and jetsam from the past are at hand to create continuity in one fluid, dance-like step. Only events interfere.

In addition to these twists and turns, Martha must struggle through male-female relationships which could stifle her at any given point. In *Martha Quest,* she must deal with a series of narcissistic young men whose need is not for her, but to assure some nagging fear in themselves—whose own hesitancy about their manhood shades every aspect of their relationships and turns most sexual episodes into mother-child encounters. With herself unfulfilled as a woman, Martha must avoid her "biological destiny," which would mean the end of all; at the same time, she finds such lack of will attractive as an alternative to setting herself constantly against her destiny. This feeling is particularly acute, as we mentioned before, when Martha views the easy compromise of the black women, who give in early to their destiny and live without seething.

Yet Martha fights off the situation in which "men seemed to press a button, as it were, and one was expected to turn into something else for their amusement"; that is, "married, signed and sealed away." In her relationship with her mother, in particular, one sees what Martha has to fight through even before she comes up against the young men. She detests her mother as only those can who have translated their hatred into pity. That is to say, she must fight against her mother in herself; she must be aware of sliding back. For Mrs. Quest is a mother, not a human being or person, and Martha must resist the same role for herself. Not only has Mrs. Quest been destroyed by racism—like most of the other settlers, she accepts a schizoid, paranoiac routine in which blacks both serve and persecute her—but she has been destroyed by her sexual, emotional, psychological repression. Having been miserable, she rejoices in her philosophy of misery; and needing to justify her own choice, she must destroy her daughter's alternatives.

Therefore Martha's rebellious assertions of will are the substance of the first four volumes of *Children of Violence*. To understand this fact is to see how contrary *The Four-Gated City* really is, for there all relationships are symbiotic. No one stands without using another as crutch; no one is sick or well without influencing the sickness or well-being of another. And these relationships are not of the sort that build a whole or unify a group which can stand together; they are an infection, a slow stain throughout the society. A good image of such suppurating love and affection comes when Mark Coldridge approaches his symbiotic other half, the mad Lynda:

> He kissed her. Lips, a slit, in the flesh of a face, were pressed against a thin tissue of flesh that saved them from pressing a double row of teeth which had lumps of metal in them. Then these lips moved to touch her own slit through which she was equipped to insert food or liquid, or make sounds. A kiss. That part of Martha which observed this remarkable ritual was filled with a protective compassion for these two ridiculous little creatures—as if invisible arms, vast, peaceful, maternal, were stretched around them both, and rocked them like water.

The imagery is remarkable for its quality of lost identity, of submergence in another, of rejection of self. From here, the novel ends with the apocalypse; the ultimate bomb goes off, and a profane society has embraced its doom.

None of this is witty, or even ironic. Perhaps because she was an outsider, Mrs. Lessing has always been earnest and has never traded on the English tradition of social comedy, or muddling through. Both Anthony Powell and C. P. Snow, in their vastly different ways, belong to that mode, as do most of the 1950s "Angries" writers. In her rather grim, relentless manner, Mrs. Lessing has tried to be both panoramic (about racism, communism, bombism, all the "ologies" and "isms") and subjective. Her length indicates as much: *The Four-Gated City* runs one quarter of a million words, and *The Golden Notebook* is about as long. And yet with all her prolixity, she has almost nowhere to go. She is getting less personal, as she suggests in her *New American Review* interview, and she has destroyed the objective world. There is always science fiction, but in that mode those intense human relationships which are the strength of her earlier work can have no outlet. One wonders as he holds these two considerable achievements in hand if still another novelist is succumbing to apocalyptic visions as a way of settling personal problems.

PATRICIA MEYER SPACKS

Free Women

In novels written by women in the nineteenth century, when social liberation was hardly a real possibility for women, the connection between imaginative vitality and psychic freedom was clear and striking. Charlotte Brontë's passionate heroines, existing in conditions of artificial social isolation—orphaned heiress, poor governess, English teacher in a foreign land—asserted their imaginations as alternative to the deadening conventionality that surrounded them. One remembers Jane Eyre: "My sole relief was to walk along the corridor of the third storey, . . . and allow my mind's eye to dwell on whatever bright visions rose before it—and, certainly, they were many and glowing; to let my heart be heaved by the exultant movement, which, while it swelled it in trouble, expanded it with life; and best of all, to open my inward ear to a tale that was never ended—a tale my imagination created, and narrated continuously; quickened with all of incident, life, fire, feeling, that I desired and had not in my actual existence." Elizabeth Gaskell, less dramatic in her evocations of the imagination's yearnings, allows Margaret, in *North and South,* to look out the window at night, see a poacher, and find herself—despite her irreproachable credentials as minister's daughter—sympathizing and identifying with him. But Charlotte Brontë's tempestuous spirits invariably find fulfillment in marriage to a dominant man, and Mrs. Gaskell's Margaret, after enduring the full experience of desertion, as her parents and guardian die, after experimenting briefly with independence in

From *The Female Imagination.* © 1972, 1975 by Patricia Meyer Spacks. Avon Books, 1972.

the doing of good works, subsides contentedly into marriage. And indeed, given the detailed exposition of the lot of old maids in Miss Brontë's *Shirley,* it is difficult to conceive other viable alternatives for these young women: they can sustain their freedom only in their imaginings.

In the twentieth century, social possibilities are greater and the image of the "free woman"—often promiscuous, often intellectual, priding herself on being emotionally undemanding but often seen nonetheless as "castrating"—has been established in fiction by men and women authors alike. The most self-conscious and elaborate study, in imaginative terms, of the "free" woman's problems is *The Golden Notebook,* first published in 1962, now read with passionate involvement by college girls who have difficulty believing that women of their mothers' generation confronted the dilemmas Doris Lessing describes, which seem to the young uniquely their own. It was the last book we read in [my] course, a fact that gave it in advance a curious special position. Because it was the last—and because I had hinted all semester that this was the book that *really* described the condition of the contemporary woman—unique expectations developed around it. This was the novel, my students hoped, that would answer their questions.

At any rate, it *asks* their questions. Five sections of the book bear the title "Free Women," a phrase surrounded by invisible inverted commas of steadily increasing emphasis. From without, from the point of view of society at large, Anna, the novel's heroine, and her friend Molly seem to lead "free lives, that is, lives like men." Anna is, in every accepted social sense, free: from financial pressures and domestic ones, from the blindly accepted restrictions of conventional morality, from traditional class-definitions, from inarticulateness, ignorance, stupidity. She is, for exactly these reasons, to men an appropriate object for casual lust: when their wives go to the hospital to have babies, they expect to be welcomed to Anna's bed. Her "freedom" thus becomes a means for her victimization.

In her own self-perception, she is bound by her physical nature as woman; every month her period makes her "feel helpless and out of control." Her emotions limit her possibilities: particularly the diffuse and irrational sense of guilt which she shares with women in general; and, even more emphatically, her felt need for love and protection. And the nature of society and of her responses to it severely restrict even her imagination of freedom. The novel's central symbol is her "writer's block," her inability to create in communicable terms, caused partly by her sense of how inadequate is any individual response to social horror. Imaginary Vietnamese peasants look over her shoulder; the challenge of reality invalidates every rendition of the real.

Anna is in fact far from free. Her personal political situation thus reflects the international one rendered in the final section of her red notebook, the one devoted to the Communist party:

> The red notebook, like the black notebook, had been taken over by newspaper cuttings, for the years 1956 and 1957. These referred to events in Europe, the Soviet Union, China, the United States. Like the cutting of Africa in the same period [recorded in the black notebook], they were about, for the most part, violence. Anna had underlined the word "freedom" whenever it occurred, in red pencil. When the cuttings ceased, she had added up the red lines, making a total of 679 references to the word freedom.

Freedom is only a word, its implications always contradicted by reality, and the idea of a free woman is illusory as that of a free society. To make freedom a fact is the central effort of all political struggle.

In Anna's personal feminine politics, one responds to felt limitation by fragmentation. Women have long been accustomed to divide their lives into compartments; Anna's mode of keeping things separate, isolating parts of her experience in individual notebooks, although more complicated, literary, and self-aware than that of most women, has the same meaning. She replies to the threat of chaos, which makes freedom meaningless, by creating limited orders, necessary, but necessarily false; recognizing their falsity, she sees herself therefore as an enemy of possibility.

But the notebooks contain also the seed of possibility, for they record not only fact but its imaginative reshaping. The black notebook—about Africa, about her writing, about her finances—offers the truth of feeling, dominated by what Anna comes to consider her "lying nostalgia" for the past. The truth of social perspective shapes the red notebook, about Anna's relation to the Communist Party; the yellow one, for fiction, offers the truth of the imagination; the blue, a conventional journal, provides the truth of detail. Truth is multiple and fragmentary, and so is fiction. Only the yellow notebook is intended for fiction, but all four notebooks contain it, since precise linguistic rendition of simple actuality is unachievable. Language necessarily mediates between fact and imagining, transforming experience into meaning. Language is for Anna the only conceivable means to freedom. Her experience produces dead ends, defeats touching nothing but hopelessness; yet writing about experience can redeem it. The lessons Anna must learn are taught her in dreams: salvation comes through the release of the subconscious. *The Golden Notebook* ends in a chaos of recorded and imagined experience, with the reader unable to tell for certain which is which. It also ends with considerable emphasis on the fact that a novel, this novel, has been written—the single clearly redemptive fact, a fact of freedom. Freedom is only a word, but the word has power.

Writing is Anna's work, for a long time her emblem of the impossible. It does not provide the freedom of escape, as Anaïs Nin claims her writing does, but of integration: the containing and ordering of experience. Partly an alternative to experience, it points up the difficulties of a woman's finding freedom directly in her life. The problem of relationship, for the fictional character, Anna, as for living women, Lillian Hellman, Anaïs Nin, Isak Dinesen, focuses the perplexities of femininity. Anna's consciousness that she needs the love of a single man dominates her understanding of all that happens to her. Recognizing that it makes her out of tune with her life and her time, she yet has no control over the need.

A complaint frequently made about *The Golden Notebook* is that its failure to depict any emotionally adequate men amounts to a serious falsification of actuality. But the paucity of good men helps to focus the problems of good women—"good" in quite a new sense. "For women like me," reflects Ella (Anna's "fictional" version of herself), "integrity isn't chastity, it isn't fidelity, it isn't any of the old words. Integrity is the orgasm." Ella, like Anna, experiences orgasm only with men she loves. And love is, for a woman, part of *wholeness*—integrity in the root sense.

To be a whole human being is the heroine's central struggle. Wholeness is, finally, the necessary condition for freedom: and it is, for Anna, unattainable. The ambiguous ending of *The Golden Notebook* records two conspicuous defeats—Molly's marriage of convenience, Anna's job at "matrimonial welfare work"—along with the partial victory of Anna's freedom-through-imagination in her writing of the metaphorical golden notebook, the novel. Molly and Anna have recognized the impossibility of wholeness, which depends for a woman, the novel suggests, on connection with another. Acknowledging the severe limitations on their freedom, they resign themselves to working within them: defeat and victory are the same. The condition that makes ultimate freedom impossible is the human condition, the same for men and women. But—so Molly's and Anna's positions imply—because women must have love, not only for orgasm but for integrity, their struggle is perhaps more intense, their triumph less conceivable, their partial freedom more entirely dependent on imagination, than those of men.

Such, at any rate, is the assumption on which much of *The Golden Notebook* rests. Molly and Anna imagine that the emotional needs of men and women are different; although they declare that this difference defines masculine freedom, their tone reveals their contempt for the emotional superficiality and exploitativeness they associate with the male. The amplitude of sexual possibility for men is, from their feminine point of view, an index of moral inferiority. The novel depicts limited men, associates such limitation with masculinity, declares it to be "freedom." The difficulty of a woman's achieving comparable freedom becomes a subtle emblem of her virtue. To differentiate between the sexes in such terms may be seen as yet another operation of defensive narcissism: self-love disguises itself as humble acceptance of things-as-they-are, betrays itself by the nature of its evaluation of the Other (i.e., the masculine), but provides protection by embracing limitation while seeming to regret it, and by defining feminine limitation in flattering terms.

> "Anna's notion of freedom isn't real because real freedom depends on a relation between two people in which responses don't have to be guarded."

My students, many of them, clung to a hope that freedom was not incompatible with love.

In *The Four-Gated City,* Doris Lessing grants that the masculine need for love is as fundamental as its feminine counterpart, but she also explicitly declares narcissism the means of salvation. What in *The Golden Notebook* seemed a link between fantasy and freedom here becomes in fact an identity. The novel's significant definition of freedom is provided—without any relieving irony—by psychotic Lynda. "I keep quiet about what I know," she says. "I have to, you see. . . . That's freedom, isn't it? Everyone has a bit of freedom, a little space. . . . That is freedom. . . . That's mine. It's all they let me have. They wouldn't let me keep that if they knew how to take it away. But if I say to them: I don't hear voices, you've cured me, the voices have gone . . . they can't prove anything. That's my freedom." Her freedom is her madness, and her privacy in it. Martha Quest, the novel's heroine, comes to believe that madness is, or derives from, true insight; her own "work," she decides, must be to achieve equivalent insight herself.

This work becomes part of the battle of being a woman. As consistently as Lillian Hellman, Mrs. Lessing in this novel employs military metaphors to describe feminine activity, here understood as largely defensive. Martha has to defend others from the petty and major ills of the world, and, more important, has to defend herself from encroachment: has to create and preserve her own freedom. Her effort involves rejection of love and marriage, finally a gladly accepted sexlessness. She expresses gratitude at the fact that young girls "borrow" her clothes, the paraphernalia of feminine attractiveness. "The rejuvenation a young girl gives her mother or an older woman is a setting-free into impersonality, a setting-free, also, from her personal past." The point foretells the ideology of *The Summer before the Dark.*

The solution to the problem outlined in *The Golden Notebook,* then, of the limitation to freedom implied by one woman's declared inability to have orgasms without love, is to eliminate sex as well as love from one's life. The solution to the restrictions implicit in all personal relations is "a setting-free into impersonality." Critics have complained about the "science fiction" final section of *The Four-Gated City,* in which dedicated "seers" and "hearers," who have developed to a high degree capacities formerly identified with madness, help to save the world, or pieces of it, from total annihilation. But the disturbing quality of this section, its sense of remoteness, its theoretical tone, in fact dominates a large part of the novel's second half. As Martha concentrates more and more on her inner life, the outer world becomes (not only to her: to the reader) increasingly attenuated. Relationships multiply, but their complexities are stated rather than felt. Sexual possibilities continue, but they are not important. The world moves toward its destruction, the political and social scene reflecting the unsureness of individuals: in a sense this is the novel's subject. But it does not feel important either, except as a weighty demonstration of the urgency of Martha's efforts toward self-discovery. Only this exploration of her own inner life matters.

Martha's external conduct is that of the "good" woman: she devotes her life to others. Her inner life, on the other hand, a life of obsessive self-concentration, denies the real significance of others and makes it clear that, in her case at least, the good woman's actions, however socially useful, do not reflect her essence. The asserted paradox central to *The Four-Gated City* is that self-obsession of Martha's kind can produce a social salvation; analogically, the horrifying physical mutations caused by radiation and other forms of contamination may involve psychic alterations which will likewise contribute to the world's redemption. But the problem of individual female salvation dominates the novel, which seems to assert a solution to that problem. Martha Quest, living a life almost entirely formed by the needs of others, lacks the external concomitants of freedom but achieves the inner dependence that comes from intense self-commitment, accepting the dangers of self-immersion. Her creator appears to claim that such solipsism, multiplied, may save the world; but the novel suggests rather that this kind of freedom, like others, may become itself a trap.

Indeed, the suspicion that here too is a trap is a subterranean theme of contemporary fiction by women. Mrs. Lessing's *Briefing for a Descent into Hell* has a masculine protagonist whose problem recapitulates Martha's, and Lynda's, in more intense form. Imprisoned in his own madness, he sees in its fantasies sources of redemption for the world, but his insight is incommunicable. He can only return to sanity and meaningless community. *Play*

It as It Lays, in which insanity means total isolation; *Up the Sandbox!,* with fantasies supporting the mundane while appearing to challenge it—such books reveal that in our era of widespread fascination with madness and romantic speculation about its power to lay hold on truth, woman novelists, sharing the fascination, also convey doubts—often apparently inadvertent, often shared with men—about its viability.

The idea that women may find their most significant freedom through fantasy or imagination need not imply any commitment to madness. Saner visions of the imagination as salvation, which underlie many pre-twentieth-century novels about and by women and at least a few autobiographies, substantiate the possibility that the liberated inner life may create new freedoms of actual experience.

The difficulties of feminine freedom, as suggested by Hellman, Nin, and Lessing, inhere in the actualities of feminine experience. To arrive at freedom, these women indicate, through direct self-presentation or fictional creation, is to triumph over actuality. The qualified triumphs they adumbrate depend at least partly on denial or avoidance: Hellman denying significant difference between the sexes, Nin avoiding self-confrontation by self-display, Lessing's heroines retreating from intolerable experience into the wider expanses of conscious or subconscious reshaping of it. But the imagination can also lead toward acceptance, as Dinesen's loving but unsentimental attention to details of the natural world suggests, providing such intense imaginative concentration on actuality that its possibilities expand. To be sure, Isak Dinesen's experience bears little relation to the "normal" lives of women—but Hellman's experience, Nin's, the careers of Lessing's heroines, are not "normal" either. Welcoming what happens to her, valuing and using her richest capacities, Isak Dinesen accepts her womanhood but insists on her freedom within it. Her capacity for acceptance repudiates the despair of such books as *Briefing for a Descent into Hell*—a despair that declares immutable the gap between the real and the imagined.

LYNN SUKENICK

Feeling and Reason in Doris Lessing's Fiction

Of all the clichés about women, the belief that they are creatures of feeling—and men creatures of reason—is one of the most ancient and persuasive. The extent of this belief has ranged from a mistrust of women's irrationality to an ardent faith in the saving power of her emotional nature. As nonreflective *bios*, woman has been seen as the root, the source, and the touchstone; she gives the surety of the natural. In her function as lifegiver woman is supposedly simple and whole; her power to give birth defies and makes unnecessary the complexities of self-consciousness.

The division between emotion and reason has been apportioned not only to men and women but among kinds of women. Jane Austen—whose freedom from inner conflicts about gender perhaps helped to supply that beautifully unruffled prose whose ironies we find so comforting—posed the terms in her novel *Sense and Sensibility*. Although there could indeed be a Man of Feeling, as Mackenzie showed in his novel of that name, it was primarily the women who enacted the iconography of tears and fainting as it appeared in novels of sensibility in the eighteenth and early nineteenth centuries. Such women were the target of Mary Wollstonecraft's *A Vindication of the Rights of Woman,* and living proof, for her, that women had to be educated out of the propensity toward exaggerated emotion which idleness encouraged. Women of sensibility were the object, too, of Austen's indicting wit in *Sense and Sensibility* and *Northanger Abbey*. To Marianne's

From *Contemporary Literature* 14, no. 4 (Autumn 1973). © 1973 by the Regents of the University of Wisconsin.

fit of nostalgia in the former book, Elinor, the sister of good sense, comments dryly, "It is not everyone who has your passion for dead leaves."

The satire of the first great female novelist did not, however, kill off the novel of sensibility; refined away from the eighteenth-century potboilers of empathy, it has emerged full-blown and serious in our century in the sensitive and lyrical fiction of writers like James, Proust, Woolf, and Mansfield. In spite of the influence of male writers (and Proust was homosexual and James sexually ambiguous), the novel of sensibility has been associated insistently with the feminine. Whether it is correct or not, Diana Trilling's statement is fairly typical: "In our own century certainly, from the time of Dorothy Richardson right down to our present-day women writers for *The New Yorker,* the female self has been the locus of all the sensibility presumed to have been left us by modern life." Women, although without perhaps the silliness of Austen's heroines or of Wollstonecraft's subjects, have maintained themselves as the caretakers of sensibility in this century as well.

Doris Lessing, whose position as one of the major women writers of the twentieth century would now seem assured, stands quite apart from the feminine tradition of sensibility. Her fiction is tough, clumsy, rational, concerned with social roles, collective action and conscience, and unconcerned with niceties of style and subtlety of feeling for its own sake. She is, nevertheless, fully aware of the bifurcation between sense and sensibility and the meaning it presents to women, and it is with an awareness of the terms that she makes her choice. In the preface to *African Stories* she writes, "*The Pig* and *The Trinket Box* are two of my earliest. I see them as two forks of a road. The second—intense, careful, self-conscious, mannered—could have led to a kind of writing usually described as 'feminine.' The style of *The Pig* is straight, broad, direct; is much less beguiling, but is the highway to the kind of writing that has the freedom to develop as it likes." The latter part of this statement is ambiguous enough; suffice it to mean that Lessing finds her freedom in a realm apart from the traditional feminine resource of sensibility.

Sensibility comes in for mockery and worse in Lessing's work. In *In Pursuit of the English,* an Orwellian memoir, one of her first encounters is with an Australian lady:

> She was a woman of inveterate sensibility. Her name was Brenda.
> . . . She wore artistic clothes. She had been crying, and was still damp. Almost the first thing she said was, "I do hope your child is sensitive. My Daphne is very sensitive. A highly strung child."
> I knew then that the whole thing was doomed. . . . Then she said

everything was too much for her, and so I went out and bought the rations and had some keys cut. While I did this, I reflected on the value of helplessness.

Lessing indulges her grudge against sensibility elsewhere as well. In *The Golden Notebook* she engages her heroine in a literary practical joke against a sensitive homosexual editor. Collaborating with a cynical young writer, she invents a journal supposedly "written by a lady author of early middle-age, who had spent some years in an African colony, and was afflicted with sensibility." The "lady" writes, of a conversation at a cocktail party:

> He suggested I should do a play . . . which should take no sides but emphasise the essential tragedy of the colonial situation, the tragedy of the whites. It is true, of course . . . what is poverty, what are hunger, malnutrition, homelessness, the *pedestrian* degradations (his word—how sensitive, how full of *true* sensibility are a certain type of Englishman, far more intuitive than any woman!) compared to the reality, the human reality of the white dilemma? . . . I went home, nearer to reality I think than ever in my life . . . to my fresh narrow bed.

Heavy-handed as the irony is in this passage, it points to a reason for the rejection of sensibility which is on Lessing's part not casual and temperamental but rather an aversion based on her commitment to something larger than private consciousness, or more precisely, a commitment to link private consciousness with historical event. She believes, in George Eliot's words, that there is no private life that has not been conditioned by a larger public life, and she is galled by those whose decorum or inclination excludes the troublingly unattractive by proclaiming it unworthy of attention. In a statement made in 1957 she chided Colin Wilson for finding starvation and illiteracy uninteresting and urged that "he and people like him should at least try and understand it exists and what a great and creative force it is, one which will affect us all." Discussing *Children of Violence,* which she had planned in 1952, she said it is

> a study of the individual conscience in its relations with the collective. The fact that no critic has seen this does not, of course, surprise me. As long as critics are as "sensitive," subjective, and uncommitted to anything but their own private sensibilities, there will be no body of criticism worth taking seriously in this country. At the moment our critics remind me a lot of Victorian ladies making out their library lists.

Victorian ladies, lady authors of early middle age—the reversion to the image of a certain kind of lady as the repository of foolishness or hysteria is an instinctive cartooning which the contemporary, rigidly ideological feminist would check. Yet this sort of lady (to use the word "woman" would be inaccurate) is very much apparent in Lessing's fiction and serves as a key to the development of the women of the generation after her, those "free women" whom Lessing describes so well.

The most fully portrayed middle-aged woman in Lessing's fiction is Mrs. Quest, mother of the central figure of *Children of Violence*. It is against her mother's vapidity that Martha Quest forms her character; her self-respect is fashioned out of her sense of difference from the woman who hovers uselessly in the margins of her life. Although it is Martha's nature to behave sensibly, her common sense is reinforced by her desire to avoid the manipulative histrionics, the mindless tabulations of inconsequential matters, the cruel helplessness, which seem to inform repeatedly the older woman's behavior.

Both Martha and her friends wage a battle against the pressing image of the older, lifeless, unfulfilled women around them. The lives of these women are suggestive, possibly prophetic, and the younger women bank their character building on their ability to outwit the future. Many succumb: in *Landlocked*, Marjorie, ashamed of her tears and her tension, says, "If I don't watch out I'll be having a nervous breakdown—imagine, I always used to despise women like me." Although there are modern variations on the older women's powerlessness, still, the women, who at thirty-five are divorced, neurotic, alcoholic, are, Lessing takes pains to point out, those "who are at twenty the liveliest, the most intelligent, the most promising." It is women, not men, who are the enemy, and in defense against any alliance with the women who fail, who give in, Martha ranges herself with the men. Working against an admission of female resemblance is the mistrust of female irrationality, an irrationality which crops up in Lessing's fiction not only as eccentricity, or paralyzing neurosis, but, as in *The Grass Is Singing*, a foaming craziness.

Lessing's hostility to the literary attitude of sensibility is based upon her commitment to large issues and to the political. Martha Quest's avoidance of the emotions is in large part a result of her matrophobia. Both Martha and the heroine of *The Golden Notebook*, Anna Wulf, resist so powerfully the claims of emotion while at the same time deploring the numbness of the society around them that we are forced to regard this not as an inadvertent or supportive theme but as a dominant subject. Let us examine the kind of attention Lessing brings to emotion in *The Golden Notebook*, *Children of Violence*, and one or two shorter works.

It is necessary to be wary, but not too wary, of amalgamating the heroines in a study of Lessing's works. Just as some critics have confused Lessing with her heroines, to the author's just annoyance, so one may accidentally combine the traits of Martha and Anna, similar in many respects, into one prototype. There is, in fact, a good deal of genuine overlapping among Lessing's characters, occurring in part from the fact that she is less interested in producing a fine, shapely, and unforgettable character than in conveying the angles and stresses of responsible consciousness, the roughened confrontations of conscience and culture, the attraction to certain ideas and the changes of mind that occur when an individual thinks, as a way of moving through life and plot. In the case of Martha, moreover, there is a complete transformation by the fifth volume of Lessing's "continuous novel"; as history becomes increasingly the protagonist, Martha loses most of the personality that has earmarked her as Martha and dissolves into the lives of those around her like some sort of intellectual Mary Worth.

What strikes us first about Martha Quest, whom we meet initially as an adolescent, is her watchfulness, her care to perceive the world accurately and without the intervention of sentiment. One of the pivotal and most rewarding passages in *Martha Quest* is Martha's experience of what she calls "the moment," which is something like the sort of "moment" that appears in the fiction of Virginia Woolf, or for that matter in the poetry of Wordsworth. This moment is, for Martha, an experience which can be repeated but not willed, one where she feels "a slow integration" with the world around her in which "everything became one, shuddering together in a dissolution of dancing atoms," and in which "her flesh was the earth . . . and her eyes stared, fixed like the eye of the sun." This moment of immersive trance soon becomes intolerable, but once out of it she tries to possess it by recollecting it. The memory changes, however, as the effort is being made, and "it was with nostalgia that she longed to 'try again.'" Martha watches herself, tempted to transform a moment of process into a keepsake of well-being, and becomes irritable: "the wave of nostalgia made her angry. She knew it to be a falsity; for it was a longing for something that had never existed, an 'ecstasy,' in short. There had been no ecstasy, only a difficult knowledge. It was as if a beetle had sung. There should be a new word for *illumination*. The emblem of her transport, then, is the dry rasp of a Rhodesian beetle rather than, say, the liquid notes of the nightingale that accompany a Keatsian moment, and the texture of value in the experience is not the unleashing of spiralling emotion that is ecstasy, but a "difficult knowledge," a "message," the access of spiritual information.

Martha is as critical of her own emotions and of potentially false feeling in the later books of the *Violence* series; often the sentiment she has not freed herself from is a bait she dangles in front of her condemning intellect. In *A Ripple from the Storm* Lessing writes of her:

> Martha watched in herself the growth of an extraordinarily un-pleasant and upsetting emotion, a self-mockery, a self-parody, as if she both allowed herself an emotion she did not approve of, allowed it and enjoyed it, but at the same time cancelled it out by mockery. ". . . It's as if somewhere inside me there was a big sack of greasy tears and if a pin were stuck into me they'd spill out."

Hysteria is as unwelcome as sentiment. In *The Four-Gated City* a more extreme Martha Quest yields to hysteria as she educates herself in the psychic lore of insanity, and the same inner division occurs: "Martha was crying out—sobbing, grovelling; she was being wracked by emotion. Then one of the voices detached itself and came close into her inner ear: it was loud, or it was soft; it was jaunty, or it was intimately jeering, but its abiding quality was an antagonism, a dislike of Martha." This particular detachment from self is a demonized and externalized version of the rigors of watchfulness which Martha Quest puts herself through. Helped perhaps by the didactic Party meetings in which mutual criticism and self-criticism are part of the program (and whose organ is *The Watchdog*), Martha also has a talent for chastising herself into a self-dislike and self-punishment which might sit well on a Charlotte Brontë heroine but which in a twentieth-century character gives the impression of a pulverizing masochism.

For many of Martha's emotions, and for Anna's as well, there is a countering intelligence, not always so devilish and punishing as this but one that insures detachment and a split between thinking and feeling. Habitually, Martha's intellect mocks her feelings. But in the deeper recesses of mental disturbance, the priority of the intellect is abolished: "She would discover herself uttering sloganlike phrases, or feeling emotions, which were the op-posite of what she, the sane and rational Martha, believed. For instance, she would find herself using the languages of anti-Semitism. . . . She floundered about in a total loss of her own personality." Rationality is personality; for Lessing it is intelligence that gives one a sense of self and preserves some approximation of integration in the face of invading irrationalities. Anna Wulf sees it quite clearly: "She could . . . feel that intelligence there at work, defensive and efficient—a machine. And she thought: this intelligence, it's the only barrier between me and . . . cracking up." Martha, too, in *Land-*

locked, "was holding herself together—like everybody else. She was a light-house of watchfulness; she was a being totally on the defensive."

Lessing invokes the intellect as sanity's guardian, and emotion is an inimical and threatening suitor to both Martha and Anna. The former thinks, in *A Ripple from the Storm*:

> Now she wanted to cry. But she would not allow herself tears. Just as tenderness, moments of real emotion with William left her exposed . . . so did tears, even brief tears, open her to a feeling of deep, impersonal pain that seemed to be lying in wait for her moments of weakness like an enemy whose name she did not know.

In the same book, the only older woman of any stature, Mrs. Van (who, in her gentleness, sacrifice, and equilibrium, resembles Woolf's Mrs. Ramsay) decides early in her marriage that "it was emotion . . . she must ban from her life. Emotion was dangerous. It could destroy her." And Martha, in a later volume, still refuses to weep: "Anguish, the enemy, appeared: but no, she was not going to weep, feel pain, suffer" (*Landlocked*). Anguish is the enemy, as is any other emotion that sets off an uncontrollable chain of feeling; any emotion has the power eventually to topple the lighthouse of watchfulness.

For Lessing's heroines, emotions disrupt the self as if they, the emotions, are outside of the self. As a Puritan might be habitually militant against evil, the figures in Lessing's novels scan the landscape for the approach of the irrational. In *Landlocked,* Martha has a "lit space on to which, unless she was careful . . . emotions would walk like actors and begin to speak without (apparently) any prompting from her." Later, she thinks again of "the stage on to which might walk, at any time, the disembodied emotions she could not give soil and roots to within herself." When emotion has rooted in the self, Lessing's heroines try to expel the organ traditionally responsible for it. Martha, in *The Four-Gated City,* tells her heart "to be quiet. . . . Her heart as it were came to heel; and after that, the current of her ordinary thought switched off. Her body was a machine, reliable and safe for walking." Lessing has, in fact, a whole story about the dislodgement of that troublesome organ. In "How I Finally Lost My Heart," a short, fanciful piece, the heroine explains, "It would be easy to say that I picked up a knife, slit open my side, took my heart out, and threw it away; but unfortunately it wasn't as easy as that. Not that I, like everyone else, had not often wanted to do it." After carrying her heart, "largish, lightish," around for awhile, the heroine passes it on to a mad young woman in the Underground as a reward for her suffering and a replacement for lost emotion. "No heart," she concludes, "no heart at all. What bliss. What freedom."

The resistance to emotion which appears so frequently in *Children of Violence* and *The Golden Notebook* is in part, of course, a resistance to pain. Yet it is not the avoidance of pain and pleasure, of the kind that numbs Tommy in *The Golden Notebook*; rather, what characterizes the emotional life of Lessing's heroines is a resistance to loss of personal will and consequent loss of freedom. Emotions, for them, are a swiftly flowing stream that can put a woman up the creek in no time at all. In *The Four-Gated City*, "Martha felt as if she were being swept fast over an edge, and by her own emotions; for the first time since she came to London, she was unfree." It is not only "sensibility" that incurs helplessness, then, but emotion itself.

Overwhelmed by or even touched by emotion, one is vulnerable, in Lessing's view, not only to the allurements of sentiment (and the attendant punishments by the intellect), or to a dangerous resemblance to the emotional women of the older generation, but to love, the resulting betrayals by men, and the trappings (and traps) of domesticity. Anna explains, in *The Golden Notebook*, "Being so young . . . I suffered, like so many 'emancipated' girls, from a terror of being trapped and tamed by domesticity." Older, Anna is wry about her freedom (and would like to marry) but determinedly aware of her need to maintain it. It is no longer the image of failed older women or the temptation to convention that has to be fought against, but the yearning to fall in love, or stay in love, at the price of loss of self and a relinquishing of identity and will to a usurping male.

Lessing has little vindictiveness toward men, and her caution about men is no greater, and often far less great, than the traditional cautions of men about women. She is enormously sensitive to the ways men do not value women and to the adjustments women make in order to increase or preserve their portion of praise, love, and comfort. It is, in fact, because her heroines like men so much, and because they make such good Galateas of themselves, that they must be so careful. It is woman's vulnerability rather than man's culpability that is stressed; both sexes are caught in a labyrinth of expectation and motivation which, although it is often of their own making, has ample precedent.

The Golden Notebook is an anatomy of woman's independence and the impediments to it, and it is in this novel that Lessing brilliantly dissects the nature of that freedom which is, paradoxically, incomplete without love, yet almost invariably undermined by it. There is, for example, the heroine of the novel-within-the-novel, Ella, and her husband George, who is a sort of Lovelace-Grandcourt-Osmond in his manipulative perversity: "The last few weeks with George were a nightmare of self-contempt and hysteria, until at last she left his house, to put an end to it, to put a distance between herself and the man who suffocated her, imprisoned her, apparently took away her will." Anna later has Ella fall in love with Paul, and "from the moment Ella . . . uses the word love, there is the birth of naïvety. . . . Again and again he put her intelligence to sleep." Such a state is, in a sense, a condition of faith, yet it is a faith that is invariably to be broken by the man, and Anna, the author-within-the-author, says of herself, "I would be incapable now of such trust."

For Lessing, intelligence is at the heart of liberation, and a fall from intelligence is, for her heroines, a cause for self-denigration. Intelligence, however, is precarious and beset by an irrational attraction to happiness. When Anna Wulf, for example, trespasses on that common enough property, obtuseness, she chastises herself severely:

> As soon as I entered their flat I realised how much I had not been using my imagination, how stupid I had chosen to be. Sometimes I dislike women, I dislike us all, because of our capacity for not-thinking when it suits us; we choose not to think when we are reaching out for happiness. . . . I knew I had chosen not to think, and I was ashamed and humiliated.

Far better then not to feel rather than not to think, since the first not only keeps one out of a stultifying dependency and consequent humiliation but better matches the capacities of men as Lessing describes them. For if there are only a few thinking women, there are even fewer "feeling" men. Each relationship in *The Golden Notebook*, whether part of the real novel or the novel within it, demonstrates the thinness of emotion on the man's part and the fuller feeling—and resulting demands—on the woman's. Ella thinks, "for the hundredth time that in their emotional life all these intelligent men use a level so much lower than anything they use for their work, that they might be different creatures." This disparity creates a sense of loss, disappointment, and loneliness for the women, and antagonism and fearful evasiveness in the men.

The closely watched relationships in *The Golden Notebook* are not, however, designed to demonstrate a Lawrentian polarity and fundamental opposition of the sexes, but rather to show the difficulties of emotional life for both men and women. The difficulties are enhanced, moreover, when the woman is a "free" woman, that is, an intelligent woman who supports her-self, whose ideas are definite, reasoned, and earned, whose activity in the world is accomplished without the assistance or intervention of a man, and who, peripherally perhaps, but not insignificantly, is not too coy to excel at the art of the retort.

Anna is well aware of "the difficulties of being my kind of woman"; she regards her condition as one without much historical precedent or present company. She also recognizes, with some irony, that free women are both saved and burdened by their intelligence. Having undergone a scene with her lover, his casualness making their coming separation more painful, Anna remarks in her diary, "Afterwards I fought with a feeling that always takes hold of me after one of these exchanges: unreality, as if the substance of my self were thinning and dissolving. And then I thought how ironical it was that in order to recover myself I had to use precisely that Anna which Michael dislikes most: the critical and thinking Anna." The new woman is both more and less vulnerable: less so because, in her victory over sexual apartheid, she has her work to resort to; more so because her intelligence is a threatening element in her relations with men and its full expression gives them a reason to abandon her. Anna thinks to herself that in this new condition "is a fearful trap for women, but I don't yet understand what it is. For there is no doubt of the new note women strike, the note of being betrayed. It's in the books they write, in how they speak, everywhere, all the time."

The betrayal Anna speaks of is in part the sexual betrayal, the lack of loyalty, she describes in *The Golden Notebook* and even more single-mindedly in *Play with a Tiger*—but it is also the betrayal of the intelligent woman by the man who refuses to honor her claims to thinking. In a memorable episode in *A Ripple from the Storm*, Mr. Van goes up to his new wife, who is waiting in bed for her husband while he has been sitting up late to prepare a case, and finds her "reading Ingersoll. He had already taken her into his arms when he saw the title of the book lying beside her pillow. At this he had withdrawn his arms and turned away, remarking in his humorously dry voice, 'I see you have better company than me, my dear. Sleep well.'" In a situation not parallel but of the same bolt of cloth, the psychiatrist in *The Four-Gated City* tells Martha, knowing it will anger her, "I think you are proud of your knowing—you are proud of that more than anything. It's your intelligence you are proud of. You are still fighting your mother with that— the masculine intelligence." The essential truth of this is overshadowed by the objectionable or questionable use of the word "masculine." Aside from insulting Martha with its obvious prejudice against the likelihood of feminine intelligence, it severs her from the heart of her identity by assuming that it belongs to another gender and threatens the female intellectual at the point where she is weakest—the question of her femininity. In her attempt to get help as an individual Martha is betrayed by a generality.

Of what is commonly thought to be "feminine intelligence"—intuition—both Martha and Anna have little, and deliberately so. Anna confesses, "It frightens me that when I'm writing I seem to have some awful second sight, or something like it, an intuition of some kind; a kind of intelligence is at work that is much too painful to use in ordinary life; one couldn't live at all if one used it for living." And the heroine of *Play with a Tiger,* also called Anna, says with indignant irritation, "Intuition!" at the suggestion that she might be engaging in a fit of this capacity.

In spite of, or perhaps because of, their vulnerability, both Martha and Anna err on the side of rigor rather than of laxity. Mrs. Van sees Martha as "too hard—almost," and Anna is described by others as "cold-brained," "too intelligent," and by herself as "over-critical and defensive." Martha, unable to respond to her father's illness with the expected emotions "thought miserably of her own lack of feeling. She only felt resentful that her father was ill. . . . She felt resentful that at any moment it might be used as an emotional argument against her" (*Martha Quest*). Anna, on a first visit to her psychiatrist, explains that she has come "because I've had experiences that should have touched me and they haven't." Looking at her daughter she thinks, "that's my child, my flesh and blood. But I couldn't feel it." And an older and improbably different Martha visits the psychiatrist in *The Four-Gated City* and is "emotionless. She had had no emotions since she had sat there last, two days before."

It is when feeling, that guest which has so often been turned away, fails to call altogether, that both Martha and Anna feel the need to invite it back. Moving from I-won't-feel to I-can't-feel, they proceed from the luxury of caution to the crucial battle for a part of themselves that is lost. Martha's essentially elitist rebellion against the mawkish feeling of an older generation begins to resemble the general numbness of the current generation. Anna, unwilling to be caught up in the decade's paralysis, sees a psychiatrist and battles her emotional indifference as if she is fighting for her conscience. Sustained perhaps by vestiges of socialist optimism, she is unwilling to buckle under to the everlasting nay which has begun to cover the culture like a deep smog:

> But it isn't only the terror everywhere, and the fear of being conscious of it, that freezes people. It's more than that. People know they are in a society dead or dying. They are refusing

emotion because at the end of every emotion are property, money, power. They work and despise their work, and so freeze themselves. They love but know that it's a half-love or a twisted love, and so they freeze themselves.

For Lessing's heroines the refusal of emotion becomes worth considering and worth opposing when it becomes a general condition, for it is then that emotion becomes attached to meaning; the absence of tears or of the completeness of loving comes to signify a configuration, a situation, higher than itself, more abstract, more susceptible to rationalization, and therefore more likely to be appreciated and understood.

It is through the rationalizations of psychoanalysis rather than through the emotional surprises of a personal relationship that Anna manages to regain her feelings. "You have taught me how to cry," she tells her analyst, typically "not without dryness." Yet in spite of the extrapolation of her personal cure into a scheme of values ("if what we feel is pain, then we must feel it, acknowledging that the alternative is death. Better anything than the shrewd, the calculated, the non-committal, the refusal of giving for fear of the consequences . . . "), the narrative ripples with caution. The message is feeling; the medium is reason. Not dispassionate, for it is concerned, yet full of a care to understand and not to relinquish an issue or situation before it is understood, the style and point of view of *The Golden Notebook* exemplify a tenacious, if fragmented, consciousness. Feeling is one of the subjects of the book, but it does not infuse the narrative.

Lessing's own predisposition, as it emerges from her statements in interviews, parallels the inclination of her heroines towards rationality. In a recent interview she describes herself as once "aggressively rational." In a conversation conducted seven years ago she declared her annoyance with readers of *The Golden Notebook* in the following way:

> When *The Golden Notebook* came out, I was astonished that people got so emotional about that book, one way or another. They didn't bother to see, even to look at, how it was shaped. . . . What I'm trying to say is that it was a detached book. It was a failure, of course, for if it had been a success, then people wouldn't get so damned emotional when I didn't want them to be.

Lessing's meaning here is not clear. For although *The Golden Notebook* is experimental in shape, it is realistic and conventional in texture, syntax, and incident, and plays on the same responses a realistic novel might elicit. Lessing is no Joyce, detaching her work into a perfection of style, a distillation of language, a floating and self-sufficient condition. Furthermore, if one concentrates on the formal satisfactions of *The Golden Notebook,* as she would like, to the exclusion of those large themes that are scrutinized through domestic relationships, or to the exclusion of interest in the relationships themselves, then one will find Lessing bulky, inconsistent, and disappointing, and be convinced that she has mistaken her gifts.

It is clear, in any case, that the response Lessing wished for was not an emotional one. In another and earlier interview, when asked for her favorite story in her collection, *A Man and Two Women,* she responded, "I like . . . 'One Off the Short List' because it's so extremely cold and detached—that one's a toughy." Again her preference is for the unemotional and the detached. Writing about an incorrigible Romeo in the story mentioned, she is perhaps proud of her detachment not so much as a feat of form as of point of view; she triumphs over the obvious pitfalls of self-pity, bitter bias, and shrillness, and manages to write in a way that no one will pigeonhole as feminine.

In a recent piece of fiction, Lessing demonstrates a mistrust of emotion that reaches exaggerated proportions. "Not a Very Nice Story" is not a very good story, yet it is worthy of notice in that it marks her extremest statement of resistance to emotion. The tone of the omniscient narrator is surprisingly, and persuasively, cynical:

> because of all this they had enjoyed a decade of profoundly emotional experience. In joy or in pain, they could not complain about flatness, or absence of sensation. And after all, emotion is the thing, we can none of us get enough of it.

> The point was not the periods of making love . . . but . . . the spilling of emotion afterward, the anguish, the guilt. Emotion was the point. Great emotion had been felt, had been suffered.

> And since none of us feel as much as we have been trained to believe that we ought to feel in order to prove ourselves profound and sincere people, then luckily here is the television where we can see other people feeling for us. So tell me, madam, what did you *feel* while you stood there believing that you were going to be burned to death? Meanwhile, the viewers will be chanting our creed: we feel, therefore we are.

In a writer of Lessing's stature, the oily, accusatory tone of the excerpts is startling. One wonders why feeling should take the blame for media greed or for the desire of people to lead lives made more interesting by intensity. The bleating objections in this story are, paradoxically, out of control and of far less value than her wry criticism of sensibility in *In Pursuit of the English.* One thing is clear, however: her criteria for acceptable and unevasive emotions are insistently, perhaps impossibly, high.

Between Lessing's aversion to the attitudinizing of "sensibility" and her caution about feeling in general, there is not much contradiction. When one turns to *Briefing for a Descent into Hell,* however, and the light it sheds on preceding novels, one has to make room for a change of direction which would seem to mark an absolute inversion of the attitudes described above. For *Briefing,* published in 1971, is a defense of insanity which follows closely the lines and at times the style laid down by R. D. Laing in *The Politics of Experience.* Writing in an abstract and aqueous style, Lessing takes her hero on a journey away from the customary responsibilities of his social role and into schizophrenia. Foreshadowed by the dull-but-combustible Martha's experiment with madness in *The Four-Gated City,* and by Thomas's journals in *Landlocked,* Lessing's novel makes her position clear, at least for the moment: it is not only the sane who are mad, as Thomas says, but the mad who are sane.

A study of madness in Lessing's work—beginning with colonial eccentricity and ending with her ideological apprenticeship to Laing—deserves a book of its own. It is necessary to treat briefly, however, the question of Lessing's conversion to irrationalism, if only because an emphatic case has been made for her rationality. Although she is hardly the first to regard suffering, melancholy, and derangement as perquisites to enlightenment, she is one of the few anti-Romantics to do so. Rationalists—Dr. Johnson, for example—have been as afflicted with mental infirmity as Romantics but usually lack the condoling belief that it is a step into a higher state. Lessing's handling of irrationality, moreover, is, as is her attitude toward dreams, typically practical, rational, and even mechanical, in spite of her respect for the subconscious. For Lessing, "dreaming," as Brewster says, "seems to be something of a discipline," and Lessing confirms this in an interview:

> Dreams have always been important to me. The hidden domain of our mind communicates with us through dreams. I dream a great deal and I scrutinize my dreams. The more I scrutinize the more I dream. When I'm stuck in a book I deliberately dream. I knew a mathematician once who supplied his brain with information and worked it like a computer. I operate in a similar way.

I fill my brain with the material for a new book, go to sleep, and
I usually come up with a dream which resolves the dilemma.

This deliberateness in dreaming, this encouragement of the unconscious to
serve conscious, problematic purpose rather than to remain an alternative to
the purposeful, is a model for Lessing's approach to madness, as Martha's
pursuit of meaning in insanity testifies.

In *The Four-Gated City,* the commonsensical, rational Martha experiences a reversal of personality: "I've been turned inside out like a glove or
a dress. I've been like the negative of a photograph. Or a mirror image. I've
seen the underneath of myself." The obverse of rationality is irrationality,
and in either case the root term for describing consciousness is rationality:
rationality is either absent or present but never negligible. In this last of the
Children of Violence series, outer violence moves in on the human personality, destroying once and for all the barrier intelligence has provided. Apocalypse and cataclysm replace skepticism, as if the implicit prophecy of doom
that lurks within every act of caution has burst the watchful bonds of reason.

Yet Martha *invites* madness and *wants* her watchfulness to be wrecked
on the jaggedness of insanity. Lessing is not writing a tale of tragic naturalism
like *The Grass Is Singing,* in which the environment presses the heroine
toward madness, but rather a bildungsroman in which the climax of education is insanity. Martha, down to the last grain of vision, battles received
assumptions about reality. She works hard at it. Madness is a task, and she
toils through it toward a higher condition of integrity, a deeper version of
self. If that version is disastrous, it is because the world is, in Lessing's eyes,
a disaster; Martha's new vision gains access, with great clarity and no in-
tervening sentiment, to that terrible knowledge. Most important, madness is
moralized into a condition of responsible consciousness—the extremes of
emotion it involves are significant because they teach, not for the release they
afford; emotions are a means, not an end.

Insanity has Lessing's sympathy and interest for reasons continuous
with her past concerns. She engages madness as a subject not because its
chaos may allow her to taste the rich peripheries of rationality but because
it is "part of the mainstream" at the center of contemporary life. Essentially
a realist, she travels parallel to the culture and keeps her eye on its movements. Madness has, moreover, a political dimension and a radical one.
Lessing is concerned with the poor treatment afforded the mentally ill, whose
dissenting perceptions make them powerless, but her aim is not only liberal
reform or social amelioration. She wants, rather, an abolition of the traditional hierarchy of the sane and insane, and a recognition of the revolutionary

nature of madness. "People who are classified as sick are becoming more and more important in England, the U.S.A., and in socialist countries too," she notes: "People who are called mentally ill are often those who say to the society, 'I'm not going to live according to your rules. I'm not going to conform.' Madness can be a form of rebellion."

Finally, and curiously, the madness Lessing describes seems to circumvent the personal, an area of experience about which she has always been ambivalent. In the cool futurism of *Briefing*, Lessing is light years away from her nostalgia for the human warmth of the nineteenth-century novel expressed in "The Small Personal Voice," a lengthy statement of literary values written in 1957. And although she mocks the doctrinal impersonality of socialist writing from time to time, her own "habit of mind," she tells us, is to see "socially, not personally." Although she says in one interview that *The Golden Notebook* "is a social novel," in a later conversation she explains:

> Since writing *The Golden Notebook* I've become less personal. I've floated away from the personal. I've stopped saying, "This is *mine*, this is *my* experience." Ever since I started writing I've wondered why the artist himself has become a mirror of society. The first novelists didn't write about themselves, but now almost every novelist writes about himself. . . . Now, when I start writing, the first thing I ask is, "Who is thinking the same thought? Where are the other people who are like me?" I don't believe anymore that I have a thought. There is a thought around.

The personal is, by definition, a private possession and may represent for the former communist a form of selfishness, a capitalist hoarding of emotional territory.

The quality of emotion expressed in the condition of madness that Lessing describes is unlike the emotions woven through our daily lives at the level of the ordinary which Lessing's earlier novels describe. It is not only much more violent and aberrant, but, most significantly, it is collective and impersonal, like the "thought" that is "around." Mark, husband of the mad Lynda in *The Four-Gated City*, says: "Sometimes it's as if . . . I don't know how to explain it . . . it's as if . . . not that *she* is mad, but there's madness. A kind of wavelength of madness—and she hooks into it and out, when she wants. I could hook into it just as easily. Or it could hook into me—it's in the air." Martha herself eventually becomes a vessel, a channel, for all the emotions seething around her, dissolving into their madness and participating in the collective psyche much as an earlier Martha had participated in the collective conscience of communism.

The appreciation and understanding which Lessing extends to insanity takes madness from the realm of the clinical, where it is domesticated and judged, confined, as it were, to an institutional attic, into the realm of the cosmic. As a new plane of perception, a coming sixth sense, it is made metaphysical, impersonal. In *Briefing,* one of the characters asserts that Charles, the protagonist, "doesn't even pay lip service to ordinary feelings," and adds, "perhaps they aren't as important as we think." Another character complains that he is "above every normal human emotion." Charles himself mentions his "new mode of feeling," and the "sympathetic knowledge" he experiences is not with other individuals but with the world itself, fused into a rhapsodic and egalitarian whole.

For Lessing to choose a male protagonist is not unusual, and *Briefing* may feature a man's consciousness simply as a preference of imagination. One suspects, however, that a man was chosen in order to give madness its fullest due and its deepest persuasion: the fact that women are more often considered irrational would give a conventional taint to a disordered female and rob madness of the novel authority it possesses in *Briefing.* In both *Briefing for a Descent into Hell* and *The Four-Gated City,* sexuality and gender begin to fade into a transcendent condition and are greatly reduced in stature under pressure of a higher androgynous knowledge. Things in general are too dire and sorrowful for the "sex war" to be important, and women can abandon their caution as their center shifts from men, their reason no longer hostage to the chemistry of attraction. Sex is only one more of those personal elements which are superseded by a greater impersonal force:

> Great forces as impersonal as thunder or lightning or sunlight or the movement of the oceans . . . swept through bodies, and now she knew quite well why Mark had come blindly upstairs to the nearest friendly body, being in the grip of this force—or *a* force, one of them. Not sex. Not necessarily. Not unless one chose to make it so.

Lessing is telling us what one of the Sufi tales she is so fond of tells us: "If you remain attached to the few things with which you are familiar, it will only make you miserable. . . ." Always pained by narrowed horizons, Lessing gives her novels a broadness of scope which is one of their most striking and enriching features, a feature with which she contradicts the conventional idea that woman's excellence in the novel comes from her habitual acquaintance with the domestic, the ordinary, the small private corners and minor nuances of existence. Like George Eliot, the exception before her who is most often praised with the assertion that "she writes like a man," Lessing writes novels with irreducibly intellectual content, strong moral commitment, thorough social description, and large temporal and geographical range.

Unlike Eliot, and as a result of historical placement, Lessing cannot enjoy the comforts of equivocal feminism. Though she is nowhere nearly so bitter as Olive Schreiner, she possesses an enlightened consciousness that is full of flashing signals and loud warnings about conformity to an image that is often pressed on women like a gift but which, when it does not fit them, is no gift but a burden. Writing out of a context of twentieth-century numbness rather than nineteenth-century enthusiasm, she is chary of those attributes supposedly natural to women but of little value in dealing with the world. "Our strongest emotions are irrelevant to the time we live in," says Ella in *The Golden Notebook*. Without the congruence of morality and feeling which George Eliot carved out in her books and which her readers regarded as practical wisdom, intuition and affect seem superfluous and threatening, except when they have diminished to a fatally low level.

In her resistance to writing the feminine novel, in the choice Lessing made of "The Pig" over "The Trinket Box," she sacrifices suppleness and gratuitous beauty; there are few admirers of her work who would defend the careless homeliness of her style, far inferior to the style of George Eliot. Yet Lessing writes novels for grown-up people, to paraphrase Virginia Woolf's remark about *Middlemarch*, and she offers an elusive quality called maturity which is far rarer than the quality of sensibility she so cheerfully ignores. Wary of being typically feminine, she becomes typically contemporary in her suspicion of emotion, and although this does not nourish our optimism, our sense of the real tells us that she is our most powerful interpreter of difficult times—past, present, and future.

NANCY SHIELDS HARDIN

The Sufi Teaching Story
and Doris Lessing

It is easier to say what the Sufi teaching story is not than to say precisely
what it is—just as it is impossible to say precisely what Sufism itself is. As
one commentator warns, the reader is not taken into the realm of Zen paradox, which is orderly in comparison:

> It would be truer to say that he is going into a messy rooming
> house, where people specialize in forgetting and remembering,
> snooping and tattling, looking askance and stealing from closets.
> It is not a realm in which it is wise to seek, still less to pretend
> to, too much accuracy. . . . They come from everywhere, in-
> cluding man's dimmest and darkest past, now "The Past Thou-
> sand Years." They come from wordplay and proverbs, from fairy
> tales, tall tales, Greek plays, Hindu epics, Tibetan jokes, infancy
> gospels, the Desert Fathers, and even common sense. At any rate
> there they are: the Magic Mirror, the Fountain of Life, the Insane
> Uncle, the head of the World, and Snow White—the belly laughs
> of the bazaar and the anguished fictions of bedeviled monks.
> "They are full of wonders and strange ideas."

The Sufi teaching story consistently parts company with many other
traditional tales. Whereas the ordinary expectations from a story of the oral
tradition are (1) entertainment and (2) a moral answer or solution of some

From *Twentieth Century Literature* 23, no. 3 (October 1977). © 1977 by Hofstra
University Press.

sort, the Sufi teaching story has as its function neither of these. Sometimes it does have a barbed, gallows sort of humor, but a moralistic solution is never the point. On the contrary, the Sufi teaching story is open-ended, depending on individual members of the audience for a variety of interpretations. Unlike most stories, the Sufi story becomes a means, rather than an end; significantly, these stories are intended to change the form of the thinking process itself. According to Idries Shah, who is the most important spokesman for contemporary Sufism, the action of the Sufi teaching story "is direct and certain upon the innermost part of the human being, an action incapable of manifestation by means of the emotional or intellectual apparatus. The closest that we can come to describing its effect is to say that it connects with a part of the individual which cannot be reached by any other convention, and that it establishes in him or in her a means of communication with a non-verbalized truth beyond the customary limitations of our familiar dimensions."

That the stories have a unique ability to survive relates in part to the fact that they are at home in Europe, in Africa, in America, as well as in the Middle East; they are not dependent on any given cultural framework. They survive as a result of their form, which often assumes the shape of the sayings and actions of a wise man. But this wise man is in disguise as an ordinary man, or even as a fool, and as such is able to criticize patterns of behavior and patterns of prejudice. These tales have been long used by the Sufis not only because "they are highly economical ways of capturing aspects of the human condition, but also because through the brief narrative form of the tale the Sufis are capable of transmitting knowledge quickly and potently rather than having to explain it away in a discursive, logical or philosophical way." Furthermore, since the average person tends to think in conditioned patterns and finds it difficult to adapt to a different point of view, the value of the Sufi tale is to be found in the unexpected juxtaposition of ideas, designed to jar the reader or listener from a more comfortable and often rigid thought pattern.

One of the most delightful forms that the Sufi teaching story assumes is that of the Mulla Nasrudin tales whose narrative voice inhabits tales both old and new. Nasrudin's zany antics and actions surprise the listener and encourage him to discover another level of knowledge found within himself. One tale that illustrates the limitations of ordinary thinking goes as follows: "Nasrudin finds a king's hawk perched on his window-sill. He has never seen such a strange 'pigeon.' After cutting its aristocratic beak straight and clipping its talons, he sets it free, saying, 'Now you look more like a bird. Someone had neglected you.'" Another story, that of Nasrudin and a Yogi who have nothing to communicate to each other, suggests that inner learning must happen through ordinary experiences:

> One day Nasrudin saw a strange looking building at whose door a contemplative Yogi sat. The Mulla decided that he would learn something from this impressive figure, and started a conversation by asking him who and what he was.
>
> "I am a Yogi," said the other, "and I spend my time in trying to attain harmony with all living things."
>
> "That is interesting," said Nasrudin, "because a fish once saved my life."
>
> The Yogi begged him to join him, saying that in a lifetime devoted to trying to harmonize himself with the animal creation, he had never been so close to such communion as the Mulla had been.
>
> When they had been contemplating for some days, the Yogi begged the Mulla to tell him more of his wonderful experience with the fish, "now that we know one another better."
>
> "Now that I know you better," said Nasrudin, "I doubt whether you would profit by what I have to tell."
>
> But the Yogi insisted. "Very well," said Nasrudin. "The fish saved my life all right. I was starving at the time, and it sufficed me for three days."

The Sufi contends that given the right time, place, and people the teaching story may have a series of developmental effects. A Sufi story reflects a certain state of mind and becomes the mirror in which one sees oneself: "Its symbols are the characters in the story. The way in which they move conveys to the mind the way in which the human mind can work." Indeed, it can be said that the Sufi teaching story encourages a holistic view of things wherein there is a unification of the brain's left hemisphere processes, which control the verbal, rational, and logical analysis of experience, and of the right hemisphere processes, such as those approaches to expression which are more spatial, abstract, and intuitive. It is then one of the functions of the Sufi teaching story to "teach" a shift in perspective from a more logical linear mode of thought process, which we of the Western world have been taught to hold in the highest esteem, to a more intuitive perception.

A Sufi can be anyone (scientist, poet, housewife, writer, shopkeeper, etc.) who has the potential to grow by the Sufi method. Indeed, there are two main objectives of Sufism: "(1) to show the man himself as he really is; and (2) to help him develop his real, inner self, his permanent part." The

Sufi teaching story assumes the first of many important functions by oper-
ating as a sorting-out process in that it serves to eliminate those individuals
who really are in need of psychotherapy or those who have come to worship.
Sufism neither encourages disciples nor is there a guru to follow as in other
Eastern ideologies. It is not an organized religion with specific dogma. Although one has a teacher, one is much more on one's own and must accept
responsibility for oneself. There are levels of conscious development to
achieve, and it is here that the teaching story can aid people to awaken from
the conditioning of their ordinary lives. The initial response of even an interested individual is to react as he thinks he should or as his background
dictates. It is only after such conditioning is cast off that other interpretations
and reactions to the stories begin to surface. Shah notes: "At last, as the
students become less emotional, we can begin to deal with the real person,
not the artifact that society has made him." Because the Sufi experiences the
world as having extra dimensions, "to him things are meaningful in a sense
which they are not to people who follow only the training which is imposed
upon them by ordinary society." To be a Sufi is to make of life an adventure,
or as Shah emphasizes, a "necessary adventure." It is then through these
stories of inner meaning that the Sufi experience can be provoked in a person:
"Once provoked, it becomes his own property, rather as a person masters
an art."

A number of Doris Lessing's novels and stories effect their meaning in
a form that shares many qualities with the Sufi teaching story. Lessing un-
derscores the notion of the Sufi experience as a series of paradoxical insights
that are not only mystical but practical. In "An Ancient Way to New Freedom" she notes:

> It does not do to say that a man, a book, an institution is Sufism,
> which is essentially something always the same, but taking dif-
> ferent forms. . . . In every part of the world, the forms of Sufism
> differ, since they are shaped to fit the people living there. The
> way Sufism is being taught in Britain now differs from what hap-
> pens in Morocco, Afghanistan, Greece, South America; the teach-
> ers and the institutions containing Sufism for this time are
> different from those in the past, and always changing . . . a far
> cry from what our conditioning has taught us to call "mysticism."
> Before you can even start on Sufic study, you must first try to
> "learn how to learn"—and everything is unexpected.

Just as in a Sufi story, Lessing's stories frequently offer the reader an opportunity to work on his mind "to enable it to make use of the story, as well
as presenting it with the story." Yet Lessing cautions about the inherent

difficulties in working with such ideas: "some people expect this material to be more sensational than it is; a Sufi would reply that our palates have been blunted; that we do not give gentle impacts a chance to operate; that people can put themselves at a remove from the Sufi operation by calling it 'banal.'"

Lessing herself has been involved with Sufism for a number of years, and she is one of the better known students of Idries Shah. From time to time she uses a Sufi teaching story to precede a section of one of her novels, as in *The Four-Gated City,* or even more frequently she incorporates Sufi teaching concepts within her novels and stories. For example, in a preface to *The Golden Notebook,* she notes that the characters "have reflected each other, been aspects of each other, given birth to each other's thoughts and behaviour—*are* each other, form wholes . . . things have come together, the divisions have broken down, there is formlessness with the end of fragmentation." Moreover, the characters "break through the false patterns they have made of their pasts, the patterns and formulas they have made to shore up themselves and each other, dissolve. They hear each other's thoughts, recognize each other in themselves." Just as Sufi teaching stories are intended to make the listener uncomfortable, so also do the Lessing stories.

Rarely does a Lessing story offer fulfillment of expectations of pure entertainment. Rather as does the Sufi teaching story, her stories give a stimulus to the imagination. A Lessing novel or story often offers a world of practical reality on the one hand, while on the other her reader is projected into a world whose dimensions are more those of *The Arabian Nights* or a dream. They require a certain willingness on the part of the reader to alter his own states of understanding. When this is done once, then there is no returning to the prior state of limited knowledge. The change has occurred and the reader is projected on a new way, even if his denial tries to protect him from the irreversible insights of such alterations.

One of Lessing's stories in particular. "Out of the Fountain," has the potential of offering nourishment for the imagination. It commences with some talk in an airport, of travelers bound together for a limited period of time, entertaining each other while waiting for the fog to lift so that their plane can resume its flight. As people will, they begin to talk about money and wealth. One man said "that he knew of a case where jewels had been flung into the dust of a public square in Italy" and he has a fragment of milk and rainbow opal to prove it. In beginning with the swirling mystery of the fog, the story is framed by an open-ended structure in which something with invisible dimensions is allowed room to exist.

Indeed, the framing device of "Out of the Fountain" contains the possibility for the story itself to assume a different form: It opens:

So he told the story. One day someone will introduce me to a

> young man called Nikki (perhaps, or what you will) who was
> born during the Second World War in Italy. His father was a
> hero, and his mother now the wife of the Ambassador to. . . . Or
> perhaps in a bus, or at a dinner party, there will be a girl who
> has a pearl hanging around her neck on a chain and when asked
> about it she will say: Imagine, my mother was given this pearl
> by a man who was practically a stranger, and when she gave it
> to me she said. . . . Something like that will happen: and then
> this story will have a different beginning, not a fog at all.

Yet something happens, something begins, and themes of time, of shape, and
of irreversible changes of perceptual energy allow us for a flickering moment
to shift our patterns of thought. It is the reality of being able to trust one's
own experience that is communicated in the closing frame of the story:

> But one day I'll meet a young man called Nikki, or Raffele; or a
> girl wearing a single pearl around her neck on a gold chain; or
> perhaps a middleaged woman who says she thinks pearls are
> unlucky, she would never touch them herself: a man once gave
> her younger sister a pearl and it ruined her entire life. Something
> like that will happen, and this story will have a different shape.

Lessing's "Out of the Fountain" assumes a form according to the time,
place, and the people, as do Sufi teaching stories. The time of the story is
varied: the late 1930s, the years of the Second World War, sometime thereafter and anytime anyone is reading the story. The place is equally diverse:
Johannesburg, Alexandria, Baghdad, a small village in Italy, and wherever
the story is being read. As for the characters—there are Mihrene and
Ephraim and Dr. Rosen, who tells the story, and there is an "I" narrator of
the author, and there is as well the reader. Not only is an audience of characters within the framework of the story, but the very boundaries of the tale
bend outward to include the reading audience. All of us share in the story,
which in itself is "ambiguous and fertile" as the ransom of a king. Potentially,
the subtle form of this story can change a reader or waken him even as
receiving the pearl altered Mihrene's life in an irrevocable fashion.

One will discover that the Lessing story contains the same components
as the Sufi story. In almost all of her later works, Lessing has focused in
some way on the importance not only of recognizing, but also of maintaining
moments of wakeful insight. Much of the difficulty arises in being unable to
acknowledge the darker, less known aspects of self as well as the more openly
accepted daylight self. But Lessing incorporates the two, making one whole:

"But it is not *or,* that is the point. It is an *and.* Everything is. Your dreams *and* your life . . ." (*Briefing for a Descent into Hell*). It is then to the dream, another open-ended form, that Lessing turns. Lessing's interest in dreams is linked with her knowledge of Sufism. Indeed, the fable-like content of her characters' dreams is reminiscent of the fable as used by the Sufis: "Do you imagine that fables exist only to amuse or to instruct, and are based upon fiction? The best ones are delineations of what happens in real life, in the community and in the individual's mental processes." Dreams, when considered as fables, bespeak another level of consciousness and as such allow a different degree of self-understanding to develop when examined: "Most fables contain at least some truth, and they often enable people to absorb ideas which the ordinary patterns of their thinking would prevent them from digesting. Fables have therefore been used, not least by the Sufi teachers, to present a picture of life more in harmony with their feelings than is possible by means of intellectual exercises."

Near the end of *The Summer before the Dark,* Lessing poses this question: "Do you think dreams are just for the person who dreams them? Perhaps they aren't?" The question has a particular relevance for Kate Brown, since she has just completed a sequence of dreams which has extended over a period of several months. As such it is a question that Lessing has confronted earlier in "The Temptation of Jack Orkney," a study of a man "facing into the dark." He, as well as Kate, is a seeker with an enterprise to complete: "Now, in spite of everything, although he knew that fear could lie in wait there, his sleep had become another country, lying just behind his daytime one. Into that country he went nightly. . . . Behind the face of the sceptical world was another, which no conscious decision of his could stop him exploring." With both of these protagonists, Lessing is one step further into her continuing exploration of an understanding of self, of life, and of Sufi knowledge.

For Kate the knowledge is within her; accessibility to that knowledge is another matter. Hers is a problem of rediscovery that her sleeping experiences matter:

> Ever since she was very small, five or six, she had been able to
> reach her hand into the country behind the daylit one, to touch
> a familiar object that lived there, or to walk through it at ease,
> not astonished, or afraid. Nor was she surprised by a dream that
> developed like a fable or a myth: she accommodated several such
> long-running dreams, and when a new stage of development of a
> familiar theme was presented to her, she would lie awake for as

long as she could, before letting it be seen that she was awake,
thinking of the ideas that were taking shape in her, and which
she could not see except in the reflections like firelit shadows on
the walls of her sleep.

In the summer when Kate's family disintegrates, each pursuing his own life-
style, Kate herself is confronted with her own programmed and fragmented
self: "The truth was, she was becoming more and more uncomfortably conscious not only that the things she said, and a good many of the things she
thought, had been taken down off a rack and put on, but that what she
really felt was something else again." Unable to free herself from her "invisible chains," Kate becomes the recipient of information from her dreams; in
her dreams she begins the journey that is to give her guidance for her fragmented life.

The first installment of Kate's dream sequence begins at a time when
she has no particular commitments and could if she chose be free. Kate
dreams of a heavy and moaning seal which she knows that she must get to
water. In subsequent dreams she struggles with problems of procedure:
"Where was the water, where was the sea? How could she be sure of going
in the right direction?" The seal becomes her responsibility, for without her,
Kate knows that it will die. Then suddenly it appears that the seal has
abandoned her dreams, and Kate feels as though "she had strayed into the
wrong room in a house, she was in the wrong dream, and could not open
the door on the right one . . . where was the seal? Was it lying abandoned
among dry rocks waiting for her, looking for her with its dark eyes?" The
seal returns again to her dream after Kate, having denied her own knowledge
of the sterility of the affair that she has begun with Jeffrey, arrives in Spain.
In her dream Kate finds herself once again on a rocky hillside and there she
finds her seal again, "slowly painfully, moving itself towards the distant, the
invisible ocean. She gathered the slippery creature up in her arms—oh, she
ought not to have left it there. It was weaker; its dark eyes reproached her.
Its skin was very dry; she must get some water for it." And from this dream,
whose flavor was that of an old tale, she learns that "going to sleep and
entering this dream was as much her business for this time in her life as . . .
wrestling with her emotional self which seemed like a traitor who had come
to life inside her. What she was engaged in was the dream, which worked
itself out in her."

Gradually the dream then merges with her waking self: "She knew that
walking into the winter that lay in front of her she was carrying her life as
well as the seal's—as if she were holding out into a cold wind her palm, on

which lay a single dried leaf." After returning to London and while recovering from her illness, Kate dreams of being abandoned by the king of her dream and sees herself "running away, in a desolation of grief. The people of the village came after her, shouting: she had become an enemy, because she had been discarded. . . . Kate had to get out of the pit, she knew that. Somewhere not far away the seal was, alone; and it was again trying painfully to make its way along the ground towards the sea. It believed she had abandoned it." Slowly, Kate understands that she must pick up the seal and walk "north, north, always north, away from the sun."

Something inside Kate insists that she must examine and incorporate entire areas of her being that she has locked off from her everyday knowledge. Whatever is inside that looks after the self has announced that hers is an intolerable situation. She forces herself to face the fact that her courage to do what she felt like doing "was what she, Kate, had lost." At Maureen's flat, Kate searches once again for the dream of the seal: "Other dreams captured her, kept her prisoner, dreams smaller and less important; in her sleep she felt like someone a couple of yards from the centre of the maze, but no matter how she turned and tried, she could not reach it. The seal was there it was being carried north by Kate, whose business it was to do this, but this was going on in a part of Kate that was obscured from her by dreams like so many parcels that she had to balance and secure." She fears that she could not remember "the dream because the seal had died. That area of her sleep was very sad, full of loss, of pain."

What Kate must come to terms with is the person that she has submerged "for all her adult life . . . she had been conforming twitching like a puppet to those strings." In her next-to-last dream of the seal, Kate sees in the snow a "silvery-pink cherry tree in full bloom." By her last dream the seal is full of life "and like her full of hope. . . . Her journey was over. She saw that the sun was in front of her . . . a large, light, brilliant, buoyant, tumultuous sun that seemed to sing." Tutored and changed by her dreams, which have spoken to the very nature of her being, Kate returns home.

So it is that Lessing, by closely examining dreams as a form of information, confronts those levels of consciousness that our world today, for the most part, has taught us to ignore. Idries Shah also points out that the self which normally one takes to be his real one is the result of conditioning: "As a consequence of Sufi experience, people—instead of seeing things through a filter of conditioning plus emotional reactions, a filter which constantly discards certain stimuli—can see things through some part of themselves that can only be described as not conditioned." In "Out of the Fountain," Lessing emphasizes that the form which the information assumes must vary according to the individual. In "The Temptation of Jack Orkney," she shocks Jack, a previously skeptical cynic, and terrifies him with the insistent power of his dreams. In *The Summer before the Dark,* Lessing uproots Kate from her conventional existence and forces her to immerse herself productively within the dark inner self of her dreams. Drawing materials from the actual world on the one hand *and* from the mental process on the other, Lessing suggests the possibilities of a single, whole experience. The secret is one of assimilation; for Lessing, as the Sufis, does not see the two as separate. One is reminded of the Sufi saying: "He who tastes not, knows not."

Yet just as the memory of taste becomes dulled or forgotten, in order to taste again one must renew the experience. As one Sufi story points out, to forget "is the way of men," until suddenly one remembers again. Lessing, too, in many of her works (especially *Briefing for a Descent into Hell* and *The Four-Gated City*) concerns herself with forgetting and remembering. Most recently in *The Memoirs of a Survivor* the nameless woman protagonist grows to understand that "one can also know something and then forget it!" Right time remains an essential part of her experiences, for she learns that by will alone she cannot move beyond "the ordinary logical time-dominated world of everyday." In this case the woman finds that she is recipient of a state of mind that allows her to penetrate a level of reality beyond the patterns of sunlight on her wall. Just as Kate learns from her dreams, the woman of *The Memoirs of a Survivor* recognizes that "what went on behind the wall might be every bit as important as my ordinary life." Consequently, she easily and unexpectedly travels within the rooms beyond the wall in "a place which changed each time" she sees it. Musing over why she never encounters the same room behind the wall again, she wonders:

> Would it be accurate to say that I forgot it? That would be to talk of that place in terms of our ordinary living. While I was in that room, the task made sense; there was continuity to what I did, a future, and I was in a continuing relation to the invisible destructive creature, or force, just as I was with the other beneficent presence. But this feeling of relatedness, of connections, of context, belonged to that particular visit to the room, and on the next visit it was not the same room, and my preoccupation with it was altered—and so with the other rooms, other scenes, whose flavours and scents held total authenticity for the time they lasted and not a moment longer.

For her these experiences alternate between personal scenes—although not necessarily personal to her—(a prison of emotions wherein pain, guilt, un-fulfilled needs and hungers are programmed) or impersonal scenes (a space of possibilities, of alternatives, of problems to be solved).

Perhaps the most significant of these problems is the continuing exis-tence of "the hidden pattern"—the ongoing work of completing a carpet of intricate design, whose colors "had an imminent existence, a potential, no more." Observing people who take pieces of material and match them with the incomplete sections of the carpet, the woman watches the potential man-ifest itself as the design of the carpet is actualized. She also seeks "for frag-ments of materials that could bring life to the carpet," and matches one to the pattern before she moves on. She realizes that other people as well "see this central activity, find their matching piece . . . and drift off again to other tasks." Even as she leaves, she cannot find the room when she turns her head "to mark where it was." She retains a sense of confidence in her knowledge that "it had not disappeared, and the work in it continued, must continue, would go on always." Just as in an earlier story, "The Other Garden," the sense of the vitality of another order of world altogether is experienced: "the place draws itself in behind you, is gathered in to itself, like water settling after a stone has disturbed it." Before it disappears it is seen as whole, "repeating and echoing like a descant." So too, in *The Memoirs of a Survivor,* one experiences "theme and descant," a sense of a world "transmuted, and in another key."

Lessing's voice—sensitive, firm with a knowledge achieved through her own experience—reaches out to her listeners, her readers. We are, she warns in that quiet but persuasive voice, running out of time. We have much to overcome before we can break out and away from contemporary condition-ing. We must look afresh to our own experience, because it is only what we learn from such experience that counts. She has told us this before at the end of *The Four-Gated City,* when Martha discovers that it is no use looking elsewhere for answers but that one must look inward: "Here, where else, you fool, you poor fool, where else has it been ever." Lessing has faith that at least some will be able to understand how "very extraordinary" is the human mind, and suggests that some can overcome the voices of authority, other people's opinions, the dogmas that have made us become conforming adults in a conforming society. It is only by experiencing ourselves as we actually are, that we can awaken from the roles to which we have been so skillfully programmed. The answers are there, but one must first pose the question. One must learn from oneself, "listening as it were to something just out of hearing; the inner tutor was wanting her to understand something, but she was being too obtuse to understand." The knowledge is within;

accessibility to that knowledge may not "be sold, or taken: it could only be earned, or accepted as a gift." Beyond that "each will perceive what he can perceive, and at the stage at which he can perceive it." The Sufi teaching stories, as the Lessing works, are a stimulus to our imagination, a route of access to "the Spy of the Heart," yet without a certain intuitive experiencing, the relating of such information is rather like "sending a kiss by messenger."

BARBARA HILL RIGNEY

"A Rehearsal for Madness":
Hysteria as Sanity in The Four-Gated City

But the most frightening thing about them was this: that they walked and moved and went about their lives in a condition of sleepwalking: they were not aware of themselves, of other people, of what went on around them . . . they stood with the masses of pelt hanging around their faces, and the slits in their faces stretched in the sounds they made to communicate, or as they emitted a series of loud noisy breaths which was a way of indicating surprise or a need to release tension . . . each seemed locked in an invisible cage which prevented him from experiencing his fellow's thoughts, or lives, or needs. They were essentially isolated, shut in, enclosed inside their hideously defective bodies, behind their dreaming drugged eyes, above all, inside a net of wants and needs that made it impossible for them to think of anything else.

These lines do not depict, as might be expected, the insanity of a grotesque and subhuman Bertha Mason; nor do they describe that troop of pathetic lunatics being marched through the streets of London to the horror of Septimus Warren Smith in *Mrs. Dalloway*. Rather, this is a description of the

From *Madness and Sexual Politics in the Feminist Novel: Studies in Brontë, Woolf, Lessing, and Atwood.* © 1978 by the Regents of the University of Wisconsin. University of Wisconsin Press, 1978.

133

"normal" members of society, the majority of humanity, as perceived by what can be termed the "psychotic" mind, that which for Doris Lessing in *The Four-Gated City* is the only mind sufficiently sensitive to apprehend reality objectively.

Lessing's rendition of this reality, apparent in the entire *Children of Violence* series of which *The Four-Gated City* is the culmination, is a world that Brontë, for all her sense of evil, could hardly have conceived; it is the world of Clarissa Dalloway's worst apprehensions now fully and socially realized. Truth, for Lessing, is first presented in *The Four-Gated City* as that nightmare vision of post–World-War-II London seen by the self-proclaimed hysteric, Martha Quest Hesse. "Martha the traveller" homelessly walks the streets, finding her way across great pits left by exploded bombs and through crowds of depressed and poverty-stricken humanity. The entire world seems to her to be numb, blinded. Martha alone perceives her own plight and the plight of others as she observes, "there's something wrong with me that I do see what's going on as ugly, as if I were the only person awake and everyone else is in a kind of bad dream, but they couldn't see that they were." Society seems oblivious to the fact that it is oppressed, that war is an unbelievable atrocity, that there are "a number of events, or processes, in this or that part of the world, whose common quality was horror—and a senseless horror . . . this barbarism, this savagery was simply not possible."

Martha is later in the novel to meet a few people, like her employer and lover, the author Mark Coldridge, who are also aware that political and philosophical oppression—which includes racism, sexism, any sort of "ism" which manipulates power—is responsible for unspeakable acts perpetrated on human beings and on the physical world in which they live. But Mark must discipline himself to learn what Martha, in her acute state of perception, already feels; he must constantly remind himself of reality by filling an entire room with maps and headlines, the physical evidence of truth:

> On the walls multiplied the charts of the death factories, the poison factories, the factories that made instruments for the control of the mind: the maps of Hunger, Poverty, Riot and the rest; the atlases of poisoned air and poisoned earth and the places where bombs had been exploded under the sea, where atomic waste was sunk into the sea, where ships discharged filthy oil into the sea, where inland waters were dead or dying.

Thus there is a kind of reverse progression from Brontë to Lessing: the individual "he" as enemy in Brontë's novel and the more universalized "He" as the quality of negative masculinity in Woolf's, become, in *The Four-*

Gated City, an even more ominous because less easily identifiable "They," responsible for the fact that the entire world is war-torn, physically and morally diseased, and, ultimately, by the end of the novel, to destroy itself through germ warfare.

Lessing, like Woolf, sees "normality" or the adjustment to such a state of affairs as itself a form of madness. A similar definition of normality is professed by R. D. Laing, whom Lessing has referred to as "a peg," a "key authority figure." In *The Politics of Experience* Laing writes that "only by the most outrageous violation of ourselves have we achieved our capacity to live in relative adjustment to a civilization apparently driven to its own destruction."

Martha can specifically identify the particular form of madness which afflicts all of society as she becomes increasingly aware that the state of normality is one of schizophrenia, of alienation; it is "a condition of disparateness," the separate parts of the mind "working individually, by themselves, not joining." Human beings by definition are mad, according to Lessing, because the human brain itself is "a machine which works in division; it is composed of parts which function in compartments locked off from each other: or 'your right hand does not know what your left hand is doing.'" In her critical biography of Lessing, Dorothy Brewster quotes Lessing's childhood memory of her father, sitting in a chair, looking out over the vast Rhodesian landscape and periodically shaking his fist at the sky and shouting, "Mad—everyone—everywhere!"

Laing's description of schizophrenia corresponds to Lessing's: he sees it as, first, an alienation from the self, which leads to an alienation from other people as well, and this condition, Laing states, is virtually universal. We live, he writes, "in an age of darkness." Lessing too sees the world as "a country where people could not communicate across the dark that separates them." Communication of any kind, verbal or sexual, is almost an impossibility in Lessing's novel, the whole of which might be seen to serve as a negative answer, at least for this time, to Laing's terrifying question: "Is love possible?"

Lessing describes sex, for example, as an act in which people temporarily "plug into" each other. "Passion," that term which has such reality and meaning in the works of Brontë and Woolf, which so permeates the consciousness and inspires such dread in the earlier works, hardly exists as a concept in Lessing's world. "We don't understand the first thing about what goes on," she writes, "not the first thing. 'Make love,' 'Make sex,' 'orgasms,' 'climaxes,'—it was all nonsense, words, sounds, invented by half-animals who understood nothing at all."

The single scene in *The Four-Gated City* which might be considered at all erotic is that enacted between Martha and Jack, who is a kind of sexual athlete and who, later in the novel, will completely pervert sexual relationships by seducing women into prostitution. Even in this scene, however, sex cannot really be considered a form of communication, the participants being locked into their own purely subjective experiences, meeting needs that are solely individual, getting from each other a compensation for personal traumas of the past. Jack has suffered terribly in the war, and now one woman serves as well as another to feed his terrible hunger for experience, for life.

Martha and Mark Coldridge also have a sexual relationship, primarily because it is convenient and serves as an outlet for the extreme pressures each is under. Mark can go from a series of premarital relationships to his wife Lynda to Martha to the brainless Rita—and it is all the same. No confrontation, no announcement precedes the end of his affair with Martha, who calmly accepts her rejection and goes on to other nondescript relationships. "When it's a question of survival, sex the uncontrollable can be controlled. And therefore had Martha joined that band of women who have affairs because men have ceased to be explorations into unknown possibilities."

Love is only a word; the reality is subjective need, and sex itself, says Martha, is a force "as impersonal as thunder or lightning." One is reminded of that African scene in Lessing's *The Golden Notebook* in which millions upon millions of copulating grasshoppers, indifferent as to their partners, frenziedly and blindly fulfill the dictates of some mad god called nature.

Martha also sees marriage as a part of this universal mockery. "The truth was, she feared marriage, looking at it from outside now, unable to believe that she had ever been in it. What an institution! What an absurd arrangement. . . ." Marriage is such an appalling situation for Martha because she sees it, like all other human relationships, as based on subjective need, selfish concerns, the use of one person by another. Women, as well as men, self-centeredly seek some impossible fulfillment. Martha recognizes and rejects this tendency toward subjectivity in herself as well as in others:

> But to herself she was able to say precisely what she feared. It was the rebirth of the woman in love. If one is with a man, "in love," or in the condition of loving, then there comes to life that hungry, never-to-be-fed, never-at-peace woman who needs and wants and must have. That creature had come into existence with Mark. She would come into existence again. For the unappeasable hungers and the cravings are part, not of the casual affair, or of friendly sex, but of marriage and the "serious" love. God forbid.

. . . when a woman has reached that point when she allies part
of herself with the man who will feed that poor craving bitch in
every woman, then enough, it's time to move on.

In her short story "To Room Nineteen," Lessing suggests that even a
"perfect" marriage, based supposedly on intelligence and mutual respect,
can become merely an animal-like struggle to meet subjective desires. In this
case the husband wins, and the wife, *her* needs completely unmet, kills herself.

Like Woolf, Lessing sees the horror of the public world reflected in the
private world of marriage. Society in Lessing's work is no more capable of
permitting the reality of Martha's dream of "the Golden Age" in which a
man, woman, and beautiful children join hands and walk "in a high place
under a blue sky" than it is of attaining the utopia of the ordered and peaceful
"four-gated city."

Perhaps, however, it is the very depersonalization of sex which, for
Lessing, contributes to the possibility of psychological survival in a mad
world. As chastity and inaccessibility operate to protect the self from annihilation in the works of Brontë and Woolf, so Lessing sees numerous sexual
experiences as precluding the possibility of total engulfment in the one. Janet
Sydney Kaplan, in her article "The Limits of Consciousness in the Novels of
Doris Lessing," states that Martha fears the loss of ego in the sexual relationship. However, if the self is not extended and made vulnerable in sex, if
"the craving bitch" is suppressed, if sex is kept impersonal, "casual,"
"friendly" (impossible concepts for either Woolf or Brontë), then the self is
protected as efficiently as if there were no sex act at all. Such a character as
Sally-Sarah, in loving a husband who is totally immersed in such abstractions
as science and communism at the expense of personal relationships, is tragic
because she does extend the self. Like the wife in "To Room Nineteen,"
Sally-Sarah ends by committing suicide. A woman who survives (at least
physically), on the other hand, is the promiscuous Jill, who most often has
no notion of the identity of the father of the current child she is bearing.

If the term "love" must be qualified out of existence in Lessing's world,
so must words like "hate," which emotion becomes merely another aspect
of the normal state of alienation, providing none of the gratification or pur-
gative function so necessary in the novels of Brontë and Woolf. Jack explains
and Martha concurs:

"You say all your life *I hate, I love*. But then you discover hatred
is a sort of wavelength you can tune into. After all, it's always

there, hatred is simply part of the world, like one of the colours
of the rainbow. You can go into it, as if it were a *place*."

"Love" and "hate" then, because each implies an object, have a limited
meaning. They are words empty of significance. All human feeling can in
essence be reduced to subjectivity, which Lessing sees as synonymous with
alienation. However, as Lessing indicates in her introduction to *The Golden
Notebook*, to recognize this subjectivity as inherent in the human condition,
as universal, is ultimately to break through the barriers which it erects:

> The way to deal with the problem of "subjectivity," that shocking
> business of being preoccupied with the tiny individual who is at
> the same time caught up in such an explosion of terrible and
> marvelous possibilities, is to see him as a microcosm and in this
> way to break through the personal, the subjective, making the
> personal general, as indeed life always does, transforming a pri-
> vate experience . . . into something much larger: growing up is
> after all only the understanding that one's unique and incredible
> experience is what everyone shares.

In the author's notes appended to *The Four-Gated City*, Lessing describes
her novel as a bildungsroman. Martha, then, "grows up" because she comes
to see her own schizophrenia and subjectivity projected into the world at
large. Only through the recognition of one's own madness as a reflection of
the world's madness can a higher state of sanity be achieved. Conscious
madness, as opposed to the world's *un*conscious madness, is the way to truth
itself for Lessing:

> Perhaps it was because if society is so organized, or rather has
> so grown, that it will not admit what one knows to be true, will
> not admit it, that is, except as it comes out perverted, through
> madness, then it is through madness and its variants it must be
> sought after.

"Madness" and "sanity" thus become, like "love" and "hate," meaningless
terms, their significance merely a matter of perception: "Better mad, if the
price for not being mad is to be a lump of lethargy that will use any kind
of strategem so as to remain a lump, remain nonperceptive and heavy."

Laing, particularly in his later works, similarly maintains that there is
a positive function for what society terms madness; that it is not "what we
need to be cured of, but that it is itself a natural way of healing our own
appalling state of alienation called normality." Normality, for Laing and for

Lessing, is the negative and truly insane state, because it implies the clinging to uncertain certainties and the dependence on a reality that is, in fact, unreal. To go mad in a positive sense is to give up all certainty, according to Laing and Lessing, to lose the distinction between the real and the not-real, between the self and the not-self. Laing and Lessing both indicate that the result of going mad in this sense may well be the emergence of a state of mind far saner than that understood by the normal world. Similarly, Woolf's Septimus in *Mrs. Dalloway* is a "saner" person than his evil physician.

Martha Quest is perhaps named for her search for this superior sanity, which she begins through a virtually self-conscious and planned inducement of hysteria, a state she describes as "a rehearsal":

> When you get to a new place in yourself, when you are going to break into something new, then it sometimes is presented to you like that: giggling and tears and hysteria. It's a thing you'll understand properly one day—being tested out. First you have to accept them like that, silly and giggly.

Hysteria thus is a rehearsal for the madness which will lead to enlightenment:

> Yes—hysteria. This country, the country or sea, of sound, the wavelength where the voices babble and rage and sing and laugh, and music and war sounds and the bird song and every conceivable sound go together, was approached, at least for her, or at least at this time, through hysteria. Very well then, she would be hysterical.

Martha also experiments with the possibilities of surrendering identity, of obscuring the distinction between the self and the not-self, not through a loss of self in the sexual experience, as Kaplan suggests, but in the more easily controlled area of her own mind. She recognizes that she has always, since childhood, maintained "as an act of survival" a second personality, a false aspect of the self, a "parody" called "Matty." Now she can clinically observe her own schizophrenia: she can "call strange identities into being with a switch of clothes or a change of voice—until one felt like an empty space without boundaries and it did not matter what name one gave a stranger who asked: What is your name? Who are you?"

Name and identity, so inextricably connected in the works of both Brontë and Woolf that the loss of one in marriage threatens the loss of the other, are also important links in Lessing's novel. Sally-Sarah, for example, is really just "Sarah," but her husband's family, seeking to disguise her Jewish background, renames her "Sally." Perhaps her inability to herself control whether she is Sally or Sarah is another contributing factor to her suicide. For Martha, however, this connection between name and identity is part of the rehearsal, a crucial factor in the experiment of surrendering identity, so serious that she refers to it as her "work":

> As for "Hesse," it was a name acquired like a bracelet from a man who had it in his possession to be given to a woman in front of lawyers at the time of the signing of the marriage contract. But who then was she, behind the banalities of the day? . . . But really, there she was: *she* was, nothing to do with Martha, or any other name she might have attached to her.

Thus madness and the loss of identity, those states which Jane Eyre and Clarissa Dalloway struggle to avoid, Martha actively seeks to confront. She realizes that she can move almost at will from "inside the empty space of self" into "ordinary living" in which the self "seemed a very far country." She experiments in this way because, paradoxically, only through the loss of self is it possible to find the self:

> Sometimes she felt like a person who wakes up in a strange city, not knowing who he, she, is. There she sat, herself. Her name was Martha, a convenient label to attach to her sense of herself. Sometimes she got up and looked into the mirror, in an urgency of need to see a reflection of that presence called, for no particular reason, Martha. She had dark eyes. She smiled, or frowned. Once, bringing to the mirror a mood of seething anxiety, she saw a dishevelled panic-struck creature biting its nails. She watched this creature, who was in an agony of fear. Who watched?

Martha's question is not fully answered until she meets Lynda Coldridge, who will, by example, guide Martha from hysteria into the insane experience where the true identity of the self is to be discovered. Perhaps it is in much the same way that Woolf perceives Septimus to have kept or even to have gained his "treasure" of the self in madness. Lynda also echoes Septimus's claim to superior knowledge, expressed in the urgent message he directs to humanity. Throughout Lessing's novel Lynda repeats: "I know things." Part of what she knows is that all people are really at least two people: "Sometimes you are more the one that watches, and sometimes that one gets far off and you are more the one that is watched." Martha too becomes aware of "the somebody in you who always watches what goes on, who is always apart."

As Brontë's Bertha can be seen as Jane Eyre's mad, bad self, so Lynda can be seen as Martha's mad, good self. She serves as both guide and doppelgänger. Martha feels this identification even before she meets Lynda:

> she had not met Lynda, save through improbably beautiful photographs, but she knew her, oh yes, very well, though she and Martha were not alike, and could not be, since Martha was not "ill" and in the hands of the doctors. But for a large variety of reasons, Lynda Coldridge, who was in a very expensive mental hospital because she could not stand being Mark's wife, and Francis's mother, came too close to Martha. Which was why Martha had to leave this house and soon.

Martha cannot, however, simply leave, being held, at least partly, by this mysterious affinity with the insane Lynda. Because Lynda cannot "stand being Mark's wife" and refuses sexual intimacy with him, Martha assumes Lynda's role and becomes Mark's surrogate wife, sleeping with him, caring for his son and nephew, managing his house, providing him with ideas for his novel and plays. When Mark turns his attentions from Martha, she moves into Lynda's apartment in the basement, where their relationship as doubles is further emphasized, where Martha comes to realize that she is "in love" with Lynda as "with a part of herself she had never even been introduced to—even caught a glimpse of." As Martha enters Lynda's mad world, both physically and emotionally, she sometimes wonders where she ends and where Lynda begins. In describing the chaos of sound which is a part of her insane experience, Martha asks, "Is it in Lynda's head or in mine?" At that point in their shared experience at which the world seems the furthest removed, Lynda and Martha together perform a kind of ritual, like a communion, Lynda kneeling on the floor and, animal-like, lapping milk from a broken saucer, and Martha drinking "symbolically" from the same saucer.

The character of Lynda could well be seen as a parody of Brontë's Bertha, not only in her function as doppelgänger, but in other areas as well. Both Lynda and Bertha are women of great former beauty, now ravaged by madness. Bertha, however, is bloated and gigantized, while Lynda has shrunk into "a creature all bone, with yellowish-smelling flesh, with great anxious globes of water tinted blue stuck in its face." Bertha is dark; Lynda is pale blonde. Bertha's laughter is maniacal and blood-chilling; Lynda's uncontrollable "giggling" is equally maniacal, but sad rather than grotesque. Bertha is violent against selected others; Lynda is only violent against herself as she deprives her emaciated body of food and repeatedly pounds her head against the walls. Lynda lives in the basement, a location perhaps more appropriate as a symbolic hell than the attic room in which Bertha is confined. Lynda gropes at the walls of her room, not seeking escape as Bertha does, but rather exploring them as symbolically representing the walls of her own mind. Bertha represents passion and sexual excess; Lynda is chaste, the imaginary Guru of the vision she shares with Martha having told her that "the Great Mother" has chosen her as "one of her daughters who had been freed of the tyrannies of the flesh—lust, he said." Bertha enters Jane's room to tear the wedding veil, her motive, Rochester suggests, being the desecration of the memory of her own bridal days. Lynda enters her husband's room on a similar errand, the destruction of her own beautiful photograph. Bertha paces and creeps in her confinement; Lynda shares a similar need for constant and seemingly motiveless movement. In a scene strikingly similar to those depicted in yet another story about a mad woman, Charlotte Perkins Gilman's "The Yellow Wallpaper," Lynda arranges her allotted space:

> around the walls there was a clear space or runway, as if there were a second invisible wall against which a table, chairs, bookcases, were arranged, a yard or so inside the visible wall. And again, all around the walls to the height of about five feet the paper had an irregularly smudged and rusty look, which turned out to be the bloodstains from Lynda's bitten finger ends.

The most important similarity between Brontë's and Lessing's mad characters is their common function as scapegoat, a role which Lynda consciously recognizes as her own. Because she is powerless and female, she, like Bertha, suffers for the sins of both father and husband. Lynda's father, frustrated in his attempts at remarriage by his daughter's strange behavior toward his intended wife, "handed her bound and helpless to the doctors, where she had struggled and fought and been bludgeoned into silence by drugs and injections, held down by nurses and dragged screaming to have electric shocks." Mark, in contrast to Lynda's father and to Brontë's Rochester, appears patient and devoted, but in reality, one suspects, he is enjoying his role as long-suffering martyr; he has played it before with other "neurotic" problem women and will assume it again with Martha and others as well. Perhaps Lynda is perceptive rather than ungrateful when she echoes Jane Eyre's cry to St. John Rivers, "Leave me alone. . . . You're killing me." Mark, after all, is a part of normal society, and therefore ill equipped to understand Lynda. He, like her father, eventually turns her over "into the hands of the doctors."

As Marion Vlastos states in the article "Doris Lessing and R. D. Laing: Psychopolitics and Prophecy," Lynda is also a scapegoat in the sense that she is "a victim of society's mistrust of the strange and the acutely sensitive."

The same description applies to Woolf's Septimus. Too, Lessing's ironically named Dr. Lamb, Lynda's psychiatrist, is a symbolic representation of that mistrusting society, in much the same way that Sir William Bradshaw represents the negative elements in Woolf's world. Like Bradshaw, Dr. Lamb is emotionless, courteous, sexless, and professional. He echoes Bradshaw's very words as he promises Martha that after her analysis she will see her problems "in proportion." He appears to Martha "like a character in a play who wore a mask which said, 'I am Wisdom.'" Lynda screams that he is the devil, and Martha perceives with horror that he is the incarnation of power itself:

> There was nobody, ever, who could approach Dr. Lamb without a certain kind of tremor. When he spoke to law courts, or advised policemen, or sat in judgement about this sick person or that: when a mortally confused human being sat before him, what Dr. Lamb said was the truth. . . . Dr. Lamb, whether benign, cruel, a secret lover of power, or a man gifted with insight, was always in a position of strength. Because it was he who knew—society had said he did—everything that could be known about the human soul. . . .
>
> The central fact here was that nobody approached Dr. Lamb unless he had to. In approaching Dr. Lamb one approached power. It was hard to think of a power like it, in its inclusiveness, its arbitrariness, its freedom to behave as it wished, without checks from other places or powers.

Sir William Bradshaw humiliates his patients by forcing them to drink milk in bed, but Dr. Lamb's medications are far more potent. Lessing, like Laing and a growing number of other modern psychologists, is opposed to many of the traditional therapeutic treatments, including the use of drugs to simulate normality. Lynda is most pathetic when she has lost control of her illness because of her addiction to and dependence on medications. Both drugs and shock treatments are, to Lessing's mind, no more than torture devices, methods used to punish and control.

Lessing also shares Laing's views regarding the dangers of the traditional analyst-patient relationship. Laing writes:

> Psychotherapy must remain *an obstinate attempt of two people to recover the wholeness of being human through the relationship between them.*
>
> Any technique concerned with the other without the self, with behavior to the exclusion of experience, with the relationship to

the neglect of the persons in relation, with the individuals to the
exclusion of their relationship, and most of all, with an object-
to-be-changed rather than a person-to-be-accepted, simply per-
petuates the disease it purports to cure.

Lessing too rejects the idea of the analyst as authority figure and sees it as
disastrous when "the patient became dependent on the doctor and was unable to free himself."

Lessing, also like Laing, deplores the existence of mental hospitals, those
institutions which, Laing says, imprison the insane person, leaving him or
her "bereft of his civil liberties . . . invalidated as a human being." Lessing
describes the politics of mental illness:

> Some years before, an act of Parliament had been passed, which
> had taken bars off windows, unlocked doors, made strait jackets
> and padded cells things of the past, created hospitals that were
> civilized. Well, not quite. Because, for this bit of legal well-wish-
> ing to work, it needed that a great deal of money should be spent
> on new buildings, doctors, nurses. This money was not being
> spent. (It was being spent on war, the central fact of our time
> which is taken for granted.)
>
> Inside the dozens of mental hospitals scattered up and down
> the country, built like prisons, were many thousands of people
> who had been strait-jacketed, forcibly fed, kept in padded cells,
> beaten (in fact, the central fact, had had their wills broken), and
> were now derelict, "deteriorated."

Normal people perpetrate such obscenities, not out of gratuitous cruelty,
according to Lessing, but out of fear that prevents their recognition of themselves as mad and out of the suspicion that the "insane" person possesses a
superior sanity:

> They are so susceptible to flattery that anything may be done
> with them; provided they are not allowed to suspect their infe-
> riority. For they are so vain that they would certainly kill or
> imprison or maim any being they suspect of being better endowed
> than themselves.

Thus, Lynda repeatedly warns Martha never to tell "them" what she knows.

Insane women of today, writes Lessing, are like the witches of former
centuries, tortured because they have superior capacities. Virginia Woolf,
too, frequently makes a connection in her nonfiction works between the

witches of history, the wise women, and present-day victims of mental illness. She writes in *A Room of One's Own*:

> Any woman born with a great gift in the sixteenth century would certainly have gone crazed, shot herself, or ended her days in some lonely cottage outside the village, half witch, half wizard, feared and mocked at. For it needs little skill in psychology to be sure that a highly gifted girl who had tried to use her gift for poetry would have been so thwarted and hindered by other people, so tortured and pulled asunder by her own contrary instincts, that she must have lost her health and sanity to a certainty.

Bertha Mason or even Jane Eyre herself with her presentiments, her prophetic dreams, her affinity with both nature and the supernatural, may be more witchlike than Lynda and Martha, yet Lessing's characters, through their mutual experiencing of insanity, do delve into the occult and emerge with what Lessing calls a "new sort of understanding":

> Yet in their own inner experience this was a time of possibility. It was as if doors kept opening in their brains just far enough to admit a new sensation, or a glimmer of something—and though they closed again, something was left behind . . . they understood what it meant that "scales should fall from one's eyes"—scales had fallen.

"Madness," according to Laing, "need not be all breakdown. It may also be breakthrough. It is potentially liberation and renewal as well as enslavement and existential death."

Certainly, what Martha feels when she comes up from the basement, after many days of sharing an intense and often terrifying experience with Lynda, is what Dante must have felt as he exited from hell, or what Woolf's Septimus experiences in his most ecstatic visions: a sense of resurrection, of rebirth. Each moment, for Martha, becomes an epiphany, a miracle:

> The words kept dropping into the listening space that was Martha's mind. She knew that if a person were to take one word, and listen; or a pebble or a jewel and look at it; the word, the stone, would give up, in the end, its own meaning and the meaning of everything.

Laing says that "our social realities are so ugly if seen in the light of exiled truth." Just as Martha has perceived through her hysteria the ugliness of reality and of humanity, so she also deeply experiences, through the "light of exiled truth," the physical beauty of the world. Like Septimus, she can perceive the universe as magnificent. The sky hangs above her "an explosion of golden light," and the world, like her resurrected self, seems new:

> The day was fresh and the world newly painted. She stood on a pavement looking at a sky where soft white clouds were lit with sunlight. She wanted to cry because it was so beautiful. How long since she had looked, but really looked, at the sky, so beautiful even if it was held up by tall buildings? She stood gazing up, up, until her eyes seemed absorbed in the crystalline substance of the sky with its blocks of clouds like snowbanks, she seemed to be streaming out through her eyes into the skies.

There are, however, also the nightmare aspects of the insane experience to be dealt with. For Martha, as for Septimus, there is the fear of losing control, the necessity to close one's eyes so that the visions do not become too beautiful, too terrifying. For Lynda and Martha, there is also the "sound barrier" to be got through, a barrage of noise which becomes excruciating and must, eventually, be sorted out and made rational. The "radio" in one's head is tuned simultaneously to a hundred stations, and one must fight to gain control.

Worst of all the mad experiences is the confrontation with what Lessing calls the "self-hater," that evil in the schizophrenic self which balances or sometimes annihilates the good. Lynda, having lost control and having been victimized by drugs and doctors, is never able successfully to combat the "self-hater," but Martha, free of impediments, eventually goes on alone to conquer it.

It is during this particular battle that Martha most clearly recognizes that the self is the microcosm and that it, like the world, is divided between victim and tormentor: Martha herself is both "the ragged bit of refuse (me) pushed into the gas chamber and the uniformed woman (me) who pushed." Woolf's Septimus perhaps experiences a similar confrontation: he feels himself guilty of terrible crimes against humanity while, at the same time, he sees himself as Christ. Lessing's description of Martha's recognition of the "self-hater" is equally paradoxical and equally imbued with religious significance:

> From the moment when Pontius Pilate washed his hands to the time when she, Martha, who was also the Devil, prepared to be bound on the Cross, because of the frightfulness of her crimes, she was as it were whipped through the ritual by the hating

scourging tongue of the Devil who was her self, her hating, self-hating self.

Recognition of and confrontation with the "self-hater" are, according to Lessing, prerequisites for knowledge of the divided self and the first steps to making it whole.

The state of insanity, then, is divided between the regions of joy and beauty, poetry and religion, and the regions of terror. Normal adult people, Lessing says, never experience these extremes of feeling because they fear any disturbance of complacency. Martha, however, strives to recall and to reattain the sensitivity and perception, the extremes of feeling, which she recalls as a part of childhood:

> The first intimations of this capacity had been in childhood, just before sleep or on awakening: a faint flash of colour, a couple of pictures perhaps, or a fragment of music, or some words, or her name called in warning or reminder: *Remember, remember.* Well, a great many people experienced this, but being well-ordered, well-trained, docile, obedient people, they heard the doctors or the priests say—whatever the current dogma ordered and that was that: they were prepared to bury the evidence of their own senses, they ran away. And like any neglected faculty, it fell into disuse, it atrophied.

Lessing's romantic idea is that children are thus somehow in touch with something mystical with which adults have lost contact. Laing, throughout *The Politics of Experience,* maintains a similar notion: "As adults, we have forgotten most of our childhood, not only its contents but its flavor; as men of the world, we hardly know of the existence of the inner world."

Both Martha and Lynda are loved by children and have a strange ability to communicate with them beyond what is possible for normal adults. Lynda, during some of her worst periods in the basement, shuts out the adult world, but admits her nephew and, later, her son. They understand her and she them, but because of her preference for the company of children, the doctors pronounce her behavior regressive.

Although Martha acts as a surrogate mother to Lynda's son, she has, before the novel begins, abandoned her own daughter. A possible reason for this action is that her relationship with her own mother has been so devastatingly disappointing, so guilt-ridden and nonloving. Yet Martha longs for maternal love. In a state of depression, dreading the approaching visit of her mother, Martha weeps "while a small girl wept with her, Mama, Mama,

why are you so cold, so unkind, why did you never love me?" Martha an-
ticipates this visit in a state, virtually, of emotional prostration, yet she provides for Dr. Lamb only the formulaic reasons for her feelings: "My mother
was a woman who hated her own sexuality and she hated mine too."

Laing, like Lessing, sees children as irreparably damaged in the mother-
child relationship which in present society, he says, is one of violence and
devastation:

> Children are not yet fools, but we shall turn them into imbeciles
> like ourselves with high I.Q.'s if possible.
>
> From the moment of birth, when the Stone Age baby confronts
> the twentieth-century mother, the baby is subjected to these forces
> of violence, called love, as its mother and father and their parents
> and their parents before them, have been. These forces are mainly
> concerned with destroying most of its potentialities, and on the
> whole this enterprise is successful. By the time the new human
> being is fifteen or so, we are left with a being like ourselves, a
> half-crazed creature more or less adjusted to a mad world.

With Laing's statement in mind, it is perhaps easier to understand Martha's
explanation for abandoning her child: "When I left my little girl, Caroline,
do you know what I was thinking? I thought, I'm setting you free, I thought,
I'm setting you free."

Martha, like Jane Eyre, is unsuccessful in her search for mother love,
but unlike Jane, Martha has a great capacity to assume the maternal role
herself, at least with others than her own child. Martha's relationship with
Mark, for example, is distinguished by a "protective compassion"; she would
like to surround both him and herself with "invisible arms, vast, peaceful,
maternal." Martha's feeling for Lynda is less a lesbian-oriented love than a
longing to mother. "Thus unknown person in Martha adored Lynda, wor-
shipped her, wished to wrap her long soft hair around her hands, said, Poor
little child, poor little girl, why don't you let me look after you?"

Perhaps disinterested, nonpossessive maternal love is the only kind of
love possible in Lessing's world; it may, in fact, provide at least a relative
salvation for all of humanity. Martha's nurturing instincts finally permit her
to assume the mother role to hundreds of special children who survive the
earth's devastation at the end of the novel. Martha knows that these "freak"
children, some anomalies born after the apocalyptic event, are really supra-
normal, highly sensitive and, like "mad" persons, able to "see" and to "hear"
things. They are, possibly, to provide the rebirth of the world; they can,
potentially, create a new world, one which might not sink into darkness and

schizophrenia, but might remain whole, perceptive, undivided, like that world ruled by the gods and goddesses of Lessing's *Briefing for a Descent into Hell*. Laing, too, sees the world's hope in children: "Each time a new baby is born there is a possibility of reprieve. Each child is a new being, a potential prophet, a new spiritual prince, a new spark of light precipitated into the outer darkness. Who are we to decide it is hopeless?"

Martha herself does not live to see any such hope fulfilled. The Edenic return possible for Jane Eyre and the self-affirmation possible for Clarissa are not probabilities in Lessing's bleaker world. Near the end of the novel, Martha is an old woman alone; however, her hysteria is calmed, her self fully discovered and recognized, if not healed:

> She walked beside the river while the music thudded, feeling her-
> self as a heavy impervious lump that, like a planet doomed always
> to be dark on one side, had vision in front only, a myopic search-
> light, blind except for the tiny three-dimensional path open im-
> mediately before her eyes in which the outline of a tree, a rose,
> emerged, then submerged in the dark. She thought, with the
> dove's voices of her solitude: Where? But *where*. How? Who?
> No, but *where*, where. . . . Then silence and the birth of a rep-
> etition: *Where?* Here. Here?
>
> Here, where else, you fool, you poor fool, where else has it
> been, ever.

Hysteria, after all, is literally a suffering in the womb. In helping to give birth to a potentially better world, Martha is left with at least a knowledge, a vision, which consoles.

ROBERTA RUBENSTEIN

Briefing for a Descent into Hell

If *The Golden Notebook* and *The Four-Gated City* can be taken as the breakthroughs in Lessing's fiction in both structure and idea, each of the novels (to date) that comes after them carries echoes of the far-ranging nexus of issues, characterizations, and patterns embraced by those two works. Yet, despite the continuity of themes, *Briefing for a Descent into Hell* initiates new formal and narrative shifts in Lessing's fiction. For the first—and only—time, the protagonist of the novel is male. Structurally, the novel is closer in conception to the experimental form of *The Golden Notebook,* with its inversion of chronology and multiple perspectives that reinforce the subjectivity of point of view. In fact, the story itself is adumbrated in the earlier work, in Ella's idea of writing a story about "a man whose 'sense of reality' has gone; and because of it, has a deeper sense of reality than 'normal' people" (*The Golden Notebook*).

Like the latter novel, *Briefing for a Descent into Hell* depends on a basic pattern of theme and variations: the "theme" is Charles Watkins's deeper psychic urge to heal the schism of his present condition of self-division; the variations include his nostalgia for union and his recognition of separation, envisioned by Lessing through a series of metaphoric or symbolic journeys. In its paring down of the density of narrative description in favor of a flowing, more symbolically saturated language, it represents a new shape for Lessing's central vision.

From *The Novelistic Vision of Doris Lessing: Breaking the Forms of Consciousness.* © 1979 by the Board of Trustees of the University of Illinois. University of Illinois Press, 1979.

In its particular exploration of the abnormal consciousness, this novel poses an even more radical critique of both "reality" and narrative realism than the novels that precede it. It is worth reviewing here the way madness itself as a particular manifestation of the abnormal consciousness has evolved thus far in Lessing's fiction. In *The Grass Is Singing* fragmentation is the response of Mary Turner's personality to the polarizations of reality along sexual and racial lines—antitheses that do exist in the phenomenal world and that are only catalysts for her own inner divisions. The resulting breakdown emphasizes the disjunction between self and world through the fact that oppression has both political and psychological modalities, both of which are divisive. Julia Barr's self-division in *Retreat to Innocence* is primarily represented through ideological and sexual antitheses. Anna Wulf's breakdown is the most thorough "working through" of the manifold implications of unconventional mental experience, with the beginnings of visionary intuition (adumbrated in the younger Martha Quest of the early volumes of *Children of Violence*) taken further until they lead to a reintegration of the personality. Thomas Stern's madness in *Landlocked* presses that connection between the dissolution of the self common to certain kinds of psychotic and mystical perceptions still further. Martha Quest's later incorporation of the meaning of his and of Lynda Coldridge's schizophrenic visions and her own explorations in *The Four-Gated City* are thus comprehensible as evolutionary stages in developing the organs of spiritual perception.

Moreover, as the "inner enemy" or shadow aspect of the self becomes more conscious and is integrated into the personality beginning with the character of Anna Wulf, breaking through rather than breaking down assumes a more central thematic position in Lessing's fiction. At the same time the emphasis begins to shift from the personal to the collective aspects of consciousness. For, while Anna Wulf wants, as she tells her therapist, to be "'able to separate in myself what is old and cyclic, the recurring history, the myth, from what is new, what I feel or think that might be new'" (*The Golden Notebook*), Martha Quest understands her personal psychological growth as a function as much of those recurring cycles as of unique events.

The changing function of "madness" thus expresses the author's conception of both social-political realities and personal development. Lessing has summarized her long involvement with abnormal consciousness in her own life, observing,

> I have spent nearly thirty years in close contact with mental illness, first through various brands of analyst and therapist and

psychiatrist, and then through people who were "mad" in various ways, and with whom I had very close contact. And still have. All this was not by any conscious choice on my part: it happened, presumably because of unconscious needs of my own.

. . . I have always been close to crazy people. My parents were, mildly, in their own ways. My father was done in by the [F]irst [W]orld [W]ar, from which he never really recovered, and my mother had what is known as an unfortunate upbringing, her mother dying when she was three or so, and she never got over that. Both were acutely neurotic people. But I do not regard this as any personal fate, far from it, I believe that the world gets madder and madder, and when I say that it is not rhetorical or because the words sound attractively eccentric.

As Lessing's protagonists turn away from the Leftist ideological framework for effecting social change, the "revolution" goes inward; the dream evolves from political to psychological alterations of the structures of reality as the novel structure correspondingly incorporates more of the motifs and narrative conventions associated with myth, romance, and speculative fiction. Breaking through one's conventional perceptions remains the primary task, with attendant risks, though even successful accomplishment of that task rarely affects the macrocosm, which continues to poison and fragment itself through self-interest, ignorance, and limited vision.

From the beginning of this next work, Lessing alerts the reader to the dual schema, as well as to the underlying Sufi inflection of its meaning, by providing a context for the novel on the frontispiece: "Category: Inner-Space Fiction—For there is never anywhere to go but in." Two epigraphs—one from the fourteenth-century Sufi Mahmoud Shabistari's poem *The Secret Garden,* and the other from Rachel Carson's *The Edge of the Sea*—describe the macrocosm encapsulated within a raindrop or a sand grain suspended in water. As in *The Four-Gated City,* the part not only represents the whole but paradoxically contains it. By analogy, the unnamed seafarer of the first pages of *Briefing for a Descent into Hell* is Everyman, rediscovering (remembering) through the explorataion of the microcosm of his own consciousness the experience of the human race.

Characteristically, the protagonist of this novel is self-divided. As one subsequently learns, the stresses of middle age and personal problems have propelled Charles Watkins, a professor of classics at Cambridge, into a mental breakdown accompanied by a temporary loss of identity medically described as amnesia. The motif of amnesia is a central one in the romance

tradition: the series of adventures of the protagonist may be precipitated by
"some kind of break in consciousness, one which often involves actual for-
getfulness of the previous state. . . . Such a catastrophe, which is what it
normally is, may be internalized as a break in memory, or externalized as a
change in fortunes or social context."

In *Briefing for a Descent into Hell* alternating sections correspond to
both ways of perceiving the psychic crisis of the central character: from
within and without his own consciousness. Accordingly, the first long portion is narrated primarily from the more immediate and subjective focus of
the perceiving consciousness, while the remaining portions are composed
primarily of letters, dialogues, and more public communications from members of Watkins's milieu and "reminiscences" provided by Watkins himself.
In the first section, however, doctors' evaluations juxtaposed with the directly
recorded subjective experiences of the protagonist emphasize the perceptual
antithesis further.

When the protagonist is most awake and aware within his own mental
experience, he is most deeply asleep from the point of view of the medical
observers. His being is split into two modes: while his body participates in
one, his mind participates in the other; they are complementary and, much
of the time, mutually exclusive. "Inner" and "outer" space become metaphors in the novel not only in the sense of the cosmic voyage doubling as
the journey of the private self but, more immediately, in the sense of disjunction between the mental and physical spaces that a person simultaneously
occupies.

Watkins is Lessing's most identifiably "schizophrenic" character. In fact,
a number of parallels can be drawn between the experiences of her protagonist and the existential phenomenology of schizophrenia proposed by R. D.
Laing, not the least of which is a ten-day psychotic journey described by one
of Laing's ex-patients, coincidentally named Jesse Watkins. One of Laing's
central (and controversial) hypotheses is that the psychotic breakdown manifested in acute schizophrenia is a natural process of mind-healing which, if
allowed to run its full course, will be therapeutic rather than destructive.
Following Bateson and others, Laing describes the "inner space journey" of
the schizophrenic as follows:

> The person who has entered this inner realm (if only he is allowed
> to experience this) will find himself going, or being conducted—
> one cannot clearly distinguish active from passive here—on a
> journey.
>
> This journey is experienced as going further "in," as going

back through one's personal life, in and back and through and beyond into the experience of all mankind, of the primal man, of Adam and perhaps even further into the being of animals, vegetables, and minerals.

In this journey there are many occasions to lose one's way, for confusion, partial failure, even final shipwreck: many terrors, spirits, demons to be encountered, that may or may not be overcome.

However, the inner journey described here is not unique to psychotic breakdown, and Lessing's apparent indebtedness to Laing accounts for only one of the multiple routes to the same archetypal experiences. The comparative mythologist Joseph Campbell has observed that the pattern of experience generated during an acute schizophrenic crisis is "the universal formula also of the mythological hero journey. . . . Interpreted from this point of view, a schizophrenic breakdown is an inward and backward journey to recover something missed or lost, and to restore, thereby, a vital balance."

As Northrop Frye has pointed out, the motifs of ascent and descent are patterns in the romance tradition in literature, wherein the worlds of idyllic and demonic experience are characteristically polarized as the narrative movement alternates between the psychological representations of wish fulfillment and nightmare. That same journey pattern also appears in esoteric traditions. The Sufis describe man's evolutionary course from the simplest form of matter through vegetable, animal, human, and suprahuman states of consciousness, to the achievement of the "total perception of the external phenomenal world." Further, phenomenologists of consciousness document similar motifs in the classical experiences described throughout the centuries in mystical and occult literature, and in the more recent psychedelic (or psycholytic) drug-induced experiences.

What all of these parallel formulations suggest is that the collective unconscious—whether reached by psychotic, psychoanalytic, psychedelic, or contemplative means—manifests itself in similar archetypal images and symbols. Regardless of the catalyst, the unconscious generates patterns which, under certain but diverse circumstances, become more readily accessible to the other layers of the psyche. That identity is central to the major motifs of *Briefing for a Descent into Hell*, the first movement of which may be read as the narrative of a spiritual, archetypal, psychotic, or even drug-induced inner journey. What determines its fullest symbolic meaning is not so much what stimulates the journey as what is attained through it, and whether or not the change in consciousness has long-reaching effects on the personality of the protagonist.

Throughout the first long portion of the novel, the images resonate on
several levels of meaning. The protagonist initially finds himself "at sea," a
figurative pun suggesting the nature of his personal crisis as well as the base-
element that symbolizes the origin of individual and collective, organic and
psychic, life. The protagonist's wanderings express other primary images and
rhythms, including heat, light, and circles. His "anti-clock Wise" direction
and his need to experience a birth in reverse suggest the circularity of his
journey backward both in time and in the development of his own consciousness as he tries to locate the center of his being. He is the archetypal
seafarer, alternately Jason, Jonah, Odysseus, Sinbad, adrift in a ship that is
inhabited temporarily by a strange unearthly light (called the Crystal) that
incorporates his shipmates but leaves him behind. (One learns later in the
novel that during Watkins's war experience he was twice the only survivor
in a group of buddies; in this section he is twice left behind by the Crystal—
an example of Lessing's refraction of events from later in the novel through
the protagonist's altered consciousness.)

   While the inner space journey traces the narrator's subsequent efforts
to reach the Crystal again, it figuratively recapitulates the cumulative history
of life on earth. The protagonist is identified with the first living organisms
emerging from the slime as they become land creatures; the psychological
and spiritual parallel is the emergence of human consciousness and its growth
toward enlightenment and wholeness. As in *The Four-Gated City,* evolution
in *Briefing for a Descent into Hell* is conceived as a dual process, both
biological and spiritual; in each context ontogeny recapitulates phylogeny.
That progress of human evolution appears in the writings of the thirteenth-
century Sufi teacher Jala-luddin Rumi as follows:

> He came, at first, into the inert world, and from minerality de-
> veloped into the realm of vegetation. Years he lives thus. Then he
> passed into an animal state, bereft of memory of his having been
> vegetable—except for his attraction to Spring and flowers. This
> was like the innate desire of the infant for the mother's breast.
> . . .
> From realm to realm man went, reaching his present reasoning,
> knowledgeable, robust state—forgetting earlier forms of intelli-
> gence.
> So, too, shall he pass beyond the current forms of perception.
> . . . There are a thousand other forms of Mind.

   Within his existential reality Lessing's protagonist accomplishes the evolutionary step from sea to land, literally and figuratively, with the aid of a

dolphin. Once on land, he establishes an intuitive communication with two gentle cat-like creatures who guide him over an apparent impasse in his upward climb. He arrives at what is at first an uninhabited archaic city. Like the mythical four-gated city of *Children of Violence,* it is organized in a circle/square configuration suggesting a sacred dimension. Later the houses are noticeably "turned inwards, to the centre," and the city itself seems to acknowledge the protagonist's presence as if also possessed of consciousness.

At first the archaic Eden-like atmosphere of the surroundings is emphasized, "as if this was a country where hostility or dislike had not yet been born." The protagonist experiences a sense of harmony and unity analogous both to the state of undifferentiated wholeness in the generic individual's personal development, and to the hypothetical primitive pre-ego consciousness in the history of civilization. However, that state is soon interrupted by the appearance of the ubiquitous "enemy" that Lessing has shown consistently as a configuration of the dark side of the mind.

The protagonist accordingly feels himself under a lunar influence, a reference not only to the pull of that dark or irrational side of the self, with its multiple metaphoric meanings, but also an ironic gloss on the "lunacy" that his rambling monologues represent to the medical staff. On the outskirts of the city he witnesses, and feels himself implicated in, a ritualistic blood-letting involving several male babies and three females whose identities are disturbingly familiar to him. He realizes that their rite destroys forever some fundamental innocence in nature by their introduction of carnality into the pure world; like Adam in the Garden, he acquires a knowledge of the flesh, and feels compelled to cover his nakedness. Just as his imagination had "invented" the city itself, "now I understood my fall away from what I had been when I landed, only three weeks before, into a land which had never known killing. I knew that I had arrived purged and salt-scoured and guilt-less, but that between then and now I had drawn evil into my surroundings, into me." The shadow further manifests itself in two species of ugly, rapa-cious animals—the negative (and further divided) counterparts of the benev-olent beasts that had earlier guided him. From the first appearance of these rat-like dogs and monkeys, the protagonist watches their mutual antagonism build and then break into open warfare, and tacitly acknowledges his own complicity in their violence.

During the time he spends on land, the voyager sees as his task the preparation of a landing pad in the center of the city, in anticipation of the return of the Crystal. Significantly, both the Crystal and the landing area are images of wholeness; in archetypal symbolism crystals and the abstract circle/square configuration often represent "the union of extreme opposites—of matter and spirit." After delays and failures in his effort to prepare himself for this crucial segment of his journey, he finally senses the presence of the Crystal. But, again, he is not ready for it: "Whatever it was that I could not quite see, but was there, belonged to a level of existence that my eyes were not evolved enough to see. . . . Beating out from that central point came waves of a finer substance, from a finer level of existence, which assaulted me, because I was not tuned in to them." The equation of extrasensory perception with the evolving organs of consciousness described by Sufi mystics underlies the formulations of Watkins's experience. The metaphoric language parallels the Sufi chemist Fariduddin Attar's description of inner transformation: "Every fiber has been purified, raised to a higher state, vibrates to a higher tune, gives out a more direct, more penetrating note." At the same time Watkins's inadequacy makes explicit the difficulty of achieving that elevated level of being.

Thus far the protagonist's journey has been on water or land. His nascent "lighter" state now enables him to move in air, through the assistance of a great white bird, and suggests his further ascent toward enlightenment. Finally, in an event that symbolically condenses the several levels of the meaning of his experience, the Crystal arrives at the center of the circle-in-the-square to receive him. His own body becomes "a shape in light" and the city changes correspondingly, "as if the city of stone and clay had dissolved, leaving a ghostly city, made in light." As the boundaries between self and world, inner and outer space, dissolve, the light is simultaneously "inner or outer as one chose to view it." The protagonist's inner being becomes congruent with the macrocosm; he understands that the mind of humanity is also a unified consciousness, of which he is an integral part. Even the war and blood-lust he has witnessed have been essential to his eventual transmutation, providing the "page in my passport for this stage of the journey . . . a door, a key, and an opening."

Formally, the movement toward a higher plane of mystical awareness suggests the ascent motif of romance and myth, in which "escape, remembrance, or discovery of one's real identity, growing freedom, and the breaking of enchantment" shape the narrative; the growth of identity through "the casting off of whatever conceals or frustrates it" typifies the positive metamorphosis of the protagonist. Thus Lessing renders the fundamentally ineffable and self-transcending experience of spiritual illumination—the event that Evelyn Underhill has called the "crystallization" of consciousness at a higher level. The Sufi teachings have it that "when apparent opposites are reconciled, the individuality is not only complete, it also transcends the bounds of ordinary humanity as we understand them. The individual becomes, as near as we can state it, immensely powerful."

In one of a series of lectures given in 1972 at the New School for Social Research, Lessing alluded to her own conversation from the rationalist position to one accommodating the connections among extrasensory perception, elevations of consciousness, and the intensification of personal energy. As she phrased it, "Now the real question is this: Where do you get your energy from? What kind of energy is it? How do you husband it? How do you use it?" And, further, concerning the ESP phenomenon—the source of apparent coincidences of like thinking between people (such as the affinity, described later in *Briefing for a Descent into Hell,* of Rosemary Baines's and Charles Watkins's ideas on education)—Lessing added, "What energy is reaching you? We don't know why, do we? There is something there to be explored . . . if we don't get upset."

Narratively, the description of this process of exploration unfolding in the consciousness of Lessing's inner space voyager is periodically interrupted by the medical staff's observations on their patient's mental condition, and their disagreements about appropriate treatment. Doctor X (deliberately nameless, like the patient) recommends extensive use of drugs and eventually electroconvulsive therapy (shock treatment), while Doctor Y is more restrained, arguing for a gradual approach with minimal intervention. Watkins perceives the doctors' different sensitivities: while he can scarcely "see" Doctor X, Doctor Y is more "visible," burning with a "small steady light." However, despite their different auras and their conflicting diagnoses, both doctors are primarily concerned to restore their patient to the same orthodox model of "normality." Monitoring his responses to the drugs, they interpret his mental condition through its physical manifestations, concentrating on such behavioral evidence as alertness, coherence, drowsiness, and other physiological signs. The reader, suspended between the image of the protagonist as Everyman journeying through the collective unconscious, and Charles Watkins as amnesiac patient, observes the same experiences as described from internal and external perspectives. To emphasize their radical disparity, Lessing juxtaposes the protagonist's approach to the pinnacle of his vision of unity with the medical records showing that he had "less grasp of reality than when he was admitted." The quintessential spiritual experience is, from the medical point of view, a religious delusion.

Consistent with the paradoxes possible at nonrational levels of consciousness, the protagonist's inner space journey is increasingly conceptualized as occurring in outer space. One recalls Anna Wulf's "game," in which the mind progressively distances itself in the direction of a more comprehensive and inclusive geography, a metaphorical statement of the cosmic perspective (*The Golden Notebook*). From deep in inner/outer space the protagonist of this novel has a similar overview of all of the earth, with its petty wars, political schisms, social insanities, divisions. Yet the index of his psychic wholeness is his perception of the fundamental unity of all things, of the interrelatedness of matter and spirit in every dimension of the cosmos. The real madness of humanity, he comprehends, is the failure to remember that unity at the base of all life, instead pursuing the courses of separation and division.

The same identification of microcosm with macrocosm, of inner with outer space, extends still further, as the enlightened protagonist finds himself at a cosmic reference presided over by an illuminated deity (the Sun). There he learns that the troubled planet Earth is in a state of First Class Emergency. The cosmic spirits—including Merk Ury, Minna Erva, and other refractions of Watkins's intellectual familiarity with the Greek classics—are being "briefed" to carry the easily forgotten message of Harmony to its inhabitants once again before it self-destructs. Though the style in this section, occasionally verging on parody of the more classic fabulations of science fiction (and also of conference rhetoric), lightens the novel's tone, the straining after humor is somewhat jarring. While Lessing frequently depends on irony and even parody (as in Anna Wulf's self-parodies in *The Golden Notebook*), humor itself is rare in her work; where it does appear, it is somewhat self-conscious. Thus, of the stylistic variations within *Briefing for a Descent into Hell,* this section and the serious but rather pedestrian verses of the earlier phase of Watkins's journey are the least successful. However, while stylistically awkward, they are nonetheless consistent with the larger design: the creation of verbal equivalents for various kinds of perception and communication, ranging from deeply interior and nearly inarticulable mental experiences to the more public messages (both implicit and explicit) that govern interpersonal relationships. To this point, Lessing has her protagonist repeat several times during his reluctant interchanges with the medical staff, "'I gotta use words when I talk to you.'"

The Forecast for Earth made by the benevolent overseers echoes the extrapolated future envisioned at the end of *The Four-Gated City* but concludes more optimistically. The "film" of the planetary crisis ends with the appearance of a new breed born with an altered mental structure promoting increased powers of perception; its members are endowed with the heritage of the previous generations, "plus, this time, the mental equipment to use it." Through the apocalyptic perspective, Lessing continues to exploit the narrative liberties of speculative fiction.

If the macrocosm and the microcosm are understood as congruent, then the anticipated cataclysm on earth that Watkins observes corresponds to the psychic crisis in his own personality; like Anna Wulf, he discovers the chaos in the outer world that is a projection of his inner state. Furthermore, for the cosmic beings who seek to revitalize the message of harmony and, analogously, for the vision of wholeness in the unconscious that seeks entry into consciousness, the obstacles are great. Even with the "brain-printed" message, the emissaries face a considerable risk of amnesia during their descent into Hell (earth); Watkins's descent into his own inner hell is manifested as amnesia to the medical observers. Symbolically, though each human being is born ("brain-printed") with the experience of harmony and wholeness, subsequent experience erodes that primary knowledge and substitutes division. As he grows older, he is more and more like a victim of amnesia, increasingly self-estranged and forgetful of the knowledge of original unity as the deepest reality of his being. Literature of the romantic tradition consistently alludes to the transcendental state of innocence (as in Wordsworth's "Ode: Intimations of Immortality"), and all mystical traditions seek the way back (or forward) to that experience of undifferentiated wholeness. Idries Shah notes in the latter case that in the Sufi dervish tradition, "remembering" is an important aspect of psychic development, beginning with "'remembering oneself,' after which the function shifts to one of harmony with the greater consciousness."

The problem given this particular symbolic form in *Briefing for a Descent into Hell* is the characteristic metaphysical one of Lessing's fictional protagonists. As Watkins formulates it, "Each individual of this species is locked up inside his own skull," unable to "see things except as facets and one at a time." Watkins himself is ironically the prime example of that propensity. Unlike Martha Quest, who ultimately fuses the opposites of her personality through diligent "work" on her self, the Watkins of the second part of the novel and the mind-voyaging protagonist of the first part do not constitute a *conscious* integrated whole personality. In his own "First Class Emergency," amnesia is the psychological manifestation of an ontological crisis, a breakdown or disintegration of his life-roles as husband, father, paramour, professor. Forgetting for a time who he "is" for others, he journeys within his own unconscious self in an effort to rescue some deeper knowledge from which his waking ego personality has become severed. Thus the hallucinations, fantasies, and visions of his inner space journey are—

from the point of view of his total personality—"unconscious." His larger task is to bring the truths discovered in the collective memory to personal awareness, to fuse the split between the generic Everyman of the inner space journey and the individual self of waking life.

In the subsequent movements of the novel the emphasis shifts from cosmic to biological and social time and their corresponding metaphorical formulations. Formally, the narrative reverses from the pattern of ascent, with its impetus toward unity, to that of descent, with its impetus toward separation. Following the rebirth that expresses his spiritual gnosis, and his cosmic briefing on Harmony, the protagonist "returns to the beginning" again, this time reliving the primary biological separation of his own physical birth experience:

> Sucked into sound, sucked into sea, a swinging sea, *boom,* shhhh, *boooom,* shhhh, *boooom* . . . thud thud, thud thud . . . one two, and the three is me, the three is me, THE THREE IS ME. I in dark, I in pulsing dark, crouched, I holding on, clutching tight, boooom, shhhh, boooom, shhh, rocked, rocking, somewhere behind the gate, somewhere in front the door, and a dark red clotting light and pressure and pain and then OUT into a flat white light where shapes move and things flash and glitter.

His first "personal" memory following birth is his initiation into the drugging of his awareness and the equation of sleeping with being a "good" baby, an expectation that prefigures the chronic spiritual torpor of adult life. Both literally and metaphorically, sleep is the norm; spiritual awakeness is the abnormal state.

Lessing has noted elsewhere that under the influence of mescaline (in her single experience with the drug) she experienced "both giving birth and being given birth to. Who was the mother, who was the baby? I was both but neither"—surely a resonant image of the creative artist giving birth to her own self. (Lessing emphasizes, however, that drugs are not the most valuable path into the mind; with discipline and patience, "if you can train yourself to concentrate you can travel great distances.") Stanislav Grof, working with psycholytic (psychedelic) drug-induced experiences and extrapolating from the psychoanalytic concept of "birth trauma," has proposed that the universal intrauterine state and the subsequent stages of labor and delivery form biological paradigms for the ecstatic and stressful extremes of psychic experiences at successive levels of consciousness; these may manifest themselves in certain aspects of both drug-induced and psychotic experiences.

Those same extremes of unity and separation permeate the conscious-

ness of the protagonist of Lessing's novel. Each framing of the journey repeats certain patterns in Watkins's split personality, as Lessing illustrates
through a variety of contexts the same emotional truths of her protagonist's
situation. That the inner journey is itself both a reflection of and an effort
to heal the division is the central assumption of the novel. As R. D. Laing
has remarked, the "cracked mind of the schizophrenic may *let in* light which
does not enter the intact minds of many sane people whose minds are
closed." The narrator of *Briefing for a Descent into Hell* describes the mental
hospitals that house the "millions who have cracked, making cracks where
the light could shine through at last."

Like Laing, whose ideology Lessing shares more explicitly in this novel
than in any of her other works (despite her own consistent disclaimers), the
author emphasizes that "mental illness"—manifested as unconventional behavior or abnormal consciousness—is a cultural label that permits the potential for vision or even self-healing to be drugged and nullified by the very
institutions that ostensibly promote recovery. The medical model of psychic
disequilibrium prevents doctors (and others) from accepting the possibility
that, in Anton Boisen's words,

> certain types of mental disorder are not in themselves evils but
> problem-solving experiences. They are attempts at reorganization
> in which the entire personality, to its bottommost depths, is
> aroused and its forces marshaled to meet the danger of personal
> failure and isolation. . . . The acute disturbances . . . arise out of
> awareness of danger. The sufferer is facing what for him are the
> great and abiding issues of life and death and of his own rela-
> tionship to the universe.
>
> . . . In some cases the charge of pathology as applied to religious
> experience is due simply to the failure to recognize that such
> phenomena as hallucinations spring from the tapping of the
> deeper levels of the mental life, and that as such they are not
> necessarily symptomatic of mental disorder but may be creative
> and constructive. But in a large number of cases the association
> of the mystical and the pathological is due to the fact that a
> fundamental reorientation is a necessary stage in the development
> of the individual.

If the first major section of *Briefing for a Descent into Hell* shows the
"light shining through" the cracked mind of the protagonist, the remainder
of the novel provides a partial explanation for the crack. As in *The Golden
Notebook,* the scrambling of chronology is essential to the novel's meaning.

Lessing provides the immediate subjective experience of Watkins's abnormal consciousness first, and only subsequently furnishes its context by showing the data of his outer world that have been translated into the particular images of his journey. The literal link between the divided layers of his being is Watkins's photographic memory (a capacity later reported by one of his colleagues). The narrative organization thus expresses two kinds of knowledge: the "information" of the external world of social interaction, and its imaginative transformations at the unconscious levels of the protagonist's psyche. Their juxtaposition both invites and expresses the implicit questions of the novel: which mode is the "real" one? And, is their synthesis possible within contemporary social and political contexts?

Once Watkins's social identity is established, by means of a photograph found in his recovered wallet, the doctors attempt to reconstruct his former identity for him. Watkins, however, categorically rejects the role and name assigned to him by his former intimates, having found his true center in the modality of psychic space he has recently circumnavigated. Concurrently, the testimonies from his wife, mistress, colleagues, and acquaintances to the doctors contribute a picture of the social persona that Watkins has vacated, and one that contrasts sharply with the illuminated Everyman of the first part of the novel. The commentaries of his familiars emphasize the ways in which Watkins—to *their* perceptions—was always somehow different, abnormal. Impervious to basic social conventions and feelings, he was "the original eccentric oddball" who did not even "pay lip service to ordinary feelings," according to his colleague Jeremy Thorne. His disillusioned former mistress, Constance Mayne, found him "above every human emotion." His wife, Felicity, who might be expected to know him best, seems to know him least, though she does volunteer the fact that he "always sleeps much less than most people." Conversely, Rosemary Baines, a bare acquaintance from one of his lecture audiences, had been so struck by his ideas and his presence that she had written an extraordinary letter, which forms a major section of the narrative (almost to the extent of straining narrative realism), to share with him her ideas on education and other matters.

Though he had initially dismissed Rosemary Baines's remarkable effort at communication, one learns subsequently that Watkins had met with her and her archaeologist friend, Frederick Larson, the night before the onset of his amnesia. Many of the ideas detailed in her letter reappear in altered form as images and events in the inner space journey that he subsequently undergoes (already narrated earlier in the novel). Rosemary discusses the problem of education—the process of indoctrinating children into social norms and thus anaesthetizing their inborn capacity for perceiving wholeness. She describes the psychic wavelength that Watkins's lecture on the topic had struck within her: the feeling of "beings briefly, on a different, high, vibrating current, of the familiar becoming transparent." Her reflections clearly parallel the experience Watkins himself lives out at the climax of his inner journey, which in turn alludes to the elevated awareness of the Sufi mystic.

Moreover, Rosemary Baines reiterates her friend Frederick Larson's archaeological speculations on the forms of life of earlier civilizations. Observations on the roofing materials of archaic houses and the implicit ethnocentric bias of archaeology resonate with Watkins's discovery of the idyllic city with roofless houses; Rosemary's long discussion of Larson's (and others') mid-life crises, precipitated by the questioning of basic assumptions about one's profession and identity, resonates with Watkins's own breakdown. Like Larson, Watkins has suffered from a stammer that is symptomatic of his inner turmoil; like Larson, Watkins is also a student of ancient civilizations, but his intellectual mastery of the heritage of Western thought has failed to develop in him any insight into the larger relationship between the collective past and his personal history. His mind journey of the first part of the novel thus acquires further meaning as a reflection of aspects of the self he has not assimilated into his mundane conscious personality. Ironically, his psychic travels make existentially real his identification with classical mythic figures and motifs from his intellectual discipline.

Though that journey is interrupted by the doctors' efforts to restore him to his pre-amnesiac identity, it is resumed in another form in response to the more sensitive Doctor Y's suggestion that Watkins recall his wartime experiences. Stylistically, this section is one of the novel's most effective passages—almost a set-piece that can be appreciated separately as the representation of an emotionally powerful experience. The sense of immediacy and detail is all the more heightened by the reader's subsequent discovery that it is a pure fantasy—neither "realistic" nor, from the perspective of Watkins's literal past life, "true." His war buddy Miles Bovey, whose death is described in the account, later confirms not only that he is still alive but that Watkins had never seen action in Yugoslavia, the location of his "recollection." Instead, these events are closer to Bovey's own war experience.

Watkins describes a number of events in a political matrix that resonate with those already encountered within a cosmic setting as patterns of his emotional reality: a briefing (this time a military one) followed by a descent (a parachute drop into Yugoslavia), and the experience of belonging to a larger collective whole (participation in the partisan Resistance). Communism is expressed in a pure, ideal form, wherein "an individual could only be important insofar as he or she was a pledge for the future." The experience of self-transcendence manifests itself through not divine but earthly harmony and union, in a love relationship with a partisan named Konstantina (an idealized fantasy of Watkins's former real-life mistress, Constance).

Again his (and the author's) nostalgia for Paradise surfaces, as he envisions "the world as it was before man filled and fouled it. . . . Those vast mountains, in which we moved like the first people on earth. . . . It was as if every one of us had lived so, once upon a time, at another time, in a country like this, with sharp sweet-smelling air and giant uncut trees, among people descended from a natural royalty, those to whom harmfulness and hate were alien." Characteristically, the antithetical shadow emerges. In a variation of the birth-in-death spasm of a rat-dog in Watkins's earlier journey, Konstantina is fatally gored by a threatened doe about to give birth. The cycle of birth and death is the paradigm for the antinomies of human experience; only in the imaginative mythic and spiritual dimensions are they reconciled.

But the more realistic necessity remains of reconciling the divided personality in the social context. In the final movement of *Briefing for a Descent into Hell,* Lessing poses the task one more time. Watkins is by then tenuously balanced midway between the two extremes of his being: the vivid experience of wholeness in its several formulations, and the urgings of his contemporaries to resume his former social identity. He is convinced that he must "remember" something that is crucial to his psychic survival, but what he must remember—the reality of unity—is antithetical to what the doctors urge him to remember—the split identity he has vacated. For a time he preserves his suspension between the two, sharing his intermediate state with a young patient named Violet Stoke. To her he describes the discrepancy in his condition as he and the doctors perceive it: "They say I lost my memory because I feel guilty. . . . I think I feel guilty because I lost my memory." Violet's status as a girl who does not want to grow up emphasizes the ambiguity of Watkins's condition.

In this context, one theory of schizophrenia suggests that the condition is the individual's response to "paradox intolerance," particularly as embodied in the antithetical emotions of love and aggression. Because of the pressure of those conflicting experiences, he seeks a "personal paradise": "a hypothetical life situation where each person can creatively express himself openly, directly, and honestly, and come to fulfillment without double-binds, games, hidden agendas, and complexes. . . . [T]he person who ends up with the appellation 'schizophrenic' is in some way more imbued with the need to find that paradise for himself, that is, he not only needs to, but has to. Such an archetype is more central to his being." Mircea Eliade describes the ambivalence inherent in the desire for paradise within the sacred context, noting that "on the one side, man is haunted by the desire to escape from his particular situation and regain a transpersonal mode of life; on the other, he is paralyzed by the fear of losing his 'identity' and 'forgetting' himself." Man must leave Eden in order to grow—but he may spend the rest of his life trying to return to it. The nostalgia for wholeness is his oldest memory, for unity is located, symbolically, at both the beginning and the end of consciousness.

Watkins submits to shock treatment in the hope that it may help him to remember the truth that hovers like a shadow on the edge of his awareness. His final insight before the shock treatment is his explanation to Violet of the phenomenon of timing at work in the level of human evolution and change:

> "It's desperately urgent that I should remember, I do know that. It's all timing, you see. . . . There are lots of things in our ordinary life that are—shadows. Like coincidences, or dreaming, the kinds of things that are an angle to ordinary life. . . . The important thing is this—to remember that some things reach out to us from that level of living, to here . . . all these things, they have a meaning, they are reflections from that other part of ourselves, and that part of ourselves knows things we don't know. . . . [W]hat I have to remember has to do with time running out."

As Neumann has observed, in mythology the sense of other-worldly knowledge that must be remembered "is usually projected into a knowledge acquired before birth or after death. . . . Man's task in the world is to remember with his conscious mind what was knowledge before the advent of consciousness."

In Watkins's long explanation to Violet, Lessing distills a number of the ideas that appear in various forms throughout the novel. In fact, their recapitulation in this segment comes precariously close to didactic excess, given the more inventive shapings of the same ideas earlier in the novel. The "message" intrudes uncomfortably upon the narrative design, and belies the occasional tension in Lessing's work between aesthetic and ideological concerns.

Despite Watkins's various illuminations, the ultimate prognosis is negative; time runs out for him as medical science preempts his personal struggle to remember wholeness. The shock treatment works with rather than against the split in his personality, and the amnesia of his earlier life merely reverses itself and becomes an amnesia of his inner journey. Watkins leaves the hospital, presumably fully recovered but in fact as split as before. His wife and friends confirm the Watkins they had known before his breakdown. The tragedy of his medical "cure" is that he has recovered his former identity only to lose, once again, the meaning of his journey.

However, in this novel Lessing suggests that the fault lies not with his choices but with the establishment iself, for its endorsement of that very state of separateness and inner division as the norm. R. D. Laing has enjoined, "Can we not see that *this voyage* [into the self] *is not what we need to be cured of but that it is itself a natural way of healing our own appalling state of alienation called normality?*" Lessing somewhat more pessimistically implies that in society as it is presently constituted, abnormal consciousness is a mixed blessing, for the self cannot exist without reference to a world. If Watkins reflects the schizophrenia of contemporary life, the cure is no better than the disease. Ultimately failing to overcome his self-division, he hovers in the perilous straits between inner illumination and the external manifestations often identified as psychosis, with no certainty as to which is "real," since the definition of reality is established by consensus. By the latter standard, the effort to relinquish the personal ego in order to embrace transcendence is a pathological one. What distinguishes between the schizophrenic and the mystic or enlightened individual, as Lessing has already suggested, is partly the capacity of unique personality to harmonize its own dissonant elements and partly the judgment of the orthodox establishment that labels it.

John Vernon has postulated that Western tradition is fundamentally "schizophrenic" in its very conceptualization of what is "real." The intrinsic dualism of logical thought shapes perception at such a basic level that not only are the patterns discerned in experience split into opposing categories (real/unreal, sane/insane, and so on), but these splits in turn create the further dichotomies in the perception of separation between the self and the world. Accordingly, the politicization of madness leads to the logical paradoxes of either the sanity of insanity, in the form of a retreat into a privately meaningful but ultimately solipsistic awareness, or the insanity of sanity, in the form of capitulation to the division endemic in contemporary life. Both are "schizophrenic," for "each mode of being, the real and the fantastic, the sane and the insane, excludes the other, and each is intolerable because of that exclusion."

Lessing's increasing use of paradox, symbolic imagery, and nonlogical frames of reference indicates her attempt to formulate an imaginative way around that logical contradiction. Though the reduction in scope, diversity of characters and events, and density of language (in contrast to the earlier major novels) result in a more schematic work of fiction with occasional stylistic lapses, *Briefing for a Descent into Hell* as a whole is an innovative and effective fusion of form with idea. The suspension between realism and fantasy retains both the metaphysical and formal ambiguity of the whole—a narrative strategy that allies the author with others for whom the "open" ending is the only way to express the uncertainties inherent in the subjective or confessional mode. One thinks of Dostoevsky's divided antihero in *Notes from Underground*, as well as of more contemporary fictions by John Barth, Anthony Burgess, William Golding, Kurt Vonnegut, Thomas Pynchon, and others who have departed from strict representational narrative, adapting conventions from fable, romance, and speculative fiction in order to render "glimmers of a reality hidden from us by our present set of preconceptions." The ambiguous tension between realism and myth, between division and unity, remains the central dynamic of Lessing's fiction. As insistently as her protagonists seek forms of consciousness that can accommodate contradiction and embrace the moment of transcendence, Lessing seeks fictional resolutions of the antinomies erected by the mind itself.

LORNA SAGE

New Worlds

The Memoirs of a Survivor (1974) does not step over into speculative fiction
any more decisively than Briefing for a Descent into Hell or The Four-Gated
City, but it does locate the threshold between Lessing's worlds a lot more
persuasively. Here, her shift in ideas is a shift in perception: the narrative
has an illusionist, teasing quality that questions the "real" with a new ex-
pertise. It is, in several ways, and for all its brevity, a stock-taking book. She
described it, on the dustjacket, as "an attempt at autobiography," doubtless
because it reconnects her with some of her oldest material (the family scenario, for instance); but it also takes stock of certain of her resources as a
writer, and in this its function resembles that of The Golden Notebook—
very distantly, of course, since now a great deal (about role-playing, about
inner space) is taken for granted. And she is not, this time, precipitating a
crisis, but rather mulling over what turns out to have happened to her. Her
tone is calm, almost elegiac: she's writing from the other side of the mirror,
as it were, chronicling the processes of dissolution with a lucid patience that
is itself shocking, almost witty.

The Memoirs of a Survivor begins with the death of a city—a London
that has lost its name, where warmth, food, water and even oxygen drain
away, until, gradually, people are left living off the corpse, scavenging, stealing, bartering. It is a picture that recalls other versions of "last days" (the
pigsties and garden plots that invaded ancient Rome, for instance), but the
writing stresses to the end the eerie persistence of a sense of normality:

From Doris Lessing. © 1983 by Lorna Sage. Methuen and Co., Ltd., 1983.

"While everything, all forms of social organization, broke up, we lived on, adjusting our lives, as if nothing fundamental was happening." Breaches in "outside" reality are quickly matched in private perceptions: the narrator, semi-besieged in her solid, ground-floor flat, turns from watching the new "tribes" gather on the pavement, to find the blank wall of her room dissolving into other rooms, other times. And still the sense of matter-of-factness persists. When a complete stranger materializes in her living room, to make her the custodian of twelve-year-old Emily, the "impossible" situation must be accepted (as if it were some kind of administrative mistake) because otherwise nothing can be trusted. So life goes on—the narrator stepping now, almost routinely, through the wall into other spaces; Emily, hungry for life, joining the tribes of the pavement, losing her identity before she achieves it:

> any individual consummations were nothing beside this act of mingling constantly with others, as if some giant rite of eating were taking place, everyone tasting and licking and regurgitating everyone else, making themselves known to others and others known to them in this tasting and sampling—eyeing each other, rubbing shoulders and bodies, talking, exchanging emanations.

As the boundaries dissolve, it seems at first that the inner space must be a refuge, a liberation to counter this repulsiveness, but no: the experience is more anomalous than that.

For example: people seem to be turning into animals (herding, migrating), but what is it to be "animal"? One of the novel's most quietly bizarre effects is to invent (along with Emily) an "impossible" creature, Hugo, a cat-dog, or dog-cat, who has all the conviction (but none of the merely whimsical appeal) of an animal in a fairy tale. Since the narrative accepts Hugo's presence with only a momentary grinding of gears, and since he's several times in danger of being eaten, we accept him too, perforce, as yet another anomaly. And one contradictory image serves to support another, so that it is with little surprise that we realize that the realm behind the wall "belongs" to both Emily and the narrator—a composite childhood. Here the "personal" life that is so under threat in the outside world is traced to its family origins, and inner space proves problematic in its turn. In fragmentary scenes from the nursery, the drawing room, the bedroom, a small girl is formed into a person: made to know her separateness, her nuisance value, her mother's resentment and weariness, her father's furtive sexuality. These ghosts are horribly solid: "tall, large, with a clean-china healthiness, all blue eyes, pink cheeks, and the jolly no-nonsense mouth of a schoolgirl";

"a soldier. . . . conventionally handsome face . . . half-hidden by a large moustache." They recall Mr. and Mrs. Quest, and, beyond them, Lessing's images of her own parents. They are "characters," and they manufacture a character—a rebellious, guilty girl, self-repressed in her mother's image.

The climactic scene on this inner stage (where everything is gigantized by a child's perspective) traces "character-forming" back to the denial of the animal, and the denial of hunger:

> Emily, absorbed, oblivious. She was eating—chocolate. No, excrement. . . . She had smeared it on sheets and blankets . . . over her face and into her hair, and there she sat, a little monkey, thoughtfully tasting and digesting.

The traumatic cleansing that follows ("naughty, disgusting, filthy, dirty, dirty, dirty,") leaves an indelible sobbing on the air. And, when the narrator next enters this realm, she tracks that down too:

> The finding had about it, had in it as its quintessence, the banality, the tedium, the smallness, the restriction, of that "personal" dimension. What else could I find—unexpectedly, it goes without saying . . . a blonde, blue-eyed child . . . reddened and sullen with weeping. Who else could it possibly be but Emily's mother, the large carthorse woman, her tormentor, the world's image?

Infinite regress. . . . Each generation has stamped its own discipline, its own wretchedly acquired boundaries, on the next. The "personal" is not the unique: its claustrophobia derives precisely from its repetitions.

This replay of the family scenario clears the stage, little by little. Intercut with the character-acting, and with the increasingly anarchic glimpses of the dying city outside, are visions of the inner space depopulated, exorcized—moving pictures that take up and transform the imagery of destruction:

> walking through a light screen of leaves, flowers, birds, blossom, the essence of woodland brought to life in the effaced patterns of the wallpaper, I moved through rooms that seemed to have aged since I saw them last. The walls had thinned, had lost substance to the air, to time; everywhere on the forest floor stood slight tall walls, all upright still and in their proper pattern of angles, but ghosts of walls, like the flats in a theatre.

Again (this is almost the determining flavour of *Memoirs*) echoes from earlier works open out/close down into mystery, anomaly: here, echoes of Lessing's blitzed London ("shock after shock . . . through brick and plaster") from *In*

Pursuit of the English; or the stage direction from her 1958 *Play with a Tiger*, where the walls vanish to show the actors against the backdrop of the city; or the scene in the basement in *The Four-Gated City* where Lynda pushes at the walls with her scarified fingers. For not the least of the illusionist effects in *Memoirs* is the gradual identification of the emptying city with the emptying inner space—so that the new barbarism without is overwritten by the transcendence of the "personal" within. In its final move, the novel crumples up its world like a sheet of paper:

> that world, presenting itself in a thousand little flashes, a jumble
> of little scenes, facets of another picture, all impermanent, was
> folding up as we stepped into it, was parcelling itself up, was
> vanishing, dwindling and going—all of it, trees and streams,
> grasses and rooms and people.

Into this vortex the narrator, Hugo (naturally), Emily, her shapeless man and a horde of gutter-children cram themselves, to meet an unimaginable future.

It is a version of space travel without the trappings. Or almost: in this last scene there is a fleeting apparition—"I only saw her for a moment, in a time like the fading of a spark on dark air"—of a tutelary being (a cosmic mother) from the "other" side. This enigmatic figure was, as it turns out, a clue to where Lessing was bound next—her future Muse. *The Memoirs of a Survivor* might have suggested a sojourn in self-consciousness, the kind of retrospective transformation of earlier works that characterized, say, late Nabokov (*Transparent Things, Look at the Harlequins*). But Lessing was not a writer to identify (she would probably say, confuse) the inner space of art—reflexiveness, self-anatomy—with the space in consciousness she was interested in. She stepped out of the mirror-world of metafiction with her wanderlust and her epic ambitions unscathed: this time, as a fully paid-up alien, into the outer space of a new series, *Canopus in Argos: Archives,* which consists to date of four novels—*Re: Colonized Planet 5, Shikasta* (1979), *The Marriages between Zones Three, Four and Five* (1980), *The Sirian Experiments* (1981) and *The Making of the Representative for Planet 8* (1982).

> *Shikasta* was started in the belief that it would be a single self-
> contained book, and that when it was finished I would be done
> with the subject. But as I wrote I was invaded with ideas for other
> books, other stories, and the exhilaration that comes from being
> set free into a larger scope, with more capacious possibilities and
> themes. It was clear that I had made—or found—a new world

for myself, a realm where the petty fates of planets, let alone individuals, are only aspects of cosmic evolution expressed in the rivalries and interactions of great galactic Empires.

This sounds more like the territory of a Kurt Vonnegut than a Nabokov—though one mischievous parenthetical reference in *Shikasta* to "(Marcel Proust, sociologist and anthropologist)" suggests that in the long view we may be surprised to find how much of the art we think of as produced in ivory towers (or cork-lined studies) turns out to be useful. Science fiction writers "have played the . . . role of the despised illegitimate son who can afford to tell truths the respectable siblings . . . do not dare."

Lessing's euphoria is clearly fuelled by joining the ranks of the unrespectable—but more than that: for the first time since the early novels of *Children of Violence* she is writing inside a genre. Admittedly a genre that can stomach nearly anything (compare Mark's line in *The Four-Gated City* about "that nasty mixture of irony and St. John of the Cross and the Arabian Nights") but, still, a containing fiction in which her anomalous points of view, divergent time-scales and characters from animals to angels can coexist without continuous tension. Space fiction is not only realism's bastard offspring, but harks back to earlier ages of storytelling—romance, for instance, in the "sword and sorcery" division; and, more broadly, the happy pre-novel formulas, like those of the *Decameron* or *The Canterbury Tales,* which haven't yet discovered the single point of view.

This, though, is to make *Shikasta* sound a lot more cheerful than it is. Lessing's tone in her prefatory "Remarks" had, perhaps, more to do with *The Marriages between Zones Three, Four and Five,* which was, she implies, already finished and waiting in the wings. *Shikasta* is about human history as an episode in cosmic "time," and much of it focuses on the wretched present and near-future (last days, as in *The Four-Gated City*), documenting our slide into pollution, starvation and near-extinction, with Youth Armies roaming a Europe threatened with genocide by the Third World (our terminology). The only sense in which, here, Lessing has found a "new world" is that she has discovered a point of view that wrenches her out of the orbit of emotional commmitment—the long, long view of the cosmic archivists, who record and collate these horrors with a cool, dispassionate eye, and for whom the end is never the end.

"Shikasta" (Earth) is colonized in its infancy by three galactic empires: technological Sirius, which operates in the southern hemisphere, and believes in removing all traces of its experiments (but fails to); vampiric Shammat, which feeds on pain (that is, most of history); and benevolent, mysterious

Canopus, which helped form humanity in the beginning, has watched over
it since, and now awaits—and "influences"—the end of history, and the
survival of the species. All along, angels were Canopean agents trying to
mitigate the effects of the Fall, the planetary dis-aster which left men star-
crossed, unable to attune their stone transmitters or build their geometrical
cities right. History is a by-product of cosmography: "We are all creatures
of the stars and their forces, they make us, we make them, we are part of a
dance from which we by no means and not ever may consider ourselves
separate." When religions told us we had a "soul," they were distortedly
echoing a Canopean instruction to retain always our "substance-of-we-feel-
ing," SOWF.

Lessing's main narrator, Johor, a reluctant Canopean expert in Shikas-
tan affairs, does, however, generate ambiguities. Is he, perhaps, affected by
the crazed atmosphere of the planet? Or is it that Lessing cannot quite, in
her anger against anger, maintain the archivist's cool? At any event, she
settles old scores—with the tyranny of ideology, with the criminal indifference of, very specifically, British governments to events in Africa, and so on.
Another voice from the past is Lynda Coldridge's, reminding us that we
usually perceive only "5 per cent" of the whole, and providing a punishing,
satiric perspective on our greeds and desires: "Love love love love love. If I
had liked it when he slobbered all over me and stuck his hands and things
into me then that would have meant I loved him I suppose." We are all much
sicker than Lynda: "To identify with ourselves as individuals—this is the
very essence of the Degenerative Disease." People of the last days learn to
contemplate their own individual extinction:

> Nothing they handle or see has substance, and so they repose in
> their imaginations on chaos, making strength from the possibil-
> ities of a creative destruction. They are weaned from everything
> but the knowledge that the universe is a roaring engine of crea-
> tivity, and that they are only temporary manifestations of it.

In this they are reaching towards the archivists' attitude, and it seems not a
bad description of Lessing's own position now. *Shikasta* is dedicated to her
father, "who used to sit . . . outside our house in Africa, watching the stars.
'Well,' he would say, 'if we blow ourselves up, there's plenty more where we
came from!'" Time is our disease, space our cure: *Shikasta* ends as it begins
with a vision of a world that lives in this awareness, with men breeding and
dying as the slow stars dictate, in stone circles, triangles, crescents (crescent
people in crescent cities), listening to the clear, minimal signals from across
the light years.

The Marriages between Zones Three, Four and Five hastens, seemingly, to assuage a certain charmlessness in this stony harmony. It has a medieval flavour, rather like those paintings and tapestries that simultaneously show you figures—the wise men, perhaps—on each stage of their journey, as if they paused now and then in attitudes that (they knew) would delight the iconographers. Except that here we have wise women: Zone Three is a magical matriarchy, sophisticated, sensual, and intuitive (they understand their animals and send messages by tree), whose queen Al·Ith is summoned by the unseen "Providers" on a mission she hates: to marry Ben Ata, the warrior king of Zone Four—which, of course, is martial, hierarchical, mysogynistic, and so on. This is the region of fable, where roles are richly fulfilled. But that is never enough, which is why Zones Three and Four must mate, to disturb them into aspiration—a degree of alienation, even. Ben Ata certainly needs Al·Ith (his country is poverty-stricken and wretched), though it is not immediately clear why she needs him. The centre of the novel is an elegant, sad comedy of sexual love, as role-playing:

> "You like red then?"
>
> "I think I like *you*," said he, in spite of himself grabbing at her—for he did not, he liked her even less than before . . . he had in fact forgotten the independence of her, which informed every smile, look, gesture.
>
> She evaded him and slid away into the room, with a mocking backward look over her shoulder which quite astounded her— she did not know she had it in her!

They do contrive to love each other, however, and gradually to see what the Providers had in mind: neither settling down nor synthesis, but an infinite extension of the repertoire of roles. The picturesque protagonists start on new journeys. Al·Ith, no longer at home in her land, looks for the first time to the high frontiers of Zone Two, where there live creatures (fairies, chimeras) a lot more mythic than she; Ben Ata moves to a wilder, more animal existence in Zone Five. "What are all these guises, aspects, presentations? Only manifestations of *what we all are* at different times." The voice is that of one of the Chroniclers of Zone Three, a wise hereditary bard, and what he points to is the proper restlessness that afflicts even the most fabulous and harmonious figures of story. Living in harmony with the Providers (always anonymous here, but presumably Canopeans in one of their guises) is to play roles, not to be entrapped by them.

It does seem, though, that there are roles it is better not to play, and moves better not made. There is a caveat about "movements" in Lessing's account of the somehow disappointing journey of the Zone Four women, newly liberated, to Zone Three. Her men and women are part of a continuum from animals to angels and beyond, and should not spend all their energies playing themselves. In fact, one of the things Lessing likes best about her matriarchy is that they talk with animals, and this is a major theme of the next *Canopus in Argos* novel, *The Sirian Experiments* (1981), where the "experiments" are in various ways (from hideous games with vivisection to complex questions of colonial responsibility) to do with the human animal. Hugo, the dog-cat from *Memoirs,* seems relevant here:

> I think that all this time, human beings have been watched by creatures whose perceptions and understanding have been so far in advance of anything we have been able to accept, because of our vanity, that we would be appalled if we were able to know, would be humiliated. We have been living with them as blundering, blind, callous, cruel murderers and torturers, and they have watched and known us.

Out of context, these animal watchers sound remarkably like Canopean agents, and it would not be surprising to find that in some sense they are.

What *The Sirian Experiments* and the latest novel in the series, *The Making of the Representative for Planet 8* (1982), do make clear is that the central theme of *Canopus in Argos* is species-consciousness—the dialectic of sameness and difference that Lessing has always been obsessed by, projected now on to galactic empires, but empires still, where colonizing cultures test out their different styles of power. Her Canopeans are the ideal colonists, who rule only by virtue of their more intimate understanding of the patterns of creation and destruction at work in the universe. In fact, they rather resemble the Sufi mystics whose writings have latterly fascinated her: the point about wandering Sufi "teachers" being that they take on the colouring of whatever culture they find themselves in, though their aim is to awaken a consciousness free of time and place. Something of their allegorizing, didactic tone has rubbed off on *Canopus in Argos* too. Lessing's writing is becoming in one sense more fantastic, more fictive, and in another more urgently admonitory. In her preface to *Shikasta,* she wrote: "Yes, I do believe that it is possible, and not only for novelists, to 'plug in' to an overmind, or Ur-mind, or unconscious, or what you will"; while, two years on, the preface to *The Sirian Experiments* protests, "No, no, I do not 'believe' that there is a planet called Shammat full of low-grade space pirates." These statements show her trying, not altogether successfully, to put her fictions into a new focus. She wants them to be disposable, emblematic and analogical, so that they convey certain imaginative moves (from the personal to the collective, from the rational to the intuitive) without getting too entangled in particular histories. Readers who suspect her of believing in diabolic space pirates are responding to something that *is* there in her tone: propaganda for "wonder," for emigration into mental space.

Perhaps she was making a private joke about her own difficulties with questions of tone and belief when she made the narrator of *The Sirian Experiments* a dry lady bureaucrat, Ambien II of the Sirian Colonial Service. The empire she serves is an enlightened technocracy riddled with existential doubt—"*who* should use *what* and *how much* and *when* and *what for?*"— which treats its subject species with clinical condescension. Ambien II, an aridly correct administrator of this policy, gradually becomes troubled by the very different methods of her Canopean opposite numbers, and the novel chronicles with deliberate but dreadful slowness her millennia-long conversion to the Canopean view. The title too is a kind of slowly dawning joke: Ambien, and through her the Sirians, have all along been themselves the object of just this "experiment" in consciousness-raising. The beginning of an answer to existential doubt is to realize that you are part of a continuous symbiotic chain, not a separate, managerial, inviolable "I." At the end Ambien II has learned enough to be shocked at what she sees from space of Earth's petty latterday empires:

> A grid had been stamped over the whole continent . . . a map, a chart, a certain way of thinking . . . made visible. . . . the mind of the white conquerors. Over the variety and change and differentiation of the continent, over the flows and movements and changes of the earth.

It is with this image of Africa that the novel's fragile fable dissolves. And it is difficult to avoid a sensation of *déjà vu*: Lessing's own mental set is showing through; *Canopus in Argos* is circling back on *Children of Violence*.

However, this return to her beginnings highlights the radical changes as well as the continuities in her imaginative life—not without attendant ironies. We note that repetition itself, for instance, is not the nightmare to her that it once was, nor is role-playing. She has settled into her alienation. Her spokesperson Ambien II, forcibly "retired" from the Colonial Service as a subversive, reflects with sad serenity that "It is not possible for an individual to think differently from the whole he or she is part of " and that, therefore, her conventional colleagues are themselves already inwardly rejecting the official line. This may sound a pacific and consoling view, but only *in extremis*: the *un*official line, the decentred, dispersed consciousness, will triumph (though that is hardly the right way to put it) in the end, as surely as death. Indeed, in *The Making of the Representative for Planet 8,* death is another name for it, and Lessing's impatience for an ending—though it is not her final instalment—has honed down the fable into a kind of rehearsal for extinction. Planet 8, dying of cold, seems hardly to have lived; the space-fiction apparatus seems ramshackle from the start, and there is something mocking about the way she details her characters' struggle for survival— building a great wall to hold the ice, keeping up morale, waiting for the space-lift—while at the same time sowing a subversive awareness that all this "machinery" is nonsense. What her people have to learn is mastery of mind-space: how to levitate into immortality, how to break down the wall in their psyches between matter and spirit, how to dissolve themselves into their "alien" elements. She turns them to frost, freeze-dries them into one collective, near-anonymous voice, their "representative."

The space-odyssey format has nearly served its purpose, which was after all to bring certain things home to us. This fourth *Canopus in Argos* novel says as much, not only by the cool speed with which it dismantles its ma-chinery, but by including, in an "Afterword," a substantial essay about self-transcendence in a quite different context—the 1910–13 British Antarctic expedition. Scott and his men interest Lessing as specimens of a long-van-ished style of heroism (and patriotism), but she is really thinking much more abstractly about changes in the "climate" of opinion, and the mysterious laws that govern them: "Is it possible that we could learn not to impose on each other these sacred necessities, in the name of some dogma or other. . . . Surely these are processes we can learn to study . . . ?" Her analysis of the mental atmosphere, presaging, at the least, a new cold war, is what is wearing her fictions thin. "No . . . ," says her Planet 8 representative, "I must not make up these tales and fabrications, comforting myself, thinking how others must be comforted."

Yet there is a shadow of comfort in rehearsing the worst, and Lessing's tone these days is oddly serene. Self-exiled in the sub-genre of speculative fiction (and rapidly using up its conventions), she has, it seems, finally con-firmed her marginality. In a spirit of irony, of course, since for her it is on the margins of the culture, and of the psyche, that imaginative life survives. She has in no sense given up her claim that the writer "represents, makes articulate . . . numbers of people who are inarticulate." Her creature Ambien II's version—"It is not possible for an individual to think differently from the whole he or she is part of "—is a teasing challenge from Lessing to her readers, as if to say: Alien or cold or even crazy as you may find me these days, I speak for you, especially for what you repress. Inner space has not escaped mapping, fencing and colonization, but there remain areas that will never be private property, that can only be visited in conjecture. What Lessing once wrote of Olive Schreiner strikes one as true also of herself, a measure, finally, both of her aspirations and of her displacement: that she seemed "the sort of woman who in an older society would have been made the prophetess of a tribe."

CATHARINE R. STIMPSON

Doris Lessing and the Parables
of Growth

From 1952 to 1969, Doris Lessing published the five novels that were to
make up the series entitled *Children of Violence*. Taking on the largest possible obligations that a novel of development might impose upon an author,
she wished to dramatize "the individual conscience in its relations with the
collective." Her example of the individual conscience, Martha Quest, has
become a character whom readers mentally lift from the page and incorporate
into their own lives as a reference point. She is a Wilhelm Meister, an Isabel
Archer, a Paul Morel, for the last decades of a monstrous century and mil-
lennium. Martha is also a woman, a possible descendant of Isabel Archer
rather than Wilhelm Meister or Paul Morel. However, Lessing would resist,
rather than celebrate, the placing of *Children of Violence* in a tradition of a
female novel of development.

Naming Martha, Lessing pointed to qualities that all her readers might
need during this century. "Martha" refers to one of the two sisters of Lazarus. She leaves home to ask Christ to raise her brother from the dead.
Explicitly she states a belief in His divinity and powers. "Yes, Lord: I believe
that thou art the Christ, the Son of God, which should come into the world"
(John 11:27). Martha personifies the principles of activity and faith, and the
conviction that history might be redeemed and changed. Christ can both
raise Lazarus and raze our sins. "Quest" is, of course, that significant jour-

From *The Voyage In: Fictions of Female Development* edited by Elizabeth Abel,
Marianne Hirsch, and Elizabeth Langland. © 1983 by the Trustees of Dartmouth
College. University Press of New England, 1983.

ney in which the process of the journey may matter as much as its end. To endure that process, to achieve that end, the quester will need magister figures who may teach benignly, but, in the twentieth century, may prove to be goblins or *idiots savants* as well.

As told by *Children of Violence,* Martha's own story is one of possible redemption and change. She begins as an estranged adolescent of fifteen on a farm in Zambesia, Lessing's composite landscape of the Africa that England colonized, with Dutch aid. She is ostentatiously reading Havelock Ellis. Her father is a failure, an attractive man whom World War I has ruined. Her mother is frustrated and bitter, an energetic woman also scarred by the war. Martha has one sibling, a younger brother whom her mother prefers. Having left school at fourteen, Martha is largely self-educated. She gets a job as a legal secretary in the colony's provincial, segregated capital. Because she thinks too much in a culture that dislikes thought, she must repress herself. To do that, she drinks too much, and plays too hard.

At eighteen, she marries Douglas Knowell, a civil servant running to pomposity and fat. Their wedding takes place in March 1939: Hitler, seizing Bohemia and Moravia, marches toward the war that will help to destroy British colonialism. Four years later, the proper Knowell marriage is a disaster. As Douggie wallows in self-pity, and threatens to rape Martha or to kill her and their little daughter, Martha leaves. Her friends and family turn against her; her mother, a betrayer, disowns her, for a while.

Martha, in her own place, has an affair with a Royal Air Force sergeant. She helps to start the Communist party of Zambesia. As an activist to whom the party is an equivalent of self and part of a vanguard group that is a central and centering presence, she is both "Red" and "kaffir-loving," characteristics equally abhorrent to colonial society. She marries again: Anton Hesse, a German Communist interned in Zambesia, whose first wife and family are dying in European concentration camps and who needs a more secure immigration status. The marriage is a sexual fiasco. Anton suffers from premature ejaculation, and, ironically, bourgeois domestic values. Both have affairs, Martha with Thomas Stern, a Polish Jew in exile. She embarks upon a Laurentian discovery of the power, joy, and compulsions of sexuality. However, Thomas will leave for Palestine, to fight for Israeli nationhood, and then for a remote African village, in which he dies.

In 1945, with peace, the patterns of Martha's life fall apart. Her father drifts, half-drugged, into death. The party flounders, as its founders move away and postwar politics rush over it. Martha and Anton have a proper divorce. Life has tamed him. Symbolically, he has learned tennis and will doubtless marry the daughter of a rich colonial businessman. Finally realizing an adolescent dream, Martha sails to England and to the London that World War II has devastated, but not destroyed. Her move is much more than a reenactment of the progress to the city by the young provincial man, or woman. For the morally ambitious white, leaving the colonies is a survival act. The women who want to go, but who do not, become what they feared they might become: anxious, emotional, self-conscious conformists who wear masks of bright cheer.

Martha finds a job as live-in secretary to a writer: Mark Coldridge, one of four sons of an elite British family. A brother, Colin, flees to Russia when he is accused of being a Communist spy. Eventually, Martha becomes Mark's lover; a surrogate mother to his son and Colin's son; and a friend of Mark's wife, Lynda, who stays in the basement with female companions when she is not in mental hospitals. At once chivalrous and obsessive, Mark loves her hopelessly. In her basement apartment, Lynda is an obvious sign of buried and ignored psychic energies.

Located in Bloomsbury, the house entertains all of postwar English politics and culture. In the late 1970s, the local government buys it. Martha alives alone, and then goes to a commune in the country to help with the children. However, for years, the inhabitants of the house have prepared for a Catastrophe. Mark has mapped the increase of atomic, biological, and chemical weapons; of fallout and pollution; of war, famine, riots, poverty, and prisons. As Lessing believes it will, the world acts out a logic of homicide and suicide. The Catastrophe does happen. Because authorities lie, and because catastrophes are such chaos, no one knows precisely what has occurred. It may have been a chemical accident, or the crash of a plane with nuclear bombs. Whatever the cause, the effects are clear.

In the brave new shattered world, Mark runs a refugee camp—before his death. He has married again: Rita, the illegitimate daughter of Zambesians whom Martha had once known. Lynda may be dead. Martha has escaped to an island off the coast of Ireland or Scotland. Her last words are in a letter of 1997 to Francis, Mark and Lynda's son. She tells him about a black child, Joseph, who has been with her on the island. In a world in which many children are deformed mutants, he may be a genuinely evolutionary one. He may have paranormal powers, even more effective than those that Lynda, Martha, and Francis have developed. Martha explains:

> He says more like them are being born now in hidden places in the world, and one day all the human race will be like them. People like you and me are a sort of experimental model and Nature has had enough of us. [*The Four-Gated City*; all further references to this text will be abbreviated to *FGC*.]

Reconstituting itself after the Catastrophe, the world may be breeding a new child, a savior. However, it may also be generating new governments, huge, quarreling, stratified bureaucracies. Joseph is to be a gardener, as Thomas was. Lessing cannot say if he will tend vegetables, or guard our dreams of paradise; if he is to be a serf, or a sage who will, as Marx promised, dissolve divisions between labor of the mind and of the hands.

Such a summary but hints at Lessing's narrative immensities, at the hugeness of her plots and subplots. She asks us to take them seriously, a request at once bolder and less truistic than it seems. Lessing acknowledges that other media—movies, television—are influential. She also assumes that speaking can mean more than writing; that logos may be livelier off than on the page. "Everywhere, if you keep your mind open, you will find the truth in words *not* written down. So never let the printed page be your master" (italics hers). However, she believes, as perhaps only a self-educated farm child can, in the moral and cognitive strength of texts. She does not revel in the post-modern theory that all verbal acts are fictions, language performances, language at play. She pays tribute to the nineteenth-century novel and to the rare book—a *Moby-Dick,* a *Wuthering Heights,* a *The Story of an African Farm*—that is on "a frontier of the human mind." Martha may thread her way through literature to revalidate its authority and to reinterpret it, but Lessing also asserts that a writer must be responsible. In essays and in *Children of Violence,* she accosts an "ivory-tower" literature and critics who acclaim it.

The writer must speak *for,* as well as *to,* others. So doing, the writer both serves as a voice for the voiceless, as a witness for the inarticulate, and helps to form a community of the like-minded. Because the writer can reveal that what we thought to be a private hallucination is actually a collective thought, literature can grant us our sanity.

In brief, despite the science fiction she now publishes, Lessing is marvelously old-fashioned, a great traditionalist. *Children of Violence* is an urgent, urging cultural achievement, a composition meant as explanation and guide. Between *A Ripple from the Storm* (1958) and *Landlocked* (1965), Lessing became a public student of Sufi, of Islamic mysticism. A scholar whom she praises has said, "The Sufi teacher is a conductor, and an instructor—not a god." With secular modesty, she seeks to conduct us to and instruct us in truths greater than ourselves. *Children of Violence* is, then, a parable—of epic proportions.

Lessing's primary lesson demonstrates the necessity of growth, particularly of consciousness. Like many moderns, she finds consciousness the precondition of conscience. Understanding must inform our will, perception, judgment. She fears repetition, the active reproduction of social and psychic conditions, and nostalgia, a mental reproduction of the past that longing infiltrates. Martha is frantically wary of "the great bourgeois monster, the nightmare *repetition*" [*A Proper Marriage*; all further references to this text will be abbreviated to *APM*]. One of the saddest ironies of *Children of Violence* is that Martha, who refuses to be like *her* mother, tells her daughter that she is setting her free. Being left, Caroline will have nothing to imitate. Yet Caroline apparently becomes a well-behaved junior member of Zambesia's elite: what Martha's mother wanted Martha to become and the antithesis of what Martha would have praised, the replication of her fears.

To picture her theory of growth, Lessing consistently employs natural imagery: a tree, a blade of grass. To conceptualize it, she calls on evolutionary theory, not of the Victorians, but of the Sufis. In *Children of Violence*, Lessing uses epigraphs to inform us of her intentions. They are annotations and shorthand exegeses. Significantly, she begins part 4 of *The Four-Gated City*, the last pillar in her blueprint of the architecture of Martha's soul, with passages about Sufi thought:

> Sufis believe that, expressed in one way, humanity is evolving towards a certain destiny. We are all taking part in that evolution. Organs come into being as a result of a need for specific organs. The human being's organism is producing a new complex of organs in response to such a need. In this age of the transcending of time and space, the complex of organs is concerned with the transcending of time and space. What ordinary people regard as sporadic and occasional bursts of telepathic and prophetic power are seen by the Sufi as nothing less than the first stirrings of these same organs. The difference between all evolution up to date and the present need for evolution is that for the past ten thousand years or so we have been given the possibility of a conscious evolution. So essential is this more rarefied evolution that our future depends on it.

Both tropes and theory reinforce the sense that growth has the force of natural law. It transcends individual choice. We may choose to obey or to neglect that law, to dwell within its imperatives or to deny them, but we cannot decide whether or not it exists.

Lessing's commitment to the expansion of consciousness tempts one to call *Children of Violence* an example of Lukács's theory of the novel: "the adventure of interiority; the story of the soul that goes to find itself, that seeks adventures in order to be proved and tested by them, and by proving itself, to find its own essence." She herself has named *The Four-Gated City* a bildungsroman:

> This book is what the Germans call a *Bildungsroman*. We don't have a word for it. This kind of novel has been out of fashion for some time. This does not mean that there is anything wrong with this kind of novel.

If the genre groups together tales of "the formation of a character up to the moment when he ceases to be self-centered and becomes society-centered, thus beginning to shape his true self "; and if one thinks of Martha as entering into, and then discarding, several societies, then Lessing's label for the last novel holds for her series as a whole. An admirer of Mann, she has produced another twentieth-century bildungsroman in which people and groups are maladjusted and ill. Images of physical, mental, and psychosomatic sickness abound in *Children of Violence*: Martha's pinkeye; Captain Quest's medicine chests; Mr. Anderson's infirmity (he is a retired civil servant who reads government reports and sci-fi pornography); Douggie's ulcers; Lynda's hands, nails bitten until they bleed; babies, after the Catastrophe, born with two heads and fifty fingers. Martha is Lessing's Hans Castorp; Africa and England her sanatorium, her *Berghof*.

Because of the nature and intensity of her sense of social illness, Lessing has grafted the Western apocalyptic tradition to the bildungsroman. For her, we inhabit a period of terrors and decadence. At its best, our age demands a stifling conformity; at its worst, it provokes fear, exploitation, oppression, violence. The End is both imminent and immanent. Like most prophets of the apocalypse since 1945, Lessing is profoundly aware of the splitting of the atom and the origins of atomic warfare. A madman, a fool, a committee—each might bring this dread upon us. In *Ecce Homo*, Nietzsche predicted the rebirth of tragedy when mankind became conscious, without any feeling of suffering, that it had behind it the hardest, but most necessary, of wars. Lessing believes that mankind has before it the hardest, but most unnecessary, of wars, and the suffering of that vision overwhelms *Children of Violence*. The apocalypse we are manufacturing may not permit anyone to survive, let alone a society to enter a reconstituted history.

In the nineteenth-century female bildungsroman, the young woman protagonist often dies—physically or spiritually. Maggie Tulliver drowns, she and her brother clasped in each other's arms. In Olive Schreiner's *The Story of an African Farm*, Lyndall "chooses to die alone rather than marry a man she cannot respect." Martha avoids such a fate. She survives the Catastrophe, and endures until she is an old woman in her mid-seventies. As a bildungsroman, *The Four-Gated City* differs from many of the genre in that Lessing describes far more than her protagonist's maturing years. The novel of development has become the novel of an encyclopedic life, as if the relations between conscience and its collectives were a part of a complex, lengthy process. Yet, Lessing hardly ignores death. Rather, our Cassandra, she broadens the drama of the death of the female protagonist until it becomes that of her culture. She rewrites the female bildungsroman to enlarge the sufferings of a young woman until they become the doom of the collective. The struggle between the woman who would be freer than her society permits her to be also changes to become a struggle between an enlightened group, a saving remnant, that would free society from its self-destruction and the larger group that is in love with its own diseaseful death.

Lessing must obviously reconcile the comic promise of the bildungsroman, that we can within history pass from youth to a semblance of maturity, with the tragic promise of the apocalypse, that history as we know it will explode. She does so through the Sufi belief in "the possibility of a conscious evolution . . . this more rarefied evolution that our future depends on." If each of us nurtures consciousness as we pass from youth to a semblance of maturity, if we join with others who are doing the same thing, then we may either avert the apocalypse, or live through it and protect those children whose minds are even more potent than our own. Lessing adapts, from apocalyptic historiography, the myth of individual and collective rebirth. Such myths have consistently attracted her. In 1957, she exulted: "I am convinced that we all stand at an open door, and that there is a new man about to be born, who has never been twisted by drudgery." *Children of Violence* tests and re-tests these myths, to retain them in a grimmer, more shadowed form. In *Landlocked*, Thomas, naked, in bed with Martha, says:

> Perhaps there'll be a new mutation though. Perhaps that's why we are all so sick. Something new is trying to get born through our sick skins. I tell you, Martha, if I see a sane person, then I know he's mad. You know, the householders. It's we who are nearest to being—what's needed.

Since the evolution of consciousness matters so much, Lessing devotes a great part of *Children of Violence* to Martha's own. The narrative is a detailed, subtle account of the methodology of growth, in which Martha is a case study, an exemplary figure, and our potential representative. The fact that she is a woman is less important than the fact that she can give the lie to official lies and ultimately exercise the paranormal psychic powers that Lessing believes are the birthright of us all. As an excellent critic says, "Ultimately, the deepest task of [Lessing's] characters is to achieve a personal wholeness that subsumes sexual identity or gender under a larger principle of growth."

Such statements embody a complication about Lessing. She is among our most brilliant, persuasive anatomists of contemporary women's lives. She writes compellingly about their friendships: that of Martha and Alice; of Martha and Jasmine, a revolutionary who stays in Africa; of Martha and Lynda; of Lynda and her flatmate Dorothy. She dramatizes the pressures on them to perform and conform. She knows about their disabilities, the need to please, the complicities, the denials and self-denials. Though Martha is incorrigibly heterosexual, Lessing has no illusions about men or male chauvinism, in conservative sets or in the radical sects more dedicated to ideologies of equality. Men exploit, patronize, and ignore women. They demand attention, nurturance, sexual gratification, and service. They seek compliant daughters, willing bodies, or mothers they can possess without complication. They use, abuse, exhaust, and bore women.

Despite all this, Lessing separates herself from the "feminine" and from feminism. She has, I suggest, several motives. Perhaps she has internalized an evaluation of women's activities, especially those of the middle class, as trivial, time-wasting, and private. If so, it might spill over onto her sense of women's politics. Certainly her fear of the apocalypse distances her from them. She has written:

> I don't think that Women's Liberation will change much though—not because there is anything wrong with their aims, but because it is already clear that the whole world is being shaken by the cataclysms we are living through: probably by the time we are through, if we get through at all, the aims of Women's Liberation will look very small and quaint.

In part because of her political history in general, Lessing also distrusts any doctrine, ideology, party, or group that holds a fragment of reality and offers it up as if it were the whole. Consistently, she deplores compartmentalizing the world, separating off those parts, and then fearing the differences we have ourselves created. In her first days in London, Martha lunches with Phoebe, a left-wing Labourite who will become a noxious combination of Mrs. Quest and bureaucrat. In one of the many scenes in which Lessing insists that privileged moments of vision occur in our daily life, in our walks down an ordinary street, Martha broods:

There was something in the human mind that separated, and divided. She sat, looking at the soup in front of her, thinking. . . . For the insight of knowledge she now held, of the nature of separation, of division, was clear and keen—she understood, sitting there, while the soup sent a fine steam of appetite up her nostrils, understood *really* . . . how beings could be separated so absolutely by a light difference in the texture of their living that they could not talk to each other, must be wary, or enemies.

(FGC)

Finally, Lessing writes out of a colonial experience. She has said that to be an African, growing up in that vast land, is to be freer than an Englishwoman, a Virginia Woolf, enwebbed in custom and the city. However, being an African also entails participation in a rigid, hierarchical social structure. Within it white men may dominate white women, but white women dominate all blacks. They have the privileges of class and color. White women subject blacks to their needs, whims, neurotic fantasies, and orders. A Myra Maynard, the wife of a powerful judge, exercises covert political power over colonial affairs and overt domestic power over her "kaffirs." In such a place the progressive conscience must first confront the presence of the "colored" or "native" problem. The treatment of the blacks is the primary structuring agent of a sense of injustice and of public guilt. For Martha, black women have a double symbolic function. Neither entails a sustained mutuality between black women and white. Icons of both a greater imprisonment and a greater spontaneity, they remind her of the injustices against which she must rebel, of the manacles she must unlock, and of a life less arid than her own. In labor in the town's "best" maternity hospital, Martha reveals that duality:

> [Martha] heard the sound of a wet brush on a floor. It was a native woman, on her knees with a scrubbing brush. . . . Martha tensed and groaned, and the native woman raised her head, looked over, and smiled encouragement. . . . [She] gave a quick look into the passage, and then came over to Martha. . . . "Bad," she said, in her rich voice. "Bad. Bad." As a fresh pain came, she said, "Let the baby come, let the baby come, let the baby come." It was a croon, a nurse's song. . . . Martha let the cold knot of determination loosen, she let herself go, she let her mind go dark into the pain. . . . Suddenly . . . Martha looked, and saw that the native woman was on her knees with the scrubbing brush, and the young pink nurse stood beside her, looking suspiciously at

the scrubbing woman. The brush was going slosh, slosh, wetly
and regularly over the floor.

(*APM*)

White men and women share more than black subordination: an ambivalent response to the "mother country," a feminized metropolitan center
to which a colonial country is tied. It, too, helps to obliterate the resentments
gender inequalities breed. Colonials feel physically superior, tougher,
stronger. They are also the romantics, the black sheep, the eccentrics who
refused to accept the manners of the mother country. Yet they feel blunt,
envious, even crude, a sense of dependency and inferiority that Australians
call "the cultural cringe." Men and women alike are the stalwart, but crass,
younger children in a global family whose power they at once disdain and
revere.

As Martha grows, then, she acts out a feminist analysis that Lessing will
not extend to an endorsement of a feminist program. Instead, Martha discovers other truths, other principles. They enable her to survive, to continue
the process of discovery, and to learn which collectives impede, and which
enhance, the self; which citizenships destroy, and which burnish, being.
Among her primary tools is a cognitive alter ego, a diligent self-consciousness, the Watcher, a capacity for apperception and self-criticism in her experiments with roles. Even during her first marriage, as she takes "every step
into bondage with affectionate applause for Douglas" (*APM*), she is still
"secretly and uneasily curious." At its worst, the Watcher devolves into
mocking, derisive self-hatred. At its best, it guards against self-deception,
wool-gathering, and bad faith. The origins of the Watcher are as obscure as
the genes that carry instructions for the child's optic nerves once were, but
they include Martha's parents' nagging reminders that she was unwanted and
the presence of multiple discrepancies in her life: between reality and what
people say about it; between reality and what books say about it; between
reality and what her dreams say about it. Each discrepancy stimulates a
sense, at once intellectual and emotional, of alienation. Any reasonable child
regards gaps between the self, the self-in-the-world, and the world warily—
if the child is to stay reasonable.

When consciousness is too watchful to accept the going interpretations
of reality, but too fragile to examine its own examinations fully; when consciousness is too vital to permit the will to lapse and collapse into acceptance
of the false and the ordinary, but the will is too weak to dictate ruptures
from them, then a person, a Martha, learns the value of negation. Saying no,
saying I will not, is halfway between submission to the life she despises

and one she might actively build for herself; halfway between conformity and authenticity. Negation is inseparable from de-education, from unlearning the formal and informal instructions of a colonial society and of its leaders, a Mr. and Mrs. Maynard.

Martha's most critical act of negation is to leave her first marriage. It proves that she can push her rejections beyond thought and speech. Abandoning Douglas, she walks out on social acceptability; on access to power; on money, comfort, and security; on the pretty, perky, willful daughter to whom she is intricately attached. A particular unfairness of a generally unfair society is the refusal of its petty elite to see Martha's pain over Caroline, which never heals, and its eagerness to rally around Douglas, who so cheerfully plays by their rules. To walk away, Martha must overcome a talent for negating her negations, for repressing her dislike of Douglas, particularly in bed. Only a few weeks before she ends the marriage, he tells her he is going away on business.

> It was a moment when the hatred between them shocked and dismayed them both.
>
> "Well, perhaps it's just as well we'll—have a break for a few weeks, eh, Matty?" He came over and stood a few inches from her, smiling in appeal.
>
> She at once responded by rising and kissing him—but on the cheek, for her lips, which had intended to meet his, instinctively moved past in revulsion. This revulsion frightened her so much that she flung her arms about him and warmly embraced him.
>
> The act of love immediately followed.
>
> (*APM*)

Because of the nature of the dominant society, Martha's need for negation will be persistent. A middle-aged woman in London, she will have to say no to Dr. Lamb, the sardonically named psychiatrist, and to the institutional power he conveys; to Jack, once her lover, and to the temptations of masochism he now holds out.

Negation demands something beyond the self to repudiate. Realizing that ego ideal of the modern period, the free and autonomous ego, Martha must also learn that the most stringent self-explorations, the most exacting and fertile meditations, begin in solitude. Her childhood in the awesome African landscape has prepared her for this. She copes with her fear of an empty historical landscape in which she has no patterns to follow. Before she leaves Douglas, she thinks, realistically: "there was no woman she had ever met she could model herself on" (*APM*). She also unravels her dependency on the cold comforts of narcissism. If having a role model means shaping identity through gazing at another's image, being narcissistic means doing so through having another's gaze. Martha has stared at her image in a mirror, or she has waited passively while men watch her. Unhappily, narcissism is as encrusted with guilt as a white dress in a field wet with mud. Guilt oozes from the belief that the recipient of a look has disappointed the onlooker. To have been seen is to be found wanting. Finally, at a Communist party meeting, in a dingy office, Martha regards a new member:

> She's what I used to be; she looks at herself in the looking glass, and she sees how her face and body form a sort of painted shell, and she adores herself, but she is waiting for a pair of eyes to melt the paint and shoot through into the dark inside. [*A Ripple from the Storm*; all further references to this text will be abbreviated to *RS*.]

In isolation, however, the naked self is not alone. Through self-analysis, Martha confronts hidden ranges of repressed material: memories, fantasies, terrors, anger, violence—the worst of which the devil personifies. Lessing accepts George Eliot's dictum that no private life has not been determined by a wider public life, a maxim compatible with her early Marxism. That public life means the French and Russian revolutions, World Wars I and II, colonialism, the Spanish Civil War, the cold war, wars of national independence. Breaking down her defenses, breaking into the unconscious, Martha understands that she wants to break up the world as well. This child of violence has internalized the thanatotic rage of global war and the looming apocalypse. Like Freud, Lessing believes we can never wholly purge the past, but seeing the experiences we have battened down helps to shake their spell.

Despite her liberal belief in the individual and freedom, Lessing, writing a bildungsroman, goes beyond the picture of the atomistic self spinning alone atop social space. If Martha rejects the nuclear family, she enters an extended family in which cords of choice replace those of blood and law. If she refuses biological mothering, she becomes a surrogate parent. Lessing is too flexible to feminize wholly the nurturing role and evoke the spirit of a Great Mother to rationalize women as mothers. Mark's son Francis is a paternal/maternal figure.

However, within *Children of Violence* is a sense of the intractability of nuclear family bonds that makes a flight toward a modern extended family necessary. The ties between mothers and daughters, particularly between Martha and May Quest, are especially taut. Martha cannot forgive May her inability to love without demands, complaints, and possessiveness. May cannot forgive Martha her unconventionality, her sexuality, her difference. Yet, because May did bear Martha, and because their disappointments in each other are intense, they cannot forget each other. Their mutual consciousness is so acute that in each other's company, they get sick. They see each other for the last time in London; May is old, Martha middle-aged. Both want to cry:

> As she vanished from her daughter's life forever, Mrs. Quest gave a small tight smile, and said, "Well, I wonder what all that was about really?"
> "Yes," said Martha. "So do I."
> They kissed politely, exchanged looks of ironic desperation, smiled and parted.
>
> (FGC)

In *Children of Violence,* irony is a useful tool for digging out sham and cant, but it is treacherous. For the disappointed, it becomes an iron rod, a staff of punishment, a mark of waste.

For Martha, the political party, like the extended family, becomes a community of choice. Deftly, incisively, dryly, Lessing dramatizes the mechanics of the small progressive party: the lobbying, maneuvering of agendas, interplay between insiders and outsiders, the desire for a charismatic leader, the gratifying sense of busyness, the feeding on ideology and hope because of the absence of real power. However, Martha is unable to find a party that fuses a radical ideology and power; vision and efficiency; prophetic zeal and historical wisdom; humanitarian ideals and humane behavior. Though brilliant organizer and analyst, Anton has neither heat, nor heart, nor humor. Martha is too modern, too mobile, too psychological to be like Charlotte Brontë's Shirley Keeldar, but Shirley's cry against a cold sectarianism is the precursor of Martha's progress beyond organized politics:

> Must I listen coolly to downright nonsense . . . ? No. . . . all that *cant* about soldiers and parsons is most offensive. . . . All ridiculous, irrational crying up of one class, whether the same be aristocrat or democrat—all howling down of another class, whether clerical or military—all exacting injustice to individuals, whether monarch or mendicant—is really sickening to me: all arraying of ranks against ranks, all party hatreds, all tyrannies disguised as liberties, I reject and wash my hands of.

Significantly, Martha's deepest discoveries about eros—that bond, at once simple and mysterious, that generates a little community—take place outside of the nuclear family and the party. Within them, she has picked up warning signals about repression; about evasive silence about sexual realities; about the sublimation of eros, not into culture, but into violence. She has also succumbed to sexual myths. Science has reassured Martha and Douggie that the rational practice of certain positions will guarantee ecstasy. Romantic poetry has whispered that "love lay like a mirage through the golden gates of sex" (APM). The patriarchy has praised her for being deferential, compliant, a Galatea before the Pygmalion of the phallus. A reaction against Victorianism has instructed her to find self-esteem in being good in bed, no matter when, or with what man. Martha begins as a modern to whom sexual competence has the gravity of grace.

Sex with Thomas, a married man, pulls down all such illusions. He is warm, direct, generous. As Martha educates herself in sheer orgasmic pleasure, she experiences both a new simplicity of will, a clarity of action, and a dissolution of the ego that serves, paradoxically, to strengthen that very simplicity of will. As the boundaries of the self blur into the other, Thomas and Martha become each other's histories. Later, with Mark and Jack, Martha will find in sex an even more expansive fusion between self and world, an access to "an impersonal current . . . the impersonal sea" (FGC). Sadly, Martha's most vital sexual experiences are with men who are flawed prophets: Thomas cannot pass beyond violence and chaos; Jack transmogrifies his knowledge of the body into sadistic domination; Mark, despite his brains and strength and kindliness, cannot transcend Western rationalism. In his camp, after the Catastrophe, he writes: "I can't stand that nasty mixture of irony and St. John of the Cross and the Arabian Nights that they all (Lynda, Martha, Francis) went in for" (FGC). Martha's most educational prophetic experiences, with a woman, are asexual.

Laying bare Martha's sexual growth, Lessing balances delicate insight and problematic theory. Both maternal and erotic sexuality can threaten freedom. Often cheerfully, the pregnant woman becomes her body. She relaxes into natural time, into the blind impersonal urges of creation. The woman in love is unappeasable, hungry, restless, dependent upon her man. For Martha, such lapses from liberation are characteristic of a "female self," a simplistic genderizing of identity that Lessing is most guilty of when she talks about female sexuality. To avoid the constrictions of the "female self," and to sharpen her capacity for insights, Martha begins to practice a willed repression of and indifference to sexual claims. She has only one biological child. Later, in London, she decides:

> When a woman has reached that point when she allies part of
> herself with the man who will feed that poor craving bitch in
> *every* woman (italics mine), then enough it's time to move on.

When it's a question of survival, sex the uncontrollable can be controlled.

(*FGC*)

Lessing has shown that same mingling of persuasive perception and puzzling theory in an earlier, more poignant picture of repression: the character of Mrs. Van. Highly intelligent, sensitive, tough, she has tutored Martha in the limits and courage of the reformist conscience in Zambesia. She has refused to rebel against her proper marriage and a maternal role. So doing, she has deliberately, if secretly, traded passion for autonomy within the system and political stature. She is a good wife to the husband who does not gratify her and a good mother—to him, her children, grandchildren, servants, clients, and friends. In return, she is an active liberal. In a quick, sad scene, she remembers her wedding night. Lessing wants us to admire her resolve, mourn for her innocence, and dislike a society in which a woman of Mrs. Van's talents must make such compromises. At the same time, she gives Mrs. Van dabs of a sexual rhetoric of swords and soft spots that Norman Mailer, Lessing's lesser and contemporary, also deploys, if far more raucously:

> Cold tears had run down over her cheeks all night . . . (an) image
> . . . filled the girl's mind through those long hours while she lay
> awake by a man who also lay awake, waiting for her to turn to
> him. The image was of something deep, soft, dark and vulnerable,
> and of a very sharp sword stabbing into it, again and again. She
> had not moved . . . and so the sword had not stabbed into her
> never again, the soft dark painful place which she felt to be some-
> where under her heart had remained untouched. She had remained
> herself.
>
> (*RS*)

Behind Martha's emerging ego, behind her relations with several communities, are her discoveries of the powers of consciousness. To become a pioneer of the mind, Martha must often crawl through swamps of primordial fear. She first learns to read her dreams. They are both hieroglyphic psychological texts and prophecies. Martha often dreams of:

> "That country" . . . pale, misted, flat; gulls cried like children
> around violet-coloured shores. She stood on coloured chalky
> rocks with a bitter sea washing around her feet and the smell of
> salt was strong in her nostrils.
>
> (*RS*)

The meaning of the dream will deepen as she grows. The sea is her passage out of Africa to England, but it will become a metaphor for the universal mind and energy in which she will learn to travel, too. Consistently, in Lessing's vocabulary, "shell" is a synecdoche for the mechanisms that protect the self from threatening pain and psychic depths. It evokes armor—of sea creatures and war. "That country" of the dream foreshadows the island on which Martha will die. Although Lessing persistently uses sleep as a metaphor for mindless oblivion, for loss of consciousness, and awakening as a metaphor for new powers of vision, sleep is the site of the dreams that minister to us and that we must monitor. Significantly, Anton refuses to admit that he has nightmares. He tries to banish memory and live glibly in the day.

Martha goes on to listen to, to hear, other people's emotions. Because of her need to know what he is going to do first if she is to react in ways that serve her best interests, and because of their intimacy, she trains herself with Douglas. She does not add new skills, but nurtures an ability that is there. During a bizarre conversation with Douggie about their divorce, she responds: "For a moment she was frightened; then she understood she was not frightened, her heart was beating out of anger. She had become skilled in listening to her *instinctive* responses to Douglas" (*RS,* italics mine). Such a refined empathy tells Martha what is special about other people, but she can also go beyond differences to appreciate a common ground of being. Psychic auditing, in league with the imagination, the ability to see worlds other than our own, can be a basis of a human ecology. Lessing can, then, speak of "colour prejudice" as "only one aspect of the atrophy of the imagination that prevents us from seeing ourselves in every creature that breathes under the sun."

Finally, Martha accepts and explores her paranormal powers, her capacities for ESP, mental telepathy, and sending and receiving messages through the mind. She first hears niggling words, phrases, and bits of music. A feature of *Children of Violence* is the coherence with which Lessing describes shards of consciousness—as if her own style reflected the sense that might lie beyond fragmentation. When Martha stops resisting such signals, she discovers that they are only apparently random: they, in fact, have meaning. Her first guide is her own adventurous spirit, but eventually she finds the "mad" Lynda. In a friendship beyond friendliness, the two "work" together. The word signifies how hard a discipline the expansion of consciousness can be, and how chary Lessing is about ordinary toil, in the home or public labor force, as a field of growth. Martha is not one of the new women whose bildungsroman includes the narrative of a career.

Lynda is Lessing's vehicle for a radical criticism of psychiatry. Rigid, officious, less sure of themselves than they pretend to be, psychiatrists are the policemen of the contemporary mind. Out of several motives, they control our prophets, like Lynda, through calling them schizoid. Though she does not go mad, Martha must experience the sensations of insanity in her rites of passage toward a greater comprehension of the mind. So doing, she lives out a statement of her father, that most defeated of her teachers, who, when he speaks, says too little, too late. As far as he can see, "everyone is mad" (*APM*). For Captain Quest, madness only explains the world. For his more resilient daughter, "the climax of education is insanity," and her bildungsroman is a text in which "madness is moralized into a condition of responsible consciousness."

As Martha's powers enable her to lose the ego but not the world; to shatter barriers but not to slump into violence, nihilism, or infantile regression, she becomes a member of another community: that of her fellow sensitives. She first enters it with Lynda:

> One night, going down to see if Lynda was all right, before she herself went to bed, she asked: "Lynda, do you ever overhear what people are thinking?"
>
> Lynda turned, swift, delighted: "Oh," she exclaimed, "you do? I was waiting for you to . . ."
>
> (*FGC*)

Such a society, far more than an esoteric cult, is the basis for a politics of mind. As a party, it transcends hardened theories and harsh practices. As an organization, it abolishes tricks, maneuvers, bureaucracies, and tyranny. It merges the virtues of anarchy and community. Learning to become a sensitive, oscillating between optimism and rage, Francis exults:

> The old right of the individual human conscience which must know better than any authority, secular or religious, had been restored, but on a higher level, and in a new form which was untouchable by any legal formulas. We quoted to each other Blake's "What now exists was once only imagined"—and did not, for once, choose to remember the dark side of the human imagination.
>
> (*FGC*)

Before, during, and after the Catastrophe, the group serves as a survival mechanism, for its members and for the mutants whose evolving consciousness may govern the future.

Lessing's politics of mind are controversial. Critics who otherwise admire her accuse her of bad faith, of sidestepping reality, of a bleak acceptance of the irreconcilability of self and society. *Children of Violence* implicitly answers that we must reread the realities of conscience and the collective. If we do, we will cultivate consciousness and accept certain laws of its evolution. Then, we will grasp what a Sufi master once said:

> For him who has perception, a mere sign is enough.
>   For him who does not really heed, a thousand explanations are
> not enough.

If we ignore Martha's reminders, we may be heedless, groggily writing out chapters in an inadequate bildungsroman, sleepwalking toward the apocalypse.

In Western culture, beliefs in the apocalypse have been entwined with utopian impulses. Both wish to wipe out time as we have clocked it. For some, the apocalypse is a prelude to a utopian world, to a New Jerusalem. Lessing, despite her belief in the apocalypse, is wary of utopian dreams, of attempts to impose them through violence and of mechanical allusions to them. In *Children of Violence*, Solly Cohen, a childish revolutionary, lives for a while in a commune named "Utopia."

Nevertheless, Martha can summon up a utopian vision, among her other powers. Throughout *Children of Violence*, her picture of the four-gated city has embodied harmony, reconciliation, integration. Her answer to Babel, it speaks against a history that has alternated centrifugal desires to separate with centripetal desires to dominate. It has been her new utopia, "rooted in the body as well as in the mind, in the unconscious as well as the conscious, in forests and deserts as well as in highways and buildings, in bed as well as the symposium." It is a collective of the future toward which the individual conscience might aspire.

Whether or not one likes Lessing's epistemology and her politics of mind in *Children of Violence*, one must respond to the appeal of her stubborn belief in an active, hopeful consciousness; to Martha's returns to a picture of a four-gated city. Lessing, dramatizing the self and society in the twentieth century, tells us what they ought to mean, as well as what they do mean. Martha's visionary rehearsals are goads to growth, that old and aching promise of the bildungsroman.

ALISON LURIE

Bad Housekeeping

A while ago Doris Lessing seemed to have given up realistic fiction in favor of a high-flown and involved futuristic fantasy. Five volumes of *Canopus in Argos* had appeared; though they were praised by some critics, many of her most devoted readers found them impenetrable and profoundly discouraging. For years Lessing had been their guide through the mazes of racism, Marxism, South African politics, feminism, Jungian and Laingian psychology, and Near Eastern mysticism. Now, struggling alone with political and sexual backlash, they felt abandoned in the hour of their greatest need.

Then, late last year, it was revealed that Doris Lessing had in fact recently published, under a pseudonym, two modest but very well-written naturalistic novels. They had been reviewed equally modestly or not at all, and soon disappeared from the bookshops. Reissued under her own name as *The Diaries of Jane Somers,* they were news everywhere; such is the effect of the literary celebrity system.

Considered in combination, however, *The Diary of Jane Somers* and *Canopus in Argos* were disturbing. They suggested that the creative high-tension in Doris Lessing between wild, imaginative energy and practical realism had finally snapped, splitting her into manic and depressive selves who produced, respectively, cloudy, optimistic fantasy and pessimistic tales of modern life.

"Jane Somers," Lessing's depressive self, was originally said to be the

From *The New York Review of Books* 32, no. 20 (December 19, 1985). © 1985 by Alison Lurie.

editor of a woman's magazine and the author of popular historical romances. The central issue of her novels was the proper relation of a successful, educated, middle-class person to the chaos and suffering that surround her. In the first, *The Diary of a Good Neighbour,* Jane Somers has emotionally failed both her dying husband and her dying mother. She becomes involved with a feisty, suspicious, dirty old cockney woman who lives in a squalid basement flat near her elegant London apartment. Through her attachment to Maudie Fowler, Jane is gradually redeemed; she also ends up furious at Maudie's family, which "had simply written Maudie off years ago . . . used her and dismissed her," and, by extension, furious with the world. "I'm so angry I could die of it," she concludes. In this novel the only solutions Lessing offers us are private charity, and a burning rage against public and private indifference.

If the Old Could . . . is a more conventional story. Here Jane Somers falls in love with a married man; he returns her feelings but is too moral either to sleep with her or to leave his wife and retarded son and marry her. She is also involved in the care of another, less attractive old cockney woman, Annie, and with her own deeply neurotic, lumpish niece Kate. Kate comes to stay in Jane's flat, steals, lies, refuses to go to school or get a job, throws up in Jane's bed, and invites her creepy friends in to wreck the place when its owner is away. Life in London today, this book suggests, is pretty hopeless, and most people, most of the time, are selfish and miserable; but true love exists, even if it must be sacrificed in the end.

In her new and far more ambitious novel, *The Good Terrorist,* published under her own name, the two Doris Lessings are happily reunited. She continues to cast a cold eye on contemporary Britain. She asks questions of the sort that must have occurred to many people there in the past few years. How could their ordinary fellow citizens—not hysterical foreigners or obvious crazies—have planned and carried out the bombings of stores and offices that have killed and injured so many? Who could set out to do such a thing, and why? Whether her answers are right or not, Lessing has succeeded in writing one of the best novels in English I have read about the terrorist mentality and the inner life of a revolutionary group since Conrad's *The Secret Agent.*

Lessing's terrorists, however, have none of the glamour and mystery of Conrad's. The shadowy atmosphere of secrets and feints is gone; in *The Good Terrorist* we see everything in icy clarity, from the fading bunch of forsythia on the revolutionaries' kitchen table to the homemade bombs upstairs, which have been cobbled together out of "cheap watches, bits of wire, household chemicals, copper tubing, . . . ball bearings, tin tacks, . . . plastic explosive, . . . dynamite," and string. "Everything . . . looked cheap, make-shift, sharp-edged, and for some reason unfinished."

Most of the members of the group, too, seem makeshift, sharp-edged, and unfinished. At the start of the novel they are not yet terrorists, only a bunch of young dropouts camping out in an abandoned London house. All but two of them are unemployed, some by choice; they live on the dole or by scrounging or stealing from their relatives, justifying this to themselves as a sharing of the national wealth.

The squatters all consider themselves socialists, but their politics range from the mild ecological and antinuclear variety to a theatrical, theoretical Marxism. Collectively, they are at odds with their origins and estranged from their families. Though they come from virtually every social back-ground, most have adopted false names and phony London working-class accents. Even the lesbian couple, Roberta and Faye, who in moments of crisis revert to the "clumsy blurting labouring heavy voices" of the northern slums from which they came, usually pose as bright, voluble cockneys.

All these young people see themselves as living in a corrupt, dishonest, and chaotic society that has no use for them. Mrs. Thatcher disgusts them, and the Labour party seems to be full of wimpy, ineffective liberals. As one of the most obsessed members of the group expresses it, they "want to put an end to this shitty fucking filthy lying cruel hypocritical system."

For some time, these people's rage and despair have been satisfied by picketing and demonstrating. As the book starts, however, most of them are beginning to feel frustrated and have fantasies of more radical forms of protest. They are not yet a revolutionary group, however; they are isolated, restless, suspicious of one another, and physically uncomfortable. The house in which they are squatting is ugly, cold, and derelict, without light or heat or plumbing, surrounded by and filled with foul rubbish.

Into this disorganized, fragmented society comes Alice Mellings, the "good terrorist" who is Doris Lessing's heroine. Alice is strong, emotionally intuitive, and sympathetic, brave, warmhearted, hard-working, and gener-ous—the sort of woman whose domestic skills and maternal sympathy have traditionally held the world together. (She also does not conceal her middle-class origins, and speaks in her own natural accent.) In nineteenth-century popular fiction Alice would have been celebrated as an "angel in the house." Louisa May Alcott or Charlotte Yonge would have admired the way she takes over the derelict building and turns it into a comfortable home. Nothing daunts her, not even the two bedrooms full of plastic buckets of excrement which the squatters have used because the water has been turned off by the Council and the toilets filled with cement.

While most of the others stand about looking on, Alice goes into an almost supernatural frenzy of cleaning and contriving, painting and hauling furniture, and persuading the local authorities to restore services. Her love for the finished product is intense and personal: "The house might have been a wounded animal whose many hurts she had one by one cleaned and bandaged, and now it was well, and whole." And Alice's maternal care is not confined to the building; she shops and cooks nourishing health-food dinners for the other squatters, who have been living on cheap takeout meals, gets a job for one of them, and tends others in their illness or grief.

There is a darker side to Alice's nature, however. She is given to slightly psychotic fugue states, hysterical lapses of memory, and uncontrollable fits of rage at the unfairness and chaos of the world:

> She exploded inwardly, teeth grinding, eyes bulging, fists held as if knives were in them. She stormed around the kitchen, like a big fly shut in a room on a hot afternoon, banging herself against walls, corners of table and stove, not knowing what she did, and making grunting, whining, snarling noises—which soon she heard. She knew that she was making them and, frightened, sat down at the table, perfectly still, containing what she felt.

Alice also suffers from a passionate asexual attachment to a good-looking but singularly unpleasant young layabout named Jasper. Jasper is neurotic, violent, dishonest (he even steals money from Alice), sulky, self-important, mean-spirited, verbally and physically cruel, absolutely no help about the house, and given to homosexual binges. He is so disagreeable that most of the other characters in the book continually advise Alice to get rid of him, but she will not listen. What seems to bind her to Jasper is, simply, his need of her. If he were more agreeable, maybe someone else would take care of him, but she knows she is his only hope. In this unwavering loyalty to an impossible man Alice, of course, also joins hands with her Victorian sisters.

Ordinarily one would expect to find someone of Alice's domestic talents and sympathy for the disadvantaged in a comfortable earth-mother situation—running Alice's Restaurant, for instance. But circumstances, or something in her own nature, lead her into a job as den mother to what gradually becomes a gang of revolutionaries. It is to Doris Lessing's credit that she does not insist on a psychological explanation, though she does point to parallels between Alice's childhood and her present life. We are told, for instance, that Alice's middle-class parents were intensely social; that they gave parties so large that Alice was often sent to stay with friends, which made her furious and miserable:

> They took my room away from me, just like that, as if it wasn't my room at all, as if they had only lent it to me. . . . It went on for years. What the fucking hell did they think they were doing?

Yet apart from their parties the senior Mellingses seem to have been model liberal parents, warm and affectionate and concerned. Until the start of the book they have steadily kept on trying to help Alice out. (Mrs. Mellings, for instance, allowed Alice, and Jasper, to live with her for four years and supported them both.) And this seems right both psychologically and artistically: as we all know, it is not only "bad," unloving parents who produce antisocial children.

One thing that differentiates Doris Lessing's terrorists from Conrad's is that most of them are female. On the other hand, the professional revolutionaries, and the policemen who make the group's lives miserable, are all men. It's not clear whether Lessing means to make a comment on the persistence of patriarchy among serious revolutionaries and their opponents. It is interesting, however, that the most violently angry characters are all women, and so are the two who, at the end of the book, manufacture the bombs and time them to go off in such a way that many people will inevitably be killed and maimed. A decade ago many of us believed that women were naturally better than men, and that if they were in power the world would be a better place; today we are not so sure. Power, even the power of an angry young woman playing with gunpowder and string in the attic of an abandoned house, corrupts.

Alice's own inclination is not at first toward public violence, though she hates the upper classes, universities, and Mrs. Thatcher. She has a romantic admiration for real revolutionaries: when she first meets a Russian agent with the improbable name of "Comrade Andrew" a thrill goes through her, "as when someone who has been talking for a lifetime about unicorns suddenly glimpses one." The existence of a Communist underground reassures and comforts her:

> All over the country were these people—networks, to use Comrade Andrew's word. Kindly, skilled people watched, and waited, judging when people (like herself, like Pat) were ripe, could be really useful. . . . Nothing was too small to be overlooked, everyone with any sort of potential was noticed, observed, treasured. . . . It gave her a safe, comfortable feeling.

As Doris Lessing says of Alice in the last sentence of the novel, "poor baby."

Alice, who otherwise feels a revulsion from sex, gets a charge from being arrested: "She yearned for it, longed for the moment when she would feel the rough violence of the policeman's hands on her shoulders, would let herself go limp, would be dragged to the van." But what she really enjoys most is going out at night with Jasper and spray-painting "No to Cruise!" on public buildings. For her friends, too, demonstrating and marching and shouting slogans and getting arrested have been a form of entertainment which also gave them a sense of social purpose. Now, however, they are becoming impatient, and beginning to agree with Alice's mother, who says, "All you people, marching up and down and waving banners and singing pathetic little songs . . . you are just a joke. To the people who really run this world, you are a joke. They watch you at it, and think: Good, that's keeping them busy." The sense of being politically ineffectual and even ridiculous drives Alice and her friends slowly but inexorably from protest toward terrorism.

As revolutionaries, however, Alice's housemates are amateurs, and not especially gifted ones. The two men who think of themselves as the leaders and theoreticians of the group, Bert and Jasper, are eager to be co-opted by some larger organization. But the professionals, as it turns out, do not want them. In a series of wild-goose chases that would be comic if they were not both pathetic and frightening, Bert and Jasper travel to Dublin and to Moscow to offer their services first to the IRA and then to the KGB; they are ignominiously turned down. Alice's abilities, on the other hand, are instantly recognized by Comrade Andrew. He tries to recruit her for the Party and send her away for training, but though Alice is flattered, she refuses to leave Jasper.

Rejected as allies by the political enemies of England, the group eventually decides to go it on their own. In a kind of awful caricature of Britain's stance in World War II, they declare: "We have to decide what to do, and we will carry it out. We don't have to ask permission of foreigners."

It is one of the most disturbing ironies of this disturbing novel that Alice's best qualities, her domestic genius, her generosity and sympathy and energy, are ultimately responsible for the transformation of a collection of dissatisfied radicals into a terrorist gang. She gives them a place to live and plot, regular meals, and a sense of community; she makes it possible for them to stay together long enough to learn to trust one another and work together to organize a "successful" bombing. Her love of order and beauty and harmony, her ideal of social justice, first destroy her, and finally destroy many innocent people.

Many of the characters in *The Good Terrorist,* with their rote revolutionary jargon and careless destructiveness, are frightening. But Alice Mellings, though she does not spout slogans or fill rooms with excrement, is perhaps the most frightening character of all, because she is, in the oxymoron of the title, both good and a terrorist. The grief and anger that many of us feel when we notice the waste, corruption, violence, and ugliness of the world is, in Alice, magnified tenfold. Unlike us, however, she does not block out this consciousness; she is almost continually consumed by rage and pain.

When a major character's name scans or half-rhymes with that of an author, it is natural to suspect some hidden connection between them. The fact that "Alice Mellings" sounds rather like "Doris Lessing" suggests that in some ways Alice stands in for her creator, and represents, in a distorted and exaggerated way, her own reactions to contemporary England.

Also, to anyone raised in the British tradition, it seems quite likely that Doris Lessing acted consciously in giving her heroine the name "Alice." After Shakespeare, Lewis Carroll is the most frequently quoted author in English literature, and we are surely meant to think of this Alice as being, in one of her aspects, the sensible, innocent, inquiring child, by turns puzzled and appalled by the ridiculous, cruel, and nonsensical adult world in which she finds herself. An inventive critic could probably find parallels between many of the incidents in *Alice in Wonderland* and those in Lessing's novel: for instance, the two nearly identical Russian agents, both badly disguised as Americans, reminded me strongly of Tweedledum and Tweedledee.

It is also possible to consider Alice as a personification of England itself. She has the traditional English sense of fairness, acute awareness of class differences, humor, courage, capacity for hard work, love of domestic cosiness, and unease about sex. Also typical is her and her comrades' amateurishness, their involvement in muddle, which doesn't always result in muddling through, and the contrast between their private affection and warmth and their capacity for public coldness and cruelty. Whether Alice's increasing lapses of memory of her own past, and her inability in the long run to face the facts of her history, should also be taken as a comment on the contemporary English character is not quite clear.

If Alice is, in a sense, England today, the prospect is bleak. By the end of *The Good Terrorist* all her good impulses have come to nothing or worse. The ruined house she has transformed into a comfortable home will be turned into expensive flats, and its inhabitants scattered; the waifs and strays she has befriended are lost or dead or in despair. Her parents' refusal to cut themselves off from her has ruined or nearly ruined their lives: her father's firm is close to bankruptcy and her mother has become an embittered alcoholic. In its conclusions, this is a deeply pessimistic book; but its energy, invention, and originality cannot help but make me optimistic about Doris Lessing's future work.

Chronology

1919   Doris Lessing born in Kermanshah, Persia, to Alfred Cook Taylor and Emily McVeigh.

1925   Family moves to Southern Rhodesia, settling on a farm in the district of Banket. Lessing attends a convent school in Salisbury, the capital.

1949   Lessing moves to London. Until this time, she has earned her living chiefly in secretarial positions. She has been married and divorced twice; Lessing is the name of her second husband.

1950   *The Grass Is Singing.*

1951   *This Was the Old Chief's Country.*

1952   *Martha Quest.*

1953   *Five.*

1954   *A Proper Marriage.* Receives the Somerset Maugham Award, Society of Authors, for *Five.*

1956   *Retreat to Innocence.* After a visit to Rhodesia, Lessing is proclaimed a prohibited immigrant, presumably because of unacceptable views on race relations.

1957   *The Habit of Loving. Going Home.*

1958   *A Ripple from the Storm. Each His Own Wilderness* performed at the Royal Court Theatre, London.

1959   *Fourteen Poems.*

1960   *In Pursuit of the English.*

1962   *The Golden Notebook. Play with a Tiger* performed in London.

1963   *A Man and Two Women.*

1964   *African Stories. Children of Violence.*

1965   *Landlocked.*

1971   *Briefing for a Descent into Hell.*

1972   *The Temptation of Jack Orkney and Other Stories. The Story of a Non-Marrying Man.*

1973   *The Summer before the Dark. Collected African Stories.*

1974   Essays in Paul Schlueter's *A Small Personal Voice: Doris Lessing: Essays, Reviews, Interviews.*

1975   *The Memoirs of a Survivor.*

1976   Receives the Prix Medici.

1979   *Re: Colonized Planet 5. Shikasta.*

1980   *The Marriages between Zones Three, Four and Five.*

1981   *The Sirian Experiments.*

1982   Receives the Austrian State Prize for European Literature and the Shakespeare Prize (Hamburg). *The Making of the Representative for Planet 8.*

1983   *The Sentimental Agents in the Volzen Empire.*

1985   *The Good Terrorist.*

Contributors

HAROLD BLOOM, Sterling Professor of the Humanities at Yale University, is the author of *The Anxiety of Influence, Poetry and Repression*, and many other volumes of literary criticism. His forthcoming study, *Freud: Transference and Authority*, attempts a full-scale reading of all of Freud's major writings. A MacArthur Prize Fellow, he is general editor of five series of literary criticism published by Chelsea House.

JAMES GINDIN, Professor of English at the University of Michigan, is the author of *Postwar British Fiction* and *The English Climate: An Excursion into a Biography of John Galsworthy*.

DOROTHY BREWSTER is Professor of English at Columbia University. Her books include *Doris Lessing, Virginia Woolf,* and *Aaron Hill*.

PAUL SCHLUETER has been Professor of English at Southern Illinois University. He is the author of *The Novels of Doris Lessing* and the editor of *A Small Personal Voice: Doris Lessing: Essays, Reviews, Interviews*.

FREDERICK R. KARL is Professor of English at New York University. His books include *The Contemporary English Novel, Joseph Conrad: The Three Lives,* and *The Adversary Literature*.

PATRICIA MEYER SPACKS, Professor of English at Yale University, is the author of *The Adolescent Idea, The Female Imagination,* and *Gossip*.

LYNN SUKENICK is Professor of Literature and Creative Writing at the University of California, Santa Cruz.

NANCY SHIELDS HARDIN is Professor of English at the University of Wisconsin, Rock County.

BARBARA HILL RIGNEY, Professor of English at Ohio State University, is the author of *Madness and Sexual Politics in the Feminist Novel* and *Lilith's Daughters: Women and Religion in Contemporary Fiction.*

ROBERTA RUBENSTEIN is Professor of Literature at American University and the author of *The Novelistic Vision of Doris Lessing.*

LORNA SAGE is Senior Lecturer in English at the University of East Anglia, England. She has frequently published in *The Observer* and in the *Times Literary Supplement,* and is the author of *Doris Lessing.*

CATHARINE R. STIMPSON, Professor of English at Rutgers University and Director of its Institute for Research on Women, has written both criticism and fiction, including *Class Notes.*

ALISON LURIE is Professor of English at Cornell University. Her books include *V. R. Lang: Poems and Plays, The War between the Tates,* and *Only Children.* She received the award in literature from the American Academy of Arts and Letters in 1978.

Bibliography

Brewster, Dorothy. *Doris Lessing*. New York: Twayne Publishers, 1965.

Brooks, Ellen W. "The Image of Women in Lessing's *The Golden Notebook*." *Critique* 15 (1973): 101–10.

Burkom, Selma R. "'Only Connect': Form and Content in the Works of Doris Lessing." *Critique* 11 (1969): 69–81.

Contemporary Literature 14, no. 4 (1973). Special Doris Lessing issue.

Donoghue, Denis. "Alice, the Radical Homemaker: *The Good Terrorist*." *New York Times Book Review*, 22 September 1985.

Doris Lessing Newsletter, 1977– .

Drabble, Margaret. "Doris Lessing: Cassandra in a World under Siege." *Ramparts* 10 (1972): 50–54.

Draine, Betsy. "Changing Frames: Doris Lessing's *Memoirs of a Survivor*." *Studies in the Novel* 11 (1979): 51–63.

———. *Substance under Pressure: Artistic Coherence and Evolving Form in the Novels of Doris Lessing*. Madison: University of Wisconsin Press, 1983.

Fishburn, Katherine. "The Dialectics of Perception in Doris Lessing's *Retreat to Innocence*." *World Literature Written in English* 21, no. 3 (1982): 416–33.

Gardiner, Judith Kegan. "Gender, Value, and Lessing's Cats." *Tulsa Studies in Women's Literature* 3, nos. 1/2 (1984): 111–24.

Godwin, Gail. "The Personal Matter of Doris Lessing." *North American Review* 256 (1971): 66–70.

Howe, Florence. "Doris Lessing's Free Women." *The Nation* 11 (1965): 34–37.

Hynes, Joseph. "The Construction of *The Golden Notebook*." *The Iowa Review* 4 (1973): 100–13.

Khanna, Lee Cullen. "Truth and Art in Women's Worlds: Doris Lessing's *Marriages between Zones Three, Four and Five*." In *Women and Utopia*, edited by Marleen Barr and Nicholas D. Smith. Lanham, Md.: University Press of America, 1983.

Knapp, Mona. *Doris Lessing*. New York: Ungar, 1984.

McDowell, Frederick P. W. "The Fiction of Doris Lessing: An Interim View." *Arizona Quarterly* 21 (1965): 215–45.

Modern Fiction Studies 26, no. 1 (1980). Special Doris Lessing issue.

Oates, Joyce Carol. "A Visit with Doris Lessing." *The Southern Review* 9 (1973): 873–83.

Poznar, Walter. "The Crisis of Identity in Doris Lessing's *The Summer before the Dark*: Who is Kate Brown?" *Texas Review* 4, nos. 1/2 (1983): 55–61.

Pratt, Annis. *Archetypal Patterns in Women's Fiction*. Bloomington: Indiana University Press, 1981.

Pratt, Annis, and L. S. Dembo, eds. *Doris Lessing: Critical Studies*. Madison: University of Wisconsin Press, 1974.

Rigney, Barbara Hill. *Madness and Sexual Politics in the Feminist Novel*. Madison: University of Wisconsin Press, 1978.

Rose, Ellen Cronan. "Doris Lessing's Città Felice." *The Massachusetts Review* 24 (1983): 369–86.

Rubenstein, Roberta. *The Novelistic Vision of Doris Lessing*. Chicago: University of Illinois Press, 1979.

Sage, Lorna. *Doris Lessing*. London: Methuen and Company, 1983.

Schlueter, Paul, ed. *A Small Personal Voice: Doris Lessing: Essays, Reviews, Interviews*. New York: Alfred A. Knopf, 1974.

———. *The Novels of Doris Lessing*. Carbondale: Southern Illinois University Press, 1969.

Seligman, Dee. *Doris Lessing: An Annotated Bibliography of Criticism*. London: Greenwood Press, 1981.

Showalter, Elaine. *A Literature of Their Own: British Women Novelists from Brontë to Lessing*. Princeton: Princeton University Press, 1977.

Singleton, Mary Ann. *The City and the Veld: The Fiction of Doris Lessing*. London: Associated University Presses, 1977.

Spacks, Patricia Meyer. *The Female Imagination*. New York: Avon Books, 1972.

Spilka, Mark. "Lessing and Lawrence: The Battle of the Sexes." *Contemporary Literature* 15 (1975): 218–40.

Sprague, Claire. "Double Talk and Doubles Talk in *The Golden Notebook*." *Papers on Language and Literature* 18 (1982): 181–97.

Stein, Karen F. "Reflection in a Jagged Mirror: Some Metaphors of Madness." *Aphra* 6 (1975): 2–11.

Stern, Frederick C. "The Changing 'Voice' of Lessing's Characters: From Politics to Sci-Fi." *World Literature Written in English* 21, no. 3 (1982): 456–67.

Stitzel, Judith. "Reading Doris Lessing." *College English* 40 (1979): 498–505.

Thorpe, Michael. *Doris Lessing's Africa*. London: Evans, 1978.

Tindall, Gillian. "Doris Lessing." In *Contemporary Novelists*, edited by James Vinton. New York: St. Martin's Press, 1972.

Valstos, Marion. "Doris Lessing and R. D. Laing: Psychopolitics and Prophecy." *PMLA* 91 (1976): 245–58.

Wood, Neal. *Communism and British Intellectuals*. New York: Columbia University Press, 1959.

Acknowledgments

"Doris Lessing's Intense Commitment" by James Gindin from *Postwar British Fiction: New Accents and Attitudes* by James Gindin, © 1962 by the Regents of the University of California. Reprinted by permission of the University of California Press.

"*The Golden Notebook*" by Dorothy Brewster from *Doris Lessing* by Dorothy Brewster, © 1965 by Twayne Publishers, Inc. Reprinted by permission of Twayne Publishers, a division of G. K. Hall & Co., Boston.

"Self-Analytic Women: *The Golden Notebook*" (originally entitled "*The Golden Notebook*") by Paul Schlueter from *The Novels of Doris Lessing* by Paul Schlueter, © 1969 by Paul George Schlueter, Jr., © 1973 by Southern Illinois University Press. Reprinted by permission.

"Doris Lessing in the Sixties: The New Anatomy of Melancholy" by Frederick R. Karl from *Contemporary Literature* 13, no. 1 (Winter 1972), © 1972 by the Regents of the University of Wisconsin. Reprinted by permission of the University of Wisconsin Press.

"Free Women" by Patricia Meyer Spacks from *The Female Imagination* by Patricia Meyer Spacks, © 1972, 1975 by Patricia Meyer Spacks. Reprinted by permission of Alfred A. Knopf, Inc.

"Feeling and Reason in Doris Lessing's Fiction" by Lynn Sukenick from *Contemporary Literature* 14, no. 4 (Autumn 1973), © 1973 by the Regents of the University of Wisconsin. Reprinted by permission of the University of Wisconsin Press.

"The Sufi Teaching Story and Doris Lessing" by Nancy Shields Hardin from *Twentieth Century Literature* 23, no. 3 (October 1977), © 1977 by Hofstra University Press. Reprinted by permission.

"'A Rehearsal for Madness': Hysteria as Sanity in *The Four-Gated City*" by Barbara Hill Rigney from *Madness and Sexual Politics in the Feminist Novel: Studies in Brontë, Woolf, Lessing, and Atwood* by Barbara Hill Rigney, © 1978 by the Board of Regents of the University of Wisconsin. Reprinted by permission of the University of Wisconsin Press.

"*Briefing for a Descent into Hell*" by Roberta Rubenstein from *The Novelistic Vision of Doris Lessing: Breaking the Forms of Consciousness* by Roberta Rubenstein, © 1979 by the Board of Trustees of the University of Illinois. Reprinted by permission of the University of Illinois Press.

"New Worlds" by Lorna Sage from *Doris Lessing* by Lorna Sage, © 1983 by Lorna Sage. Reprinted by permission of Methuen and Co., Ltd. and the author.

"Doris Lessing and the Parables of Growth" by Catharine R. Stimpson from *The Voyage In: Fictions of Female Development* edited by Elizabeth Abel, Marianne Hirsch, and Elizabeth Langland, © 1983 by the Trustees of Dartmouth College. Reprinted by permission of the University Press of New England and the author.

"Bad Housekeeping" by Alison Lurie from *The New York Review of Books* 32, no. 20 (December 19, 1985), © 1985 by Alison Lurie. Reprinted by permission.

Index